ALL THE ANIMALS OF
THE BIBLE LANDS

ALL
THE ANIMALS
OF THE
BIBLE LANDS

by

GEORGE CANSDALE

B.A., B.Sc., F.L.S.

Foreword by

John R. W. Stott

ZONDERVAN PUBLISHING HOUSE
Grand Rapids

ALL THE ANIMALS OF
THE BIBLE LANDS

Copyright © 1970 The Paternoster Press

Library of Congress Catalog Card No. 76–120040

First Edition

Printed Offset Litho in Great Britain

Contents

List of Illustrations

ACKNOWLEDGEMENTS: *All the colour illustrations are by the Author, with the exception of the Harvester Ants' Nest, facing page 145, which is reproduced by kind permission of Rev. Julian Charley. Appreciative acknowledgement is made to the British Museum for the illustrations facing pages 64, 65, 80 (bottom). 81 (top), 97 (bottom) and 160; to M. H. Woodford for the illustration facing page 80 (top); to Peter Merom for illustrations facing pages 96, 97 (top), 112, 113 (bottom), 161, 176, 177, 208, 224, and 225 (top); to Uri Tson, of Israel Nature Reserves Authority (facing page 81, top), and to the Moody Institute of Science for the illustration facing page 208 (bottom). The illustration facing page 225 (bottom) is a "Shell" photograph; remaining black and white illustrations are by the Author.*

Foreword

I DO NOT HESITATE TO SAY THAT EVERY CHRISTIAN SHOULD TAKE AN interest in natural history. Yet comparatively few seem to. I once had a curate whose hobby was trains. Since mine is birds, we often teased one another about the respective fascination of train-spotting and bird-watching. But I think the trump card was in my hand, since I could remind him that whereas trains are the works of men, birds are the works of the Lord! 'Great are the works of the LORD, studied by all who have pleasure in them' (Psalm 111:2 RSV).

The truth is that many of us have a good doctrine of redemption, but a poor doctrine of creation. We become so absorbed in God's works of grace, that we tend to forget His works of nature. But the Bible does not forget them. It presents the living God as equally Creator and Saviour. No lesser authority than Jesus Christ Himself told us to consider the birds of the air and the lilies of the field, so that we may learn from them about God's providential care.

There can be no better qualified author to write on this theme than George Cansdale, for he combines the two essential qualifications. First, he is a knowledgeable and travelled zoologist. Secondly, he is a professing and practising Christian. His interest in wild life developed while he worked for the Colonial Forest Service in Ghana. During this period of fourteen years he caught many species and sent them to the London Zoo, whose Superintendent he became in 1948. Soon afterwards his popular television programmes began, in which he exhibited numerous animals.

But he is also a Christian. For twenty years he has been an active member of All Souls Church in London, for nineteen of them as church-warden. He has been a keen Bible student all his life, while his visits to the Holy Land in 1960 and 1962 enabled him to study at first hand some of the biblical fauna. Julian Charley, a former curate of All Souls (though not the one mentioned above!), whose help is acknowledged in the author's preface, accompanied him on one of these trips, and George Cansdale, he and I have enjoyed many bird-watching expeditions together.

I hope and pray that this excellent and comprehensive book will stimulate the interest of natural historians in the biblical record, of Christians in natural history and of all readers in the essential relations which God has established between the two.

JOHN STOTT

9

Preface

IT IS HARD TO SAY JUST WHEN THE IDEA OF WRITING SUCH A BOOK AS
this first came to my mind. It can hardly be less than twenty years ago,
when I returned from the jungles of West Africa to become Superintendent of the London Zoo. For years I gathered material and wrote
briefly about the various animals that could be identified in the Scriptures,
and in 1960 my wife and I spent a month wandering through the Lebanon,
Syria, Jordan and Israel. But I was still no nearer to finding a form in
which to cast my book and my family began to wonder if it would ever be
finished. A request to write the animal articles for the Zondervan Pictorial
Encyclopedia of the Bible finally gave me the spur that I needed. This
meant that I had to study every animal name in the Hebrew and Greek
texts, a fundamental task that I had so far avoided and one that was possible
only with the help of Young's monumental *Analytical Concordance*. There
are nearly 3,000 mentions of animals in the canonical books and very
many of the passages involved have been examined in AV, RV and RSV,
as well as in several commentaries. The root meanings of numerous
ancillary words have been studied and the history of many animal names
traced through the *Oxford Dictionary of English Etymology*. It has been a
fascinating task and I am left deeply impressed with the consistency that I
have found; this is particularly noticeable with such important animals
as the ass and the horse (see pp. 64–79).

There are many people to be thanked in many fields. First of all my
wife, who has read and criticized the MS at all stages; she is as relieved as I
am that it is now complete. The people who helped make our 1962 Israel
tour a success are too numerous to name in full, but they include Professor
Shulov, of the Department of Zoology at Jerusalem University, and
'father' of the Bible Zoo, with his assistant P. Amittai, expert on vipers
and scorpions; Professor Mendelssohn of the University of Tel Aviv,
whose study collection of Israel animals allows a visitor to see Palestine's
fauna in a day; Uzi Paz, chief executive of the Nature Reserves Authority,
who took us to see gazelles, hyraxes and many other animals; the officials
of the Ministry of Agriculture and Fisheries and the Department of
Information, who supplied transport and provided many facilities,
including a night's fishing on the Lake of Galilee, and Julian Charley and
Ion Trant, who were my colleagues on that trip. Dr. John Taylor, the Rev.
Michael Green and Professor F. F. Bruce have helped on many Hebrew
and Greek linguistic points; any errors are in sections on which I was not

able to consult them. My thanks are also due to Mr. F. Nigel Hepper, author of the companion volume on *Plants of Bible Lands*, for his help in reading Chapter I in manuscript and for his line drawings; and to the Rev. John R. W. Stott for writing the Foreword. Though perhaps best known as Rector of All Souls, Langham Place, he is a keen ornithologist, and has photographed birds in most countries where his extensive travels have taken him.

In the past thirty or forty years animal life in Palestine has been steadily losing ground and a detailed account of it could quickly become out of date. The political situation is still far from settled and much depends on this, but we can see factors which could give wild life a better future. I shall be happy if the status of the wild animals in thirty years' time is still as I have described. With increasing national awareness of the need for conservation this is quite possible.

Introduction

Scope of work. Sources of material – Biblical text, history, archaeology, etc. Present-day fauna. Outline of treatment. Problems of translation and identification.

THE BIBLE INCLUDES THE NAMES OF MANY ANIMALS. NEARLY 180 Heb. words, some still listed as 'uncertain', and just over fifty Gr. words represent a wide range of animal life. Some words have been translated in widely different ways in the various versions, and while modern research in a number of fields has helped solve certain problems, some identifications remain in dispute. Both AV and RSV mention about 150 animal names, including the male, female and young of some more familiar kinds, so the total species involved is less than this. On the other hand, Heb. names tend to refer to groups of species and often have no precise equivalent in English, though they might compare with genera or even families in the zoological sense. This list is the material on which this book is based; where authorities differ, some attempt is made to discuss all the suggested species; also to include some of the obvious present-day animals, even though they are not specifically named, and a few others, like the elephant, which are mentioned indirectly, through their produce, in OT and NT.

The word 'animal' is here used in its wide and correct meaning, i.e., for any living organism endowed with sensation and voluntary motion (SOED). It thus includes the whole range of animal life from mammals to the minute creatures without backbones that build coral reefs.

While it would be unrealistic to search the Scriptures for anything in the nature of a check-list of Palestine animals in Bible times, it is likely that most of the obvious and important forms then native find some mention. It must be stressed that these animals are present as an integral part of the life of ordinary people, even if they appear only in figurative contexts, and the frequency with which any animal's names occur is some indication of its status. Parallel with this is the range of names given to one species, which can be equally meaningful as an index of its economic and ceremonial importance. For instance, the sheep has twelve Heb. names and is mentioned about 400 times; cattle, with ten Heb. names, are mentioned over 450 times. No other kind, wild or domesticated, can compare with these two.

Because animals appear in the Scriptures largely in this incidental way, they fall roughly into four classes:

1. **Domestic stock,** both working and edible, and wild animals specially named as suitable for food. Although limited in number they range widely from mammals to insects.

2. Animals that were a **danger to human life,** stock, crops and other possessions. Those mentioned are not numerous, but they vary from lion and wolf to flea and clothes-moth.

3. Familiar **wild animals** seen along the roadsides and around houses, etc. These would include the swallow, sparrow, harvester ant, etc. Some falling in the second part of (1) above and in (4) below could also be included here.

4. A group of **unclean animals** specifically forbidden as food to the Hebrews. This apparently arbitrary prohibition is discussed in more detail where some of these animals are described and it is shown often to be based on sound hygiene not understood or properly practised for another 3,000 years.

Many names offer no difficulty. They occur frequently, often in contexts which confirm identification, while some Heb. names are derived from roots of known meaning or are found today in cognate languages. Gr. names are generally easier for they are known through literature of classical Greece. These remarks are especially true of classes one and two. In contrast, class three contains many 'neutral' animals, often rather small, with little help in the contexts, and not all can be named with certainty. Some names, such as those normally tr. sparrow, are probably group-names in both Heb. and Gr. and may cover many species as understood now. Class four offers most problems. These names make up lists in Leviticus and Deuteronomy, arranged in series which are usually assumed to indicate rough relationships, but there is often little in the context to help, and some of these names appear nowhere else.

It will be seen that there is wide disagreement about some of these unclean animals, even as to the zoological Order or Class to which they might belong. Even so, philology can sometimes help, and the Heb. *peres*, (tr. ossifrage AV, following the Latin Vulg.), is a good example. This comes in a list of birds of prey, and the name 'bone-breaker' describes precisely the strange habit of two scavengers still found in Palestine. These are the Bearded Vulture, or Lammergeier, and the Black Vulture, which drop clean-picked bones on to rocks and then swoop down to extract the marrow. Some names are from roots now lost or not identified, and modern Heb. cannot always be relied on, for a few words have been applied to animals different from those to which they were once given. Some names are found only in figurative passages, often in poetical, wisdom or prophetic books, and these can be difficult. However, there are few cases where at least a tentative name cannot be suggested, or several possible alternatives. There will inevitably be a little repetition as the problems of each group are discussed, especially where several widely different translations have been suggested.

The modern reader, and especially the naturalist, should not be disappointed that some Bible animals are hard to name. Accurate study of animals really began only in the nineteenth century; there had been a few notable exceptions, such as the elder Pliny, but in the ancient world, as in most under-developed countries today, animals were largely of objective interest only, as the above discussion about classification suggests. This was certainly my experience in Ghana, where I did much of my field work on animals; the villager was concerned mainly with two groups – those he could eat and those that might endanger him or his crops. These were known in some detail, and named with an accuracy that often varied with size and importance. Other animals needed to be bizarre or conspicuous to merit a name. This is not unlike the situation in Palestine in biblical times. Failure to appreciate this point has perhaps allowed some writers to suggest individual names for animals which would probably not have been distinguished. If the ordinary person in Palestine today does not recognize two animals as being sufficiently different to have separate names, it seems likely that this was also true then.

A comparison of AV, RV, and RSV shows many variations. In some cases, especially in the use of words such as beast, kine, fowl, etc., this is due solely to changes in English usage. Elsewhere both philological and zoological research has shed new light on the problem as, for instance, where roe-buck is now correctly tr. gazelle. This work continues, but by no means all results have been incorporated in modern VSS, as will be noted as the species are discussed.

Even within each VS the translation of Heb. names is uneven. This is perhaps most obvious in the AV; the RSV is often better and takes account of many changed meanings which allow greater precision, but its treatment is by no means uniform. As regards animals the RV is rather disappointing for it corrects only some of the words which had long become obsolete and, contrary to its usual policy, does not always translate animal names consistently.

Examples of all these problems will be found in most chapters and their complex nature can perhaps be illustrated briefly with a general word such as 'creature', which starts at some disadvantage, for SOED gives five definitions! Today the generally accepted meaning is an animal as distinct from man. The first five uses of this word in the RSV are from five different Heb. words, qualified as living, wild or swarming. The AV renders them moving creature, beast of the field, creeping thing and living thing. The treatment of 'animal' is just as complicated; its first twelve uses in the RSV are from six Heb. words, which the AV tr. beast, cattle, of the herd and of the flock. The latter is still not consistent, but is often nearer the original. These are analysed in more detail in Appendix B. It is hoped that all animal names in the AV, RV and RSV are treated, if only briefly or by reference to another.

A major source of evidence about the biblical fauna is the increasing volume of ancient material processed by scientists. The palaeontologists' field is mostly too far back to be relevant, for they deal with faunas that probably lived in climatic conditions so different as to have only academic interest, but it is sometimes useful to know that certain species once occurred within the area.

Archaeological finds are becoming of increasing value, thanks largely to the pioneer work of the late F. E. Zeuner, who worked out new methods of investigating animal remains found in human contexts that previously had been taken mostly for granted. Above all, he tried to differentiate the bones of truly wild animals from the domesticated forms derived from them, a line of research that has proved most productive. It is fortunate that much of his work necessarily concerns Palestine and nearby lands where civilization was born. By its nature this data is more or less limited to three groups:

1. Domestic animals and, earlier, their wild forbears.
2. Wild animals, whose meat was eaten and whose skins, bones, horns, antlers, etc., were used for clothes, weapons and tools.
3. Other animals connected with superstition and religion.

Zeuner's work is of tremendous value to anyone studying domestic animals and their wild ancestors and relations, and it is perhaps the most important entry in the bibliography at the end of this volume.

Alongside this comparatively new work is a much greater amount of accurately dated and localized pictorial and written material resulting from excavations in Egypt, Palestine and Mesopotamia. Many of these records show animals in settings that are informative; others, though sometimes highly stylized, show unique features which allow precise identification; e.g., the hump of zebu cattle, and the load or harness on a camel proving its domesticated status. Prehistoric cave drawings and paintings are of less value here than in some other countries.

Another main source of information is the countryside today, with its often pathetic relics of plant and animal life. Since man first lived in these lands he has had a devastating effect on them – their soils and streams, as well as their flora and fauna. In isolation these last two would often be of little help in reconstructing a Bible natural history, but studied historically they have much to tell. The first chapter therefore describes the important regions that are found within our limits and attempts some comparison with the position some 2,000 to 4,000 years ago. The second chapter looks in greater detail at what man has done – and is still doing. For most of the time his interference has been disastrous to everything, including man himself, but it will be noted that some of his recent activities have been more beneficial, for some people may at last have recognized the true cause of the trouble. Together these two chapters should make it possible to suggest the potential of the various natural regions, which has probably changed little for some thousands of years.

Apart from these two introductory general chapters treatment is in logical sections. Where possible, animals are considered in natural groups – cattle, sheep and goats; canines; birds of prey, etc. Others have a common use – the beasts of burden; or a common habit – the migratory birds; or a common habitat – the waterside birds. While the widely varying nature and importance of these animals call for differing detail and emphasis, the following aspects will be treated as far as possible, though not always in this order:

> identification; description;
> natural history, i.e., habits, breeding, food, etc.;
> status, former and present;
> economic and religious importance;
> place in metaphor and symbolism.

While this book is for the layman and the general scholar, and is for the most part written in popular language, some technical terms and conventions are unavoidable and these are now explained.

The major geographical divisions, called natural regions, are described in Chap. I. Many animals and plants are typically found within one or other region but it is likely that the living space of any one kind will be more closely defined than this, and we refer to this as its habitat – the type of place in which it normally lives. Some animals are said to have narrow habitats; e.g., the hyrax (coney) in certain rock formations and the jerboa in sandy desert. Others are less demanding and they have broad habitats; e.g., the Palestine viper which may be seen almost anywhere outside the desert and swamps, and the Palestine gazelle, which can find a living in several regions.

Scientists classify animals and plants into natural groups which are systematically sub-divided. The backboned animals, the vertebrates, constitute a *Phylum* divided into a number of Classes – the mammals, birds, reptiles, etc. These are further broken down progressively into orders, families, genera, species and perhaps sub-species. This is best explained by taking the Syrian bear as an example:

Class:	*Mammalia.*
Order:	*Carnivora* (flesh-eating animals).
Family:	*Ursidae* – the bears.
Genus:	*Ursus* – Brown and grizzly bears.
Species:	*Ursus arctos* Brown bear.
Sub-species:	*Ursus arctos syriacus.* Syrian (Brown) Bear.

This may sound very complicated, but precise naming is as essential for every species of wild animal as a registered kennel name is for a pedigree

dog. *Ursus arctos* is known as the specific name; it can also be compared
with a man's name, except that the surname comes first.

Many of these Latin names are derived from old Gr. or Latin words
and are to some extent descriptive; others, especially the second and third
parts, are based on names of people or places. This is seen in the above
example: *Ursus* (Latin); *arctos* (Greek); *syriacus* (country). The convention
is that the whole of this name is in italics; the first part (genus) always has a
capital, the others never, even if based on proper names. A person's name
in ordinary print at the end of this Latin name indicates the one who
first described it, and thus allows a final check to be made on the identity
of the animal. To save space, if two members of a genus are mentioned,
in the second the genus is shown by the capital initial only, e.g., *Ovis aries*,
the domestic sheep, and *O. musimon*, the mouflon.

The word race is sometimes used in connexion with a species; it is almost
the same as a sub-species but usually means that the differences are not
enough to warrant giving formal sub-specific names.

Animals with initials in capitals, e.g., Short-toed Eagle, indicate agreed
English names for individual species. To avoid excessive use of capitals in
the text this is usually confined to the first use of the full name.

Unless otherwise indicated all translations are from the AV.

The precise transliteration of Heb. and Gr. words into English is never
possible, for the alphabets do not correspond in either number of letters or
their values. For Hebrew the simple transliteration of *Young's Analytical
Concordance* is used. Those readers who, like myself, know little or no
Hebrew, will not be worried by problems of pronunciation. The experts
should have no trouble in recognizing the words and going on from there.

I

The
Geographical
Background

Topography, geology and climate as they affect soil, flora and fauna. Natural regions of Palestine – Desert, Coastal Sand Dunes, Lowland and Plain, Rift Valley, Hill Country, Trans-Jordan Hills, Marshland. Their present flora and fauna, with some attempt at assessing the position in Biblical times.

MANY AND COMPLEX CHANGES HAVE TAKEN PLACE IN BIBLE LANDS since 2000 B.C., not least in political boundaries. These have been altered so much, especially in recent years, that geographical reference is complicated. Palestine is often spoken of as the 'Land of the Bible', but its meaning has varied over the centuries and as a national unit it is now obsolete. However, for the purposes of this book only and in default of a more precise and convenient name, Palestine is taken to have its old meaning, indicating the 1919 Palestine, with the adjacent deserts west of the Rift and Jordan valleys. But I give it no political significance and use it solely because this book is concerned with the animal life of earlier times.

The changes in vegetation and land use have been even greater and these are of a more permanent nature. These will best be understood if the area is discussed by regions, a word used here as a technical term to indicate each large natural unit into which a major geographical area can be divided. It is useful that Palestine, where most of the Bible narrative is set, has a small number of fairly well defined regions which will be considered one by one. Mesopotamia, whence the Hebrew stock first came and where many were later taken into captivity, will be mentioned briefly, as also will Egypt, where the growing nation of Israel spent some 400 years.

Several factors work together to produce these natural regions. The topography, in which the shape of the land surface, geology and soil are basic and inter-related; the climate is in part determined by topography and, in turn, can modify it, thus having a major influence on soil formation. Assuming that there is no basic change in climate and in the absence of human interference, a stable position is finally reached and a type of vegetation is established. This, with the factors mentioned above, largely decides the pattern of the fauna, though this seldom fits at all points into the regional pattern. Unfortunately, human interference is never absent! In this corner of the world it has been drastic and far-reaching; parts of some natural regions – those lending themselves most fully to occupation by man – have been changed beyond recognition and no traces of the original cover are left. Some regional boundaries are now completely masked or have been shifted, while some regions, such as the swamps, have just disappeared. The object of this chapter is to describe briefly the physical features of the areas – position, major features, geology, soil and climate – and then to discuss the various regions in the light of these man-made changes. The next chapter examines in more detail the different ways in which man has made – and is still making – himself felt.

I. PALESTINE

Palestine occupies a unique position, on the crossroads of Europe, Asia and Africa, a narrow strip of country running more or less north and south, with the Mediterranean on the west and desert on the east. It has thus always been a passageway for man and, as we shall see in Chap. XI, some migratory birds also find it a convenient route. Within a small area there are extremes of country – deserts and swamps, hills and plains, both high and low. A topographical map shows depths of more than 1,200 ft. b.s.l. and, not many miles to the east of this lowest point on the earth's surface, equally barren hills of 5,000 ft. Only a relief map can give any impression of its complexity and variety, the detailed analysis of which is beyond the scope of this chapter, but will be found in a book such as Denis Baly, *The Geography of the Bible* (1957).

Palestine's geology is complicated by the giant fault known as the Rift Valley running almost its whole length, and the resulting patchwork is equally hard to describe. Great areas of sandstone underlie the eastern deserts and hills; this is the material out of which the rose-red city of Petra was carved. There are extensive outcrops of granite in the south and basalt in the north, the latter used for the buildings in the long-ruined city of Chorazin, giving evidence of very early volcanic activity. Most of the land, however, is composed of rocks formed in marine conditions; the hill mass from Hebron through to Ephraim is made of hard limestone, flanked by larger expanses of later chalks and softer limestones. Between the hills and the sea lie the only recent beds – of sands, alluvium, etc. Soils, and especially their structure, are largely the result of climatic influences, but the parent rock is important, for it is the source of most of the nutrient salts. This varied geology and topography, and the resultant local climates, produce a range of soils, many of which are potentially fertile and have lack of water as their main limiting factor.

The climate is essentially Mediterranean in pattern, with the summer so hot and dry that plant growth may cease for weeks or even months, and the winter mild; frost is rare except in the higher hills. The bulk of the rain falls between October and April, and while the hills are the main factor in deciding where it falls, there are two general rules that apply here – the rainfall decreases as one goes south and also as one goes inland. The rain varies so much from year to year that averages may be meaningless, especially in the drier zones. The wettest parts of the hills enjoy up to 32 in., and on the border with the Lebanon upwards of 40 in. South of Beersheba 12 in. is the most farmers can ever hope for, and they cannot be sure of even half of that. Readers who live in temperate climates and complain of summer rain may find it hard to understand why water in the Scriptures is a picture of life. A summer spent in modern Israel would soon teach them!

The Desert

Large areas in the south and east consist of desert, whose low rainfall is caused by the above factors. While the average is from 2 to 8 in. per annum, this is very erratic and the rain often falls in a few winter storms; it is not unusual for a year, or even two, to pass without rain over large areas, and this possibility of drought over the country as a whole is a problem often referred to in the OT. These winter storms are severe enough to cause local flooding. I shall never forget my astonishment at finding signs on the Beersheba–Eilat road, in the middle of the Negev, telling visitors in several languages to 'Beware of Flood Damage'. These floods occur both where the surface is bare rock and also, mostly on lower, more or less flat ground, where the soil quickly becomes almost impervious when beaten hard by heavy rain, which then runs off; some of this finds its way underground into strata from which oases get their water, but much of it goes into *wadis* leading to the Dead Sea or into broad open *wadis* where it evaporates. It is estimated that in most areas no more than 3 % of the rain penetrates the surface. As is explained in Chap. II, limited occupation of the desert is made possible by enterprising use of such rain as is received.

The surface of the desert varies widely. Deep sand is not widespread and there are few areas of extensive moving dunes such as characterize parts of the Arabian and Sahara Deserts. The wind is often so continuous that the sand is blown away, leaving only rock or gravel in all but protected sites. On the higher ground and steep slopes bare rock is the commonest surface. Nights can be cold for much of the year, but frost is unusual. These rocks are therefore subject to little erosion other than wind, which often carries sharp sand and eats out the softer material, leaving a gaunt skeleton; this action is particularly obvious on the cliffs around the Timna copper mines a few kilometres inland from Eilat. The desert topography includes everything from almost flat plains to steep escarpments, such as the Maktesh Ramon which cuts right across the Negev, and there is a wealth of colour in the various rocks. Altitude varies from 1,250 ft. b.s.l. at the Dead Sea to rather over 2,000 ft. a.s.l. on the big escarpment.

Life in the desert is made difficult by wide fluctuations in temperature. In spring the annual range of 60° to 70° F. (mean) may almost be felt in one day. In summer the ground surface by day becomes far too hot for bare feet and it would be lethal for any small animals, whose activity must then be confined to the night. Winter nights are bitterly cold and even in spring some small animals may be found to vary their time-table and have periods of activity between the heat of the day and the cold of the night. There are no patches of dense vegetation in the desert, but few large areas are entirely bare of shrubs, which can draw water from deep in the ground, and there are also a few very widely scattered trees. Pockets of soil accumulate in holes or clefts, even in large expanses of bare rock, whether sloping or flat, to be colonized by shrubs. Most *wadis* are more or less lined with specialized woody plants, some of which remain green throughout even the hottest weather. Some desert soils are fertile, especially in some of the loess areas, and after rain these quickly become covered with grasses and flowering plants, mostly annuals; perennials, whose root systems can survive long resting periods, take over later in the year when the annuals have died. These provide the only greenstuff available to the livestock around the desert edge and the Bedouins' intimate local knowledge allows them to make good use of it.

Conditions are so extreme that only specialized forms can live permanently in the desert; there are areas where no animals can survive and, throughout, the average density of animal life of all kinds is very low. In such surroundings gazelles are now the only large animals. They are never common and need grazing/browsing grounds reckoned in square miles per head; they are big and fast enough to cover such vast territories in search of food, and they stand high enough to keep above the fierce ground temperatures, which do not harm their horny hoofs. The pale coat is to some extent protective camouflage but it also reduces the absorption of sun heat. Even so gazelles try to find some shade against the midday heat. Their most important asset is a special metabolism which wastes little water, mostly obtained from their food, which includes tuberous roots. The other ruminant of the desert is the Nubian Ibex, but this is confined to the hills, including those around En Gedi, just above the Dead Sea, where it is now fully protected. Asses are still used around the desert edge and for short journeys into it, but only camels can serve as beasts of burden in the desert itself; they are often left to range more or less freely until

...lt and during this time thorny plants provide most of their food, but ...ed regular, though not daily, access to water, and when used heavily loaded on long desert routes they must also be well fed. Camels are still a familiar part of the landscape but modern transport is making them less and less essential.

Small mammals are more numerous and varied, but their distribution is patchy. The most famous of all is the Egyptian Jerboa, familiarly known to the troops in N. Africa as the Desert Rat, though in fact it belongs to a different rodent family from the rats. It spends the day in burrows, where the temperature stays more or less the same day and night, and air is moister, and it emerges at night in search of seeds, fruit and succulent roots. It seldom or never needs to drink. Other small rodents – gerbils, jirds and sand-rats – are perhaps more typical of the desert edge and need a rather higher rainfall.

The beasts of prey are necessarily much rarer than their prey, and the only true cat of the desert seems to be the Caracal or Desert Lynx. A race of leopard, small and pale, lives around the desert edge and in the hills rather than in the open desert, but the Fennec Fox is found in very dry country; it has huge ears, presumably for locating insects and other small prey, and it is paler and smaller than the true foxes. The slow-moving Arabian Hedgehog is seen much more often than these; it feeds largely on invertebrates and small lizards.

The large vultures are in a special position, for although they live off the desert they are not limited by it. Very small numbers are enough to scavenge a great area of desert, which they survey while cruising or soaring slowly at great heights, skilfully using rising currents to maintain position. Large birds of prey would have been a familiar sight to the Israelites on their desert wanderings; some of the big vultures are resident but during the spring migration many other large birds of prey, including eagles, kites, buzzards and other vultures, go through, riding the thermals and gliding north.

For several months of the year migrant birds are by far the most conspicuous animals of the desert. Most large birds go straight over, though a few, such as Ospreys, Black Kites and harriers, often move in shorter stages and may be seen perched on telegraph poles along the Eilat–Beersheba road. The small birds – swallows, pipits, wagtails, buntings and warblers – tend to travel more in stages, visiting oases for food and water, but this pattern has been encouraged in recent years by the increase of desert irrigation. Like quails, which still fly north in numbers, these migrants are travellers across the desert rather than resident in it. One other notable resident needs mention. The Rock Dove, ancestor of all tame pigeons, nests on steep rock faces, such as in the deep gorge of Ein Avdat, but it flies great distances to the desert edge every day, or to oases or new farms, for both food and water.

Although their density is always comparatively low, the desert has a surprsingly large variety of reptiles; none is very large and most are cardivorous, but one lizard – the Spiny-tailed – is partly or wholly vegetarian. Having little or no internal means of regulating body temperatures, reptiles are even more limited than the small mammals in their periods of activity and may be forced to spend not only the hot parts of the day – which may be from before eight a.m. to nearly six p.m. – but also the cold nights safely underground, where the daily temperature range is much reduced. Small lizards may use their tongues to take some moisture from dew condensed on leaves, but it is likely that some desert snakes are independent of water and obtain all necessary moisture from their victims. The Egyptian Sand Boa is found mostly in sandy desert and 'swims' back into the sand if placed on the surface. The skinks dive into the sand, using their tapered noses to force a passage. At least four vipers are widely distributed in the deserts from Egypt through to Persia, and these are discussed under 'Serpent'. Most desert snakes probably take a range of prey but may depend, at least to some extent, on casualties from the flocks of small migrant birds which pass twice a year over a total period of some five months. Many snakes can survive without food for months at a time, and during the hottest weather they go into a resting state, called aestivation, underground.

Within the desert are oases of various sizes and types. Yotvata, in the southern Negev, and Jericho, just north of the Dead Sea, depend on wells sunk into the strata over which they stand, and many small oases have similar supplies. The *kibbutz* of En Gedi, among the hills on the west side of the Dead Sea, is serviced from a natural spring higher up the hill, from which the water formerly ran to waste in the Dead Sea. An increasing area is being irrigated by the six-foot pipeline bringing water from central and N. Israel, and wherever water is distributed, tiny leaks give many animals the opportunity of a free drink. Small patches of garden and orchard are made possible by the sewage effluent at small desert settlements, such as at Mitspe Ramon, on the high escarpment of the Negev, where there is a hostel for the workers in the gypsum mines. The resulting cover and crops attract a bird fauna not typical of the surrounding desert. Some species are resident, such as Tristram's Grackle, at the ancient oasis of En Gedi, where other birds also nest, but small passing migrants are even more obvious; they may stay for a few days to feed and recuperate before passing on, and their chances of survival must be increased by the extension of these areas.

The Dead Sea is more truly desert – to both plants and animals – than the surrounding dry hills, for its high mineral content makes it utterly useless either for drinking or as a habitat for any kind of life.

Few regions are demarcated by sharp lines and this is especially true of the desert, around which there is what can best be described as a buffer zone, of varying width but usually many miles wide. Conditions here are marginal; better than average rainfall means fair crops, while less than average spells failure and hunger. It is in such areas that irrigation is most useful for it can more or less guarantee a crop; in effect it pushes the frontier farther into the desert.

Coastal Sand Dunes

Shifting dunes such as are normally associated with the great deserts are a familiar feature of the coastal country today; they stretch from around Gaza in the south to beyond Haifa in the north, in a discontinuous belt up to 150 ft. high and usually not more than two or three miles wide, though there are a few larger patches and they cover some 10 per cent of the coastal land. These dunes usually enjoy a fair rainfall but they provide, in effect, a desert habitat, for the water cannot be retained by the almost pure sand; only specialized plants can thrive, mostly with an extensive root system, and they include both Mediterranean and desert species. The typical animals are those of the sandy desert, especially the small rodents whose tracks and burrow entrances are seen everywhere; they are, in fact, more plentiful and varied than in the desert dunes where vegetation, and therefore food, is very sparse or entirely lacking. Hedgehogs are typical, the eastern and western species meeting somewhere in this area.

This region cannot be identified in the Bible. Many of the dunes may be more recent, but there is some evidence that the Roman aqueduct near Caesarea may have been moved after a section had been blocked by moving sand. Such coastal dunes are well known in other parts of the world and they are to some extent, if not entirely, the result of human activity in destroying woody cover and so allowing the easier movement of sand by the prevailing westerly winds. Man is now reversing the process by fixing these dunes, using various mechanical devices and planting selected grasses and trees. This will recreate a habitat more favourable to both agriculture and animal life generally, but it should be noted that in the process some interests may suffer, for the rainfall will then be used on the spot instead of penetrating under the sand and travelling underground for drawing elsewhere. This would be important only in country where every drop of water is precious. This region has been described in some detail largely because the ordinary visitor could easily confuse it with the desert.

Lowlands and Plains

The two major areas comprising this region are the plains of Sharon, on the coast behind Jaffa, and Esdraelon, extending south-east from the foot of Mount Carmel. Perhaps one should also include the plain of Asher, north of Carmel, and the much drier plain of Philistia, which adjoins the Negev, though they do not compare in fertility, and the following remarks apply largely to the first two. These areas have been farmed since the dawn of history; most of their original vegetation was destroyed long ago and in post-war years these plains have been occupied so intensively that little trace of it now remains. Rainfall is fair though marginal, for the heights are not enough to cause heavy precipitation from the westerly winds. Formerly covered with forest, scrub and marshland these plains are now a great complex of towns and smaller settlements (including *kibbutzim, moshavim* and co-operatives) with their fields and orchards, mostly irrigated to the limit of their water supplies. The woodlands were once the home of Red and Fallow Deer, but these were driven out long ago, possibly well before the end of the Biblical period. They survived much later in other habitats, but the nearest of their kinds today are probably in Persia and Turkey. Lions and leopards hunted there, though they were more typical of the broken hill country and the lower ground beyond the hills. While mammals, except small ones, have become much rarer it is likely that bird life is more plentiful today, for mixed farms may shelter and support a richer and larger bird fauna than virgin scrub or woodlands. Many birds are resident, and they are small rather than large. Some are recent additions to the fauna; such, for example, as the African Bulbul which has moved into orchards and gardens in search of fruit. Migrants also pass through but they are less obvious here, for they are travelling on a broad front and have more cover. In modern Israel, where farming is often ruthlessly efficient, it is surprising to find many road verges and odd corners left fallow to become filled quickly with dense beds of milk thistles, whose seed heads fall straight down and are not widely dispersed by wind. They provide shelter and food, especially for goldfinches. It is likely that most animals familiar to the hill shepherds also went down to the plains at some seasons.

The Rift Valley

From above the Lake of Galilee nearly to Jericho (from about 300 ft. above to nearly 1,000 ft.b.s.l.) the Jordan valley forms a semi-tropical tract where many plants flourish that are more typical of the upper Nile valley. Papyrus, the bulrush of the Bible, is one such; today this valley is its only habitat north of about 7°N latitude on the River Nile, though in Ancient Egypt it grew in the delta and was used for making writing materials. One of Galilee's most important fishes is the *Tilapia*, a genus of Cichlid widespread in Central Africa, where it is the most important food fish of the great lakes. The lush vegetation has been gradually cut back and now the main area of Huleh has been drained, but the deeply-cut valley is still lined in parts with almost impenetrable jungle in which Wild Boar, Fishing Cats and perhaps other large animals survive. Up-to-date information about parts of this region is scarce, for much of it lies along a frontier which naturalists have not been encouraged to visit.

The Hill Country

Much of the Bible narrative is set in the hills – around Galilee in the north, through Samaria and Jerusalem to Bethlehem and beyond. It is a gross over-simplification to consider this as a unit but it can reasonably be so treated as regards animal life. The rainfall is generally above 24 in., increasing steadily from south to north, falling off rapidly on the east, or leeward, side to a very low figure at the foot of the hills. Nights are cool in summer and cold in winter, when frost and snow are unusual but not unknown. In the north large oaks of several species can grow, but are now rare. Over much of this region the climax vegetation is mostly scrub, with taller trees growing in sheltered places and pockets of deeper soil. Large areas of the hill country have suffered severe erosion through bad farming, over-grazing and goat damage, and the cover in such places is very degraded or non-existent. Olives and tall cypresses are the commonest planted trees.

This region once supported a wide range of animal life, for it offered both grazing and browsing, as well as nuts and fruits of various trees. The rock formation, with many holes and clefts, gave shelter to mammals as varied as the Syrian Brown Bear and Rock Hyrax, the coney of the Scriptures. Deer were probably the most numerous wild ungulates, with the Palestine Gazelle, which is much smaller than the Red and Fallow Deer. The deer have gone but the gazelle survived in drier country to the south and in recent years, under protection, it has made a good recovery; so much so that it now lives in fair numbers in the Judaean hills and even on the plain of Esdraelon, where gazelles may be seen close to tractors working in the fields. Bears and lions have disappeared, but the Striped Hyena and Wolf remain. The Leopard, too, has been driven out of the hills but a very few are left in the Jordan Valley. It is probable that the status of small carnivores has changed much less; the Fox, Jackal, Badger and Mongoose are locally common and when I have travelled by road I have several times seen a run-over corpse. The most obvious resident in this, and much other, country is the Mole-rat, which pushes up its untidy heaps of soil in irregular lines wherever the soil is deep enough, but never itself appears above ground.

The general comments about birds in the lowlands and plains apply here too. The Rock Partridge is heard daily in some months but is seldom seen, for it prefers to run through cover rather than fly. The Palestine Jay, with a black cap, and the Hooded Crow, identical with the British form, are often seen and heard, the latter waiting on the roadside to pick small animals knocked down by cars, just as it does in the Scottish Highlands. The large resident birds of prey are now rare, partly because of poisoning, and the main scavenger is the conspicuous Egyptian Vulture which still frequents garbage-tips outside towns. However, the Griffon Vulture is not

extinct and still nests among crags high above the lake of Galilee, and on
one of my spring visits I saw a pair of Verreaux's Eagles in Upper Galilee,
one of the few times when this splendid bird has been recorded in Israel.

Locusts were once a potential danger everywhere but this pest is now
largely under control and the only ones that I found were in the University
laboratories in Tel Aviv! The only insect worth mentioning is the
Harvester Ant, which is busy in spring and early summer gathering food
supplies for storing underground; the nest entrance, with well-worn paths
and a trail of husks, is very obvious.

The Rainbow or Agama Lizard, eight to ten in. long, is more often
seen than any other reptile – on the roadside, on ruins, and even on occupied buildings – and it is at once recognized by its habit of doing 'press-
ups'. In spring the big geckos may be seen warming themselves on walls
and boulders after the chilly night. The largest venomous snake – the
Palestine Viper – is found among the hills as well as in most habitats other
than desert; reaching a length of over 4 ft. and a thickness of 1 in. it can
inflict a serious bite, and because it lives in inhabited areas it is considered
responsible for more human casualties than any other snake.

Sheep and goats have always been the main domestic stock in the hills,
the latter being able to live off country too poor for sheep; they can even
climb trees in search of browsing. The rolling hills of N. Galilee are more
suited to cattle-raising. The hills are not really ideal for camels but they
are still kept in small numbers, notably in Samaria, around Nazareth and
in the Druse country north of Carmel, where they look strangely out of
place in the green countryside.

The Hill Country of Trans-Jordan

To the east, beyond Jordan, are further ranges of hills and broad plateaux.
These were once the home of Ammon, Moab and Edom, traditional
enemies of Israel, and this area therefore barely comes within the limits
of this book. The highest points are over 5,000 ft., high enough to make the
westerly winds drop more rain, but much of it has already been extracted
by the western hills in Palestine. Conditions in these hills are more
extreme and the rainfall lower, with the desert never far away. Lions and
leopards were once well known, though it is hard to speak about their
prey. Gazelles lived here then, as now, and the country perhaps suited the
Persian race of the Fallow Deer, which liked poor scrub and dry woodlands. The Onager was near the western edge of its range here, but a
century ago it was still common in places though soon after that it became
extinct. It may have come only to the foot of the hills, but it would
have been within range of the lions; in Africa the Zebra is the favourite
prey of lions, and the same could have been true of the closely related
onager.

The vegetation had not then become impoverished, so that great numbers of sheep could be kept in Ammon and Moab; evidence for this is the annual tax that Mesha, King of Moab, had to pay Solomon – 100,000 lambs and the wool of 100,000 rams (II Kings 3:4, 5). If the land could carry such numbers, however well managed, presumably there had once been plenty of wild grazing animals and suitable beasts of prey in attendance. Camels formed the basic transport, though perhaps they were more at home on the lower ground than right up in the hills, and they were used by the traders whose routes ran through these lands.

The Marshlands

Perhaps it would be more correct to regard these as islands within other major regions. All have now been drained and put to good use; some owed their origin to human activity, by impeding drainage and filling valleys with silt, but those on the Plain of Sharon were caused by the low sand hills parallel to the coast. There were once considerable areas of marsh on the plains and in a few places on the coast, which probably dried out in part during the hot dry summer but served as useful barriers against invading armies. Another area surrounded Lake Huleh and gradually increased as the lake became silted up; the River Jordan flowed through it and kept it permanently wet. Most of these areas were breeding-grounds for the mosquitoes that carried malaria, for many centuries perhaps the most important disease of the E. Mediterranean and the basic cause of the collapse of Ephesus. Both mosquitoes and malaria disappeared when these marshes were reclaimed.

The marshes made an ideal habitat for the Fishing Cat, and a safe retreat for the Wild Boar when it was driven out of other regions; its main stronghold today is still around the old site of Lake Huleh. Frogs of several kinds and water tortoises were common; fish abounded in the open areas of water left in Huleh. These frogs and fish were the food of many aquatic birds that bred there or passed through on migration. Herons were the most conspicuous but they also included ducks and terns. Countless numbers of waders stayed for varying periods of passage, while in winter these marshes were a vast refuge for ducks and coots. A large complex of brackish fish ponds at Ma'agan Mikhael – on the coast between Tel Aviv and Haifa – covers what was once a useless swamp. This area is now a fully protected sanctuary where a colleague and I spent several days when the spring migration was in full flood. In just under a month we had already 135 species on our list and new birds were hard to find, but we quickly added another fifteen at Ma'agan. They included many of the waders in breeding plumage, especially the Curlew-Sandpiper and Spotted Red-shank, and we identified and photographed the Grey Phalarope – the first record for Israel – but the bird that gave me the biggest thrill was the White-winged Black Tern in its summer dress, for previously I had known it only in its winter haunts in Central Africa.

II. EGYPT

The only part of Egypt that need be mentioned is the Nile Delta, for it is generally agreed that the land of Goshen which the pharaoh gave to Joseph for his brethren was somewhere here, probably in the north-east sector. Climatically the lower Nile Valley and the Delta are desert, with virtually no rain except for a little along the Mediterranean coastal strip. The key to the fertility which made possible the continuous occupation and cultivation of this area, and the advanced civilization based on it, is the Nile itself, which in its annual flood not only waters the land but brings silt to replenish and build up the soil, raising it perhaps a foot in three centuries. Occasionally the water failed to rise high enough, as witness the famine for which Joseph made provision, but usually the rains of Central Africa and Ethiopia supplied adequate water to flood the land and silt to fertilize it. Ancient Egyptian records show that by the time the Hebrews moved into Goshen, water control and irrigation had long been practised and they must have found a settled land from which any large native fauna had disappeared and the only animals of any size were domestic stock. Most of these were already developed into a range of breeds, but the status of the camel is still unknown and this is discussed in Chap. V.

The wild animals that the pharaohs hunted or trapped for training were found only in Upper Egypt and even farther south. The flora and fauna of the desert enclosing the riverain strip would be comparable to that of the Negev, but not many miles from the river no rain falls, and the desert becomes almost lifeless. The lakes and flooded areas of the Nile have always been the haunt of waterfowl, especially in the autumn, when the river is at its highest and the southward migration in full swing. The pictorial records of Ancient Egypt show many kinds of birds that the Hebrews must have known – and probably enjoyed as food: these include the Mallard, and the Egyptian and Red-breasted Geese. The great barrage schemes now being completed will bring changes, for though more water will be available, it will be supplied throughout the year and it is not clear how the controlled waters will carry down the fertile silt on which the land largely depends. The animals responsible for the plagues are not peculiar to Egypt and are treated in detail elsewhere.

III. MESOPOTAMIA

The 'land between the rivers' Tigris and Euphrates provides the only other setting for parts of the OT story. Abram came from Ur, in the south of this vast alluvial plain, and travelled to Canaan in a long arc nearly touching the Turkish mountains. More than a thousand years later conquering armies brought back groups of Hebrews and kept them captive for varying periods. The earliest human settlement was in this area and occupation was almost continuous. Long settled periods, at home if not abroad, allowed the development of great cities with advanced cultures, based on an elaborate irrigation system that was applied to all suitable land. Throughout the biblical period Mesopotamia was, like Egypt, a largely man-made habitat, a gigantic, artificially maintained oasis surrounded by desert and hills, but before man took over the area must have been similar to parts of the N. Negev, with complexes of marshes in parts of the delta.

The great alluvial plain was flanked by mountains where forests grew and the woodland animals were safe, either in wild inaccessible country or in hunting preserves which the kings guarded carefully for their own pleasure, but it is doubtful if the exiles saw much wild life other than birds and lizards – and perhaps a few captive animals such as the lions to which Daniel was introduced. The area today is very different from the land where great cities once flourished. Climatically it was desert, with the deep soil made fertile only by irrigation. In contrast to the narrow Nile Valley, the broad plain gave the rivers great scope for wandering, while wasteful methods of farming sometimes led to soil desiccation and the build-up of harmful salts. By the time the Greeks took over, Mesopotamia had seen over 4,000 years of civilization and soil and water resources were beginning to run out, but life went on at a decreasing pace for another 1,500 years or so until finally, in A.D. 1258, the Mongols smashed the great canal system and the land reverted to the patchwork of desert and marsh that it is today.

II

Man—

Farmer,

Herdsman

and Destroyer

A historical consideration of man's complex effects on the countryside and fauna since the land was first occupied, but especially from the arrival of Abram in Canaan. An examination of the factors now operating.

FOR THOUSANDS OF YEARS MAN HAS BEEN BUSY MODIFYING, EXPLOITING and destroying the surface of the earth, sometimes deliberately, sometimes unwittingly, and few large areas now remain unaffected. Deserts, with their sparse plant life, have resisted most attacks, but modern irrigation and the discovery of oil have now led to their deeper penetration. At the other extreme the Siberian tundras of the far north, enjoying a brief but active summer, are largely protected because the ground is permanently frozen a few inches beneath the surface; now these too may have to yield to Russian attacks. Of the few tropical jungles that may still be virgin, none is likely to remain so indefinitely.

Man has left his mark all over the world, but the lands of the Bible have been occupied and used since the birth of civilization, so it is not surprising that he has done more damage there than almost anywhere else, leaving great areas of soil impoverished or even eroded down to bare rock. This is reflected in the flora, poor in species and thin on the ground, and this in turn in the fauna. The status of many animals has changed for the worse, and there is ample historical evidence that some have been exterminated either from the area as a whole or from large parts of it. Before considering the more detached causes of all this change and what modern man is doing about the problem, one possible complication should be examined.

Human interference alone would explain the state of affairs in fully occupied areas, but is this the complete answer everywhere? Has Palestine's climate perhaps become less favourable since the biblical period? Has the rainfall decreased, increasing the extent of the deserts and causing

MUCH OF THE CENTRAL NEGEV is rocky and hilly. This heavily eroded mass is west of the main road near Side Boker (p. 22).

THE DEAD SEA is surrounded by almost rainless desert. Many flowering plants take root along the course of tiny streams flowing from the hills above (p. 24).

THE LEEWARD FACE of a coastal dune south-west of Tel Aviv. Great efforts are now being made to anchor these moving dunes and so stop further land from being covered with sand (p. 25).

THE VALLEY OF JEZREEL as seen from the hills south of Nazareth in mid-April. The patchwork pattern points the intensive cultivation of this fertile area, helped by irrigation from the Jordan system (p. 26).

growth everywhere to be less lush? This theory has often been put forward, though seldom by scientists on the spot, and if it were true it would confuse the assessment of the flora in, say, the days of the Patriarchs, for the earlier potential would have been different from today's; it could have included some plants and animals, not on our present lists, that need moister conditions, and excluded others, the ones that thrive in drier surroundings. A marked change of climate would affect the division into regions, for rainfall in these lands is the main limiting factor.

The suggestion about a poorer climate comes from two sources. First, there is the school claiming that destruction of tree cover reduces rainfall, while planting new forests increases it – and it is undeniable that forest destruction on a large scale has taken place. This is, in fact, a confusion of cause and effect, for it is the rain that makes forest growth possible. Land with ample woody cover certainly makes better use of rain, in that the water is more likely to penetrate the protected and anchored soil and go underground rather than run off out of control, to cause erosion and flood damage, and then to be wasted. Trees also give shade and protection from the wind and they are therefore beneficial to animals and crops, but their influence on rainfall is negligible. It would be felt only if a plantation of trees on a hill-top increased the effective height by enough to make a moisture-bearing wind drop its rain. The second school argues on different lines, that Palestine, with its present climate, cannot be regarded, even potentially, as a land 'flowing with milk and honey'. Further it claims, if the N. Negev was successfully occupied and farmed, as it was during at least two long periods, it must have enjoyed a higher rainfall than it gets now.

Israeli scientists who have considered this problem, which is vitally important to them, seem fully agreed that there has been no significant climatic change, but that the vegetation of the various regions is still potentially what it was when Abram moved into Canaan. The division into regions is therefore still the same, except where man has moved the boundaries, and man alone must be blamed for the damage. As regards the Negev, botanists and agriculturists, led by Professor Evenari of the Hebrew University, have reconstructed the earthworks of the old settlement at Avdat from which the Nabateans were driven out around A.D. 120. There was a further period of activity in the Byzantine period starting c. A.D. 300 and reaching a peak in the sixth century. The town and its farmlands were abandoned in A.D. 634 when the Muslims conquered Palestine, and remained in ruins for about 1,300 years. These heaps and lines of stones which had long been misunderstood are now known to have been part of a complex irrigation system, where many acres of bare slopes were used to supply water to a few acres of soil collected in a valley bottom. Some farms and orchards have been successfully established, which is fair proof that the rainfall now is no less than it was 2,000 years and more

C

ago. When man used the same skill and worked as hard he got the same results, even though such labour may not be economic today. We thus assume that we are dealing with an unchanged climate and the same climax vegetation on which the fauna depended. This somewhat simplifies the interpretation, even though man's effects have been both destructive and uneven, and have caused some changes which can hardly be rectified.

Man's influence on the land and its flora and fauna is both indirect and unconscious on the one hand, and direct and deliberate on the other. The first results simply from his occupation of the land; forest, scrub and prairie are cleared and burnt to prepare the land for farming or housing; before coal and oil began to come into use less than 200 years ago, the only regular fuel was wood, for which further large areas were raided. These activities change any habitat so markedly that many animals leave the area, either because conditions are no longer suitable or because they will not tolerate human disturbance. In general the larger species are worst affected and most grazing animals move away, but there are exceptions, such as the gazelles which now take little notice of the Israeli tractors. Smaller animals are often helped by such changes, which give easy access to food crops: some may become more numerous and others may take advantage of the situation and move in, even becoming pests that must be controlled.

Man acts directly against animals by killing them or driving them away, and here several different classes must be recognized. The grazing and browsing animals – antelopes and wild cattle, swine and horses – may compete with domestic stock and must therefore be cleared from an area larger than what is occupied fully. Many of these, and others too, are good for food, or in demand as trophies or totems, or for making weapons and tools, so they are hunted or trapped. The beasts of prey may be dangerous to man himself as well as to his stock, so they are attacked at all times. Other animals, not actual predators, are a nuisance or danger to life or health, ranging from venomous snakes to disease-carrying insects, though the latter are seldom recognized as deadly enemies by primitive peoples. The smaller and more resilient animals may not suffer so much, but there is drastic reduction in the range and numbers of many species once widespread. This is, of course, a world-wide problem. For instance, of five species of rhinoceros in Asia and Africa two are almost extinct and two others are in danger, not just because their ranges have been reduced but, even more, through hunting for their horn which is used as a quack medicine. The lion, described in Chap. VII, is another striking example.

Man began doing this damage as soon as he became a settled farmer but he never foresaw the possible consequences, because he just assumed that earth's resources were inexhaustible. Mankind had to learn the hard way that this was not so; unfortunately the lesson usually came far too late for the individual to profit from experience, largely because in most parts of the world, for century after century, the process was working too slowly for a single generation to notice it. In many countries this dangerous lesson has still not been learnt. The ancient civilizations of the Fertile Crescent were born very early, and major damage to the countryside was done as far back as the Bronze Age, the rate of progress varying widely from place to place.

The chain of events in Egypt and Mesopotamia has already been described in Chap. I. Palestine's pattern is very different, for it has a varied terrain and, as a whole, enjoyed no such periods of settled rule as Mesopotamia and Egypt knew. In fact, Palestine's longest spell of peace seems to have begun towards the end of David's reign and was over before Solomon's death. For hundreds of years, both before and after this, there was unrest and guerrilla warfare, with occasional massive campaigns. Trouble came from almost every side and the centre of fighting moved around, so that except perhaps for the plain of Esdraelon, which was fertile but more vulnerable than the hills, few parts were occupied intensively or continuously, even though farming under these conditions was often wasteful. However, there was some local damage and serious erosion even before the Israelite invasion. Kirjath Sepher, later known as Debit, was a city in the Judaean hills; it is now known that the forest and scrub had been destroyed by about 2200 B.C., for the first Amorite city was built on the bare rocks of the eroded hillsides.

Throughout this time the wild fauna was probably less affected than in most nearby lands. These wars, often with heavy losses and, later, with several successive periods of deportation and scattering, kept the population far below the potential. Even under Greek and then Roman rule Palestine continued to be a disturbed area until well into the Christian era. This argument is from history and, if it is correct, we can assume that much of the natural vegetation remained untouched, or at least not severely damaged, and provided a sanctuary for wild animals.[1]

With such a small population the land was not under pressure, and flocks and herds could be led over wide areas to find pasturage and other feeding, but they were limited in numbers and always controlled and protected, against both beasts of prey and raiders from surrounding nations, and some frontier areas were too dangerous to be used. Under such conditions the hillside soil remained stable and safe, with little serious erosion. Some of the naturally rare animals had suffered but there

[1] Since this section was drafted I have read a passage in Bodenheimer's *Animal and Man in Bible Lands* that I had not noted previously, quoting from Taylor (1946): 'Early pilgrim reports and study of soil levels confirm that there prevailed in Palestine well-balanced soil conditions and good agricultural practices from very early times, going on during Roman and Byzantine times up to the Moslem conquest, and perhaps somewhat later. Then came the great increase in numbers of goats, the Bedawi invasion and Moslem civil war, when the terraces broke down and vast quantities of earth were washed down from the hills and were spread by the *wadis* over the plains.' The approach is different but the conclusion is very similar to mine.

was probably little change in the basic flora and fauna from the days of the Judges until towards the time of the Crusades. The wild life which the Bible writers, from Moses onwards, knew was richer and much more prolific than what is there today, and though it is true that by NT times more people lived in towns, Palestine remained an agricultural country and the fauna still came quite close to the everyday lives of the ordinary people.

The real deterioration began after the Crusades, and before the nineteenth century ended it seems that more damage had been done than in all the preceding centuries. It is hard to suggest a precise time for its beginning but, as is explained below, the whole process became a vicious circle. The damage from which Palestine and many other Mediterranean countries have suffered had three main immediate causes, all related and all man-made:

1. Livestock, especially goats, were allowed to range uncontrolled, destroying plants of all kinds and exposing the steep hillsides to erosion by the fierce winter storms. This lack of control continues in many Arab countries today and there is heavy over-stocking locally. In places along the Israel–Jordan frontier, as seen from the Jerusalem–Tel Aviv road in 1960, the green spring vegetation on the west side, where goats must now always be tethered, was in marked contrast to the brown on the east. In this respect the goat is far worse than other livestock, for it takes woody plants by preference. Serious efforts are now being made in Jordan to limit or even eliminate roaming goats, but this affects ancient rights and the problem is a very difficult one.

2. As soil deteriorated, whatever its situation, the unit yield dropped, forcing farmers to bring larger and larger areas into cultivation, gradually working up the steep slopes as lower ground became exhausted. This can be reasonably safe when conservative methods of farming are used; otherwise the usual result is progressive erosion. The abuse of the hillsides in Upper Galilee helped to fill much of the Huleh Valley with silt and create extensive marshes. It seems that the Phoenicians were the first people to cultivate steep slopes – in present-day Lebanon – and so create the problem of hill erosion, which they countered by contour-working and building stone retaining walls. This was in the second millennium B.C. but the principle was not generally understood and most of the terraces were later destroyed.

3. Many trees, both within and outside the farmed areas, were cut for firewood and charcoal, thus leaving the soil more open to the storms and also destroying the root systems which helped to bind the soil. During one period of Turkish rule a tree tax was imposed as a means of taking

further tribute from the Arabs – who retaliated by cutting down some of the trees! The disappearance of trees and shrubs sometimes caused a fuel shortage; this further resulted in the drying and burning of dung that would have been far more valuable dug into the soil.

In such comparatively hot lands, where the rain falls mostly in sharp storms in winter and spring when the ground has least cover, damage is done which will astonish folk from temperate lands such as Britain and some parts of the U.S.A.

The twentieth century has introduced several new factors, some favourable and some very dangerous, which complicate the present position and may cause further changes. These are:

1. Until the invention of accurate rifles, hunters could hardly get within range of the larger desert animals and their more primitive methods had little effect on numbers, but rifles on their own did only limited damage in some regions, though this became serious enough. The danger point was quickly reached when fast motor transport let soldiers and oil-rich sheikhs wander freely over the desert, and within a few years the Desert Oryx was high on the world list of threatened species, and the Palestine and Dorcas Gazelles seriously reduced in numbers and range.

2. The creation of the State of Israel attracted zoologists and naturalists from European countries with a long tradition of wild life conservation and study. This conception was quite new to a part of the world where even human life was lightly thought of and wild animals, large and small, were just something that Allah had provided for men to eat – and would go on providing! This disregard for wild life generally has added markedly to the other damage the fauna has suffered in recent centuries. In contrast, the setting aside of Nature Reserves and sanctuaries, under the administration of a keen scientist naturalist, has now made Israel an area where animal life is less harassed than it had been for a long time; while the gazelles are safe again, this has come too late to help the Desert Oryx, of which the nearest survivors now are well over 1,000 miles away, in southern Arabia. Even recent immigrants do not seem to look on every small bird as something to be trapped and eaten, as it is in most lands around the Mediterranean. It is good to record that in the neighbouring Kingdom of Jordan the Azraq Desert National Park has been royally proclaimed and will soon be fully established.

3. The extensive tree-planting programmes, in forests and shelter-belts as well as in huge fruit orchards, and the irrigation of marginal and desert land have created new habitats which some species, especially birds, have

found much more to their liking and their numbers have leapt up. For instance, the Palm Dove, a largely African bird, has colonized towns and villages until it has become a nuisance. The African Bulbul has also come from the south to live in gardens and orchards; like many 'soft-billed' birds it is useful to man when it catches insects to feed its young, but later in the season it does so much damage to ripening fruit that it is a pest. Between the wars large areas of poor hillsides were afforested, and since World War II many hundreds of miles of roadside have been planted with double rows of eucalypts.

4. Many different land reclamation and improvement schemes have been started since the beginning of the Mandate. More-or-less bare hillsides are being rehabilitated by terracing and the establishment of cover plants. Sand dunes are being 'fixed' and colonized with suitable vegetation, so producing new acreage as well as stopping further damage to leeward. Sometimes the original cover will be restored; sometimes the final crop will be a different one, and more useful to man; almost everywhere it should be a better home for animals than what it replaces. The drainage of marshes has resulted in a massive change of land usage that is not so favourable to wild life. In the Huleh Valley, for example, some 6,000 acres were drained to form highly productive arable land, ringed with a network of fish ponds where the passing water is put to work, and with 400 acres of marsh and open water set aside as a Nature Reserve. The whole area is still a resting-place for passing migrants, especially White Storks and Pelicans; it is no longer such a refuge for larger wild animals or for the great flocks of water birds that once lived there, though the Reserve provides a home for many of them. One useful side effect is that by draining these Huleh marshes evaporation has been reduced and enough water saved to irrigate a further 20,000 acres.

All the operations described in (3) and (4) are done for man's benefit, whether improvement (of the desert) or reclamation (of the eroded slopes); it is good that with the exception of the drainage schemes the result is also helpful to the fauna, especially birds. But history has a warning to give; all these projects call for technical skill and continued hard work in maintaining the position. The margin is a narrow one, as witness the dust-bowls and 'bad lands' in the U.S.A. and elsewhere, and the collapse of civilizations based on the artificial farm lands of Mesopotamia and N. Africa.

5. To set against these two largely beneficial factors is a sinister one that adds point to the above warning. Intensive arable farming, often on a large scale in the reclaimed marshes, has encouraged serious plagues of rodents, especially voles, and these have often been attacked by such

permanent poisons as thallium sulphate. The dead and dying voles have been taken by small birds and beasts of prey; these in turn have died, to be eaten with equally fatal results by jackals, hyenas, vultures and other scavengers. This danger was soon spotted by the naturalists, but the scientists on pest control were hard to convince and the breeding population of the species worst hit was soon down to 10 per cent. Even worse, many of the numerous migrant birds of prey were either killed or permanently affected. Years of protection will be needed to restore the position, for these larger Raptores are slow breeders at the best of times. A similar chain of damage has also been started by the use of the durable insecticides about which there was such a storm in America and Europe in the early 1960s.

6. Lastly, man has affected the fauna of Palestine by the introduction of animals and plants from other lands. The plants include all crops, trees and garden flowers, even though some may have been bred from wild native plants. The animals include all livestock, which can have an impact far more damaging than the wild native ancestor. However, these two groups are an integral part of farming and this has been discussed already. Weeds are described as plants growing where they are not wanted. Some come in by accident; others are introduced species that have found a suitable niche and got out of control, sometimes with disastrous results, such as Lantana in India and prickly pear in Australia. Both these are used in Palestine for hedge-making, so far without trouble, but in certain conditions they can form vast, almost impenetrable thickets useless to most animal life.

The introduction of exotic animals has been on a much more limited scale than in many temperate countries, where such species as the rabbit and musk rat have become serious pests. There have been a few gate-crashers travelling in ships, such as the plague-carrying Black Rat from the East, but most animals taken into Palestine were for strictly practical purposes; their new land was a hard one, with few comforts and many enemies, so it is not surprising that none has become a problem. (Insect pests of farm and orchard crops are outside this discussion.) Only two species need mention as escapees. The coypu is a large aquatic rodent kept on fur farms; a few have escaped and are living around the fish farms, feeding on reeds and other plants and doing no damage, and because it is large and edible it is worth catching. The carp is a cultured form that has been kept for centuries in the fish-ponds of Europe and Asia (see Chap. XVII) and is now the main species reared in artificial ponds for the Jewish market. Some find their way into the Jordan and its carriers, where they may be caught by rod-and-line anglers; a few reach the lake of Galilee where they may grow large before being caught in nets. The carp fills a man-made niche; it is not predatory and it is not likely to affect adversely either other species of fish or animals of other classes. As with the coypu, control should never be difficult.

These varied and complex factors have been described in some detail for they all combine to produce the modified and impoverished fauna that a visitor to the Holy Land sees today. The birds, especially the small migrants, have probably changed least of all and they perhaps have an easier passage than ever before. The larger mammals are down to a tiny remnant, seen at present only by the energetic enthusiast, but in places responding to protection. Livestock continue to be the most conspicuous animals, but even here a major change is taking place in the 1960s. Intensive, highly efficient animal husbandry is beginning to put cattle, sheep and even chickens more or less permanently into stalls or under cover, which is where the Friesian herds of the large desert oases in Israel are already being kept. Draught animals, too, are decreasing. The tractor is taking over for pulling the plough and farm cart, and even Bedouins are moving tent in ex W.D. Lorries instead of on camel back! It will be a long time before the donkey retires altogether but its life should become a bit easier, for the light motor-cycle is proving ideal for personal transport around the desert edge.

III

The Cattle upon a Thousand Hills

The phenomenon of domestication. The prime importance of the ruminant animals. Goats, sheep and cattle, their origin and development; their importance in Hebrew economy and religion. The humane content of the Mosaic Law.

THIS CHAPTER IS CONCERNED WITH THE IMPORTANT DOMESTIC ANIMALS that for thousands of years have been man's chief providers of protein food and a wealth of other products. The twentieth century has seen great changes resulting from the invention of artificial materials and their replacement of leather and wool for many purposes, but no substitute for meat has yet been found acceptable by most people, and milk with its many derivatives is still in universal demand. Factories and quarries now supply much of the nitrates and phosphates needed to grow our crops, a job largely done until last century by sheep and cattle, which still play a valuable rôle in maintaining soil fertility in many parts of the world – including Britain – and their droppings will never be completely replaced by artificial manures.

The taming of these animals is a striking fulfilment of the prophetic command to man, 'Have dominion over the fish of the sea, and over the fowl of the air, and over every living thing that moveth upon the earth' (Gen. 1:28). Over the course of years man has brought into a domesticated state a wide range of animals, including insects, fish, birds and above all, mammals. 'For every kind of beasts and of birds and of serpents (creeping things) and of things in the sea is tamed and hath been tamed of mankind' (Jas. 3:7). Many that have been brought into the service of man have in turn become largely dependent upon him, if only because he has gradually developed them into extreme forms, useful or pleasing to him, that cannot survive on their own.

The whole problem of domestication is fascinating and can only be

41

hinted at here. The late Dr. Zeuner, who was both archaeologist and zoologist, made a lifetime study of it: his writings, not all of them highly technical, cover nearly all the animals that man has enlisted over the years and pay special attention to their early history, as far as it can be discovered.

It is essential to stress that domestication does not just mean taming. Every year all over the world various wild animals are hand-reared and become tame – but only as individuals. With most of these the margin between tame and wild is a narrow one. Few remain docile all their lives; most either are released to revert to the wild or else end their days in zoos neither fully tame nor fully wild. Domestication occurs when a whole species, or part of one, becomes permanently amenable, resulting from a change of temperament in the whole unit, when man is accepted as the new leader of the group who must be obeyed. What greater contrast could there be than between the true wild ox of Chap. V and an Ayrshire cow quietly making her own way to the milking byre? Or, at the other end of the scale, between a wild brown rat, which is reckoned one of the most unpleasant and intractable creatures, and a tame hooded rat, derived directly from it only about a century ago, that is perhaps the most reliable and easily handled of all rodent pets?

The ability of man to have dominion over his environment, often only to destroy it, was discussed in Chap. II, but in his efforts at domestication he is not entirely unique. Throughout the animal world one finds examples of what is called symbiosis – living together. The sponge that is found only on the shell of a crab; the coral fish which makes its home around the deadly tentacles of the giant sea anemone; and the parasitic cuckoo that leaves other birds to incubate its eggs and rear its young. The latter is a one-sided affair; the others are more mutual arrangements though one cannot attribute intentions to either side. If we turn to the ants, which are insects with senses utterly different from our own and with little capacity for learning, we find a complex social organization which includes using aphids as 'cattle', some of them even confined in underground pens. We find colonies where other nearly related ants are enslaved and kept to produce food, the nearest approach to the notion of oxen ploughing our fields.

Even so, this cannot properly be compared with the domestication by man of cloven-hoofed animals, for these were really the foundations on which civilizations were built. Until the extra labour from beasts of burden was available, as described in the next chapter, and the production of meat and milk guaranteed, his time was fully occupied in surviving and his capacity to develop systems of government was limited. It is notable that many of the backward peoples today live in places where, for a variety of reasons, keeping domestic stock on any scale has never been possible, and that slave-raiding and -keeping was typical of such areas.

The origin of each of these animals will be discussed as far as we have evidence and its development studied, but there is one great unanswered question that must be mentioned briefly here. The animals really important for production and labour were enlisted during the Stone and Bronze Ages. How did these men do it? Using only their primitive tools and working in country where large beasts of prey were still active, how did they obtain control over these intractable animals and then keep them until they were docile enough for use, perhaps generations later? In how many places did some native genius see the possible advantage to be obtained from such prodigious labours? All this took place before the peoples concerned had any written records, nor do the various cave paintings tell us much. The tools provided by modern science are helping scientists to answer such questions as when? and what? but they cannot dig up evidence to settle the much more difficult questions why? and how?

Few animals have been added to the list in the past thousand years, most of them small and none comparable to the basic food producers; perhaps the most important are the turkey and rabbit for their food, and the rat, golden hamster and budgerigar as laboratory animals and pets. The fact remains that the animals on which man's welfare has depended entered his service before or at the dawn of civilization. Long before the end of Genesis they were all hard at work.

Goat, sheep and ox are all described as cloven-hoofed ruminants, which were the only mammals allowed for food under the Mosaic Law. In addition there were their wild relatives, the antelopes, gazelles and deer. Their cloven hoof is easily described, for the basic five digits of the foot have been reduced and only two functional ones are left; these end in hoofs and the animals are, in effect, walking on two toes of each foot. This horny hoof makes ideal 'footwear' on rocky and hard ground for it is springy, hard-wearing and always growing; so much so that if a zoo animal does not get enough exercise the hoof may over-grow until it looks like a wooden shoe and has to be trimmed back.

Chewing the cud is a complicated matter. The bulky vegetation on which ruminants feed is not very nutritious; they must work over a large volume and if this were chewed and swallowed normally they would perhaps be exposed to danger for long periods. Further, ordinary methods of digestion do not give the maximum yield from such herbage. Chewing the cud solves both problems. A mass of grass, leaves, etc., is swallowed after little chewing and stored in the paunch or rumen; this is the largest of the four stomach compartments. Once this is full the ruminant goes to a safe place and, after a short while, starts chewing again. A ball of moist greenstuff is sent back to the mouth, masticated well for perhaps a minute and again swallowed, this time to be passed slowly through the second and third to the last compartment, where many digestive juices are added and the greatest chemical breakdown takes place. This goes on until all has been processed. Meanwhile the rich bacterial content of the stomach is at work: by the time the finely ground mixture reaches the intestines the food content is ready for absorption and only hard fibres and waste products pass right through; the latter with the urine, containing the nitrogen and other chemicals, provide food for plants.

Pigs and hippos are related to this important group and are cloven-hoofed but do not chew the cud, whereas the camels, which are without hoofed feet, have a modified form of chewing the cud. The subjects of this chapter and their relations are regarded as the true ruminants and will be referred to as such.

Goat

The goat is taken first for it is generally accepted as the first of this group to be domesticated; probably it came second only to the dog, whose beginnings go back much further still. The tame goat is known as *Capra hircus*, a name that is not very meaningful for there are now many breeds that vary widely in colour, size and some anatomical features, as well as in type of hair, and it is reckoned that it had several wild ancestors, of which the main one is thought to be *C. aegagrus*, the Bezoar or Cretan wild goat. Some zoologists differ and give the name *C. hircus* to both wild and tame forms. The overall range of the bezoar is still from India to Crete but its numbers are everywhere reduced, and it has disappeared completely from many areas and elsewhere it is so rare as to be in danger. A few survive in the mountains of Crete and also in the island of Antimilos in the Cyclades. It is reddish brown in summer and grey brown in winter. The distribution of other wild goats farther to the north-east has been modified by man but it seems likely that some of them have interbred with the main stock. These do not include the Nubian Ibex, the wild goat of the Bible which is still found in Palestine; this has never been domestica-ted. All these goats are hill animals, sure-footed and able to live in rugged country. By choice they are browsers rather than grazers.

Two factors add to the difficulty of tracing the early history of the goat. Firstly, the goat has always been virile and rather independent, and for a long time the tame form did not differ markedly from the wild. Secondly, although skeletons complete with head and horns are easy enough to name, in some cases even experts cannot distinguish the long bones of sheep and goats. The earliest accepted evidence for domestication of the goat is from the New Stone Age pre-pottery levels of Jericho; carbon gives a reading of 6000–7000 B.C. Some of the finds show horn damage suggesting that they had been confined. Material from N. Mesopotamia is of about the same period and if both are truly domesticated forms they may suggest a rather earlier common origin. Among the early goats two types are already recognizable – with corkscrew and with scimitar horns, both of which are seen today. As mutations occurred, in type of hair, head and ear shapes, etc., they were fixed and recombined by careful breeding. Goats with long pendent ears are illustrated as early as about 2000 B.C. in Mesopotamia. However, these varieties were few compared to the wide range of breeds which are of modern origin, with the large ones weighing perhaps three or four times as much as the dwarf types.

Colour varieties are known from the earliest illustrations in Egypt and elsewhere; the only clear Scriptural mention of colour pattern is in Gen. 30 – the spotted and speckled goats that Jacob bred – but the Heb. word for flock (*tson*) applies to both sheep and goats, and the 'brown of the flock' of v. 40 could include goats. Today, they are in black, grey, brown and white and a range of patterns and mixtures.

It is likely that goats were first kept as milk-producers. The meat of an adult, especially of the male, is tough and strong-smelling, but the kid is very edible and this was the standard meal prepared for a stranger or, in fact, for any small feast, e.g., 'Gideon went in and made ready a kid' (Judg. 6:19). Lambs were mostly kept until well grown, while the fatted calf on which the elder brother commented bitterly in Luke 15:30 was reserved for bigger occasions, partly because of cost and size, and was rated highly. A goat skin became the standard water-bottle in countries where this had to be carried and it was the only container suitable for travellers. The larger and heavier jars were used for storage and for carrying over short distances only. To make one of these bottles the skin was removed in one piece after cutting off head and legs. The neck served as the mouth, and the other holes were sewn up before the whole was filled with tanning liquid until the skin was cured and set in the right shape. The hair was left on the outside to serve as padding. These containers were used for milk and also wine from early times; wine bottles feature in one of our Lord's parables (Mark 2:22). Skin bottles stayed in regular use until tins and then Jerry-cans from World War II began to replace them.

All kinds of skins were prepared and then made into simple clothes, e.g., 'they wandered about in sheepskins and goatskins' (Heb. 11:37). Tanning is an ancient craft but it is hard to find a definite record before *c.* 1500 B.C. in Egypt and we do not know when roughly treated hides were replaced by dressed leather. There are only two direct mentions of leather – II Kings 1:8 and Matt. 3:4 speak of Elisha and John the Baptist wearing leathern girdles. The rams' skins dyed red that were used for the Tabernacle are tr. 'tanned rams' skins' (RSV), which is probably more accurate, for they would be coloured by the use of some tanning materials of plant origin. Heavy leather was used for shields which seem to have been treated with oil either to make them glisten or to preserve them. Tanning was presumably an unclean trade and had to be practised outside the town; Paul stayed with Simon a tanner 'by the sea side' (Acts 10:32, etc.). As early as *c.* 1288 B.C. in Egypt goat and sheep-skins were made into writing parchments: a manuscript of Isaiah dated *c.* 150 B.C. is on this material, which was in wide use by NT times and Paul asked Timothy to bring his books and 'especially the parchments' (II Tim. 4:13). Goat's hair was woven into cloth and also used for stuffing pillows – 'a pillow of goat's hair for his bolster' (I Sam. 19:13).

In addition to the common cloth made into tents and warm rough cloaks for the shepherds in winter, the goat's hair was also woven by the women into a special fabric for the covering over the Tabernacle (Exod. 26:7). The setting of scarlet and fine linen for these furnishings may suggest a cloth of greater quality, perhaps comparable to that of Cashmere goats today. Long-haired races from farther east became widely distributed and it is obvious from the account of Jacob's manipulation of Laban's flocks (Gen. 30) that something was known about breeding for special qualities.

The sheep came on the scene fairly soon after the goat; its meat was better at all ages, with plenty of fat, and its soft wool was preferred to the coarse goat's hair, so the sheep began to replace it wherever the ground was suitable, i.e., where it had good grazing. The goat was still valued for its rich milk, and continues to be, but when the cow arrived the milk from this proved even better and then the goat was pushed back into the drier and rougher areas where the grazing sheep would not thrive. By the time of the Patriarchs sheep and cattle probably outnumbered goats, but the use of *tson* for small cattle makes this uncertain. Milk is mentioned more than forty times in OT, only four times referring specifically to goat's milk, 'Thou shalt have goat's milk enough for thy food' (Prov. 27:27). The prohibition against seething a kid in its mother's milk is found three times (Exod. 23:19, etc.) and it was imposed because this was a Canaanite fertility custom. This precept has been taken to extremes by some ortho-dox Jews today, for whom milk and meat must be cooked in separate pans and served at different meals. This contrasts with Abraham's custom as recorded in Gen. 18:8, 'He took butter and milk and the calf which he had dressed . . . and they did eat.'

When man domesticated the goat he recruited an assistant second only to himself in destructive powers, as already explained in Chap. II. The goat is hardy and well able to fend for itself, and if several are released they can soon form a feral race. Sometimes goats have been liberated on uninhabited islands to provide a supply of fresh food for passing sealers and whalers, but the final result may be the destruction of all the plants and the death of the herd. This is because the constant browsing kills the ground cover and causes severe erosion. Goats will even climb trees to get at leaves and twigs, as we found them doing in Arab areas in N. Israel and as is illustra-ted in ancient art. This fondness for the shrubs whose roots keep the hillsides stable is seen when a shepherd leads his mixed flock on the hill-side; the sheep concentrate on the patches of grass while the goats range a little higher up the hill, among the rocks, reaching for the tender shoots and leaves of trees and shrubs.

The many references and the range of Heb. names are some proof of the goat's importance in OT times, and these words will now be examined. The basic word for goat is 'ez, with pl. 'izzim, which is rendered 'goat' or 'she-goat' sixty times. This is the word normally used in non-ritual passages but it is occasionally given to sacrificial animals, especially the sin offering, where it cannot be differentiated from the other common word sa'ir, which means 'hairy one'; though this might be assumed to mean an adult, it is most often translated kid. With its fem. form se'irah this is about as common as 'ez. With the single exception of its first mention in Gen. 37:31, where it is the goat whose blood was put on Joseph's robe, it is used only for the sin-offering and scapegoat. (The word sa'ir, mostly as plural se'irim, is also used in another sense and translated satyr; this is discussed below.)

Another common word is 'attud, tr. he-goat, goat and ram. This really refers to the leader which each flock has – and by derivation 'chief one', as in Isa. 14:9. This is most often used for the peace-offerings made by the various families after the completion of the Tabernacle. Most other mentions of 'attud are in sacrificial contexts. Tayish is also the he-goat, found only four times in literal and proverbial verses, and likely to be a nickname, for it may mean 'the butter'. The common Arabic word for goat is from this root. Tsaphir is a late word, probably Aram., for he-goat; it is used three times for the sin-offering and four times as a symbol of the Greek empire in Daniel 8; gedi is a kid, probably of up to only a few months old and therefore too young for general sacrifices; however, it features once as a special burnt offering (Judg. 13:19). Apart from the prophetic passage in Isa. 11:6, 'the leopard shall lie down with the kid', it is used only literally, especially for the kid prepared for the stranger's meal. It gives the name to En Gedi – the Spring of the Kid – but in this case the kid of the Nubian Ibex is meant.

The three Gr. words occur too rarely to merit much comment; they are tragos the he-goat, which in Heb. 9 and 10 refers to the sin-offering; eriphion, young kid, and eriphos, kid.

The collective names tson, the flock, and seh, a member of it, are best tr. small cattle, for they may apply equally to sheep or goats or a mixed flock. The context often helps. (See under 'sheep' for further discussion.) Another collective name, 'eder, translated flock, drove or herd, refers mostly to sheep but sometimes to goats, e.g., 'a flock of goats' (Cant. 4:1).

Our English words today have just the same meaning as in AV. The sexes are properly called he-goat and she-goat, but billy and nanny are often heard. The young is known only as a kid.

Both sheep and cattle had an even greater variety of Heb. names; they are mentioned more often and obviously were kept in greater numbers, especially the sheep; goats are only once spoken of in terms of thousands. 'The Arabians brought . . . 7,700 he-goats' (II Chron. 17:11). One of the very rare metaphorical passages is Matt. 25:32, and to most Westerners this separation would present no difficulties, for our sheep and goats are quite different and seldom run in mixed flocks. This is not so in Palestine, where the Arabs still keep the two together and where the local breeds may be alike in both colour and general shape. They provide no problem to the owner or herd-boy, but the outsider looks for the usually upturned tail of the goat. The symbolic reference in Daniel 8 has been noted. Apart from that the goat has little figurative significance, in marked contrast to the sheep; some 70 per cent of the words, even in the Prophets, are in the context of sacrifice, and to the Hebrews this must have become the goat's main purpose.

The Heb. *sa'ir* is found in four verses where it cannot possibly be tr. goat. It is rendered satyr in Isa. 13:21; 34:14; and devil in Lev. 17:7 and II Chron. 11:15. It is generally thought that these represent the heathen woodland spirits that the people pictured as half-man, half-goat. Some commentators regard them as related to Egyptian deities which the Hebrews must have known and it is never suggested seriously that they were wild animals.

Sheep

The origin and early history of the sheep, known as *Ovis aries*, is complex and disputed. Many different views have been expressed over many years and once it was generally thought that the wild ancestor of the sheep had long since become extinct; some authorities still hold this view and give the above technical name also to this supposed ancestor. This whole subject was examined in great detail by the late Dr. Zeuner, and his work is unlikely to be superseded unless some entirely new material is unearthed, whether actual remains or written records or illustrations, or some radically new method of assessing data is found.

While it is thought that several wild sheep have contributed to the stock it seems that two species are the main ancestors, of which the Urial, *O. orientalis*, is the more important; this is a central and W. Asiatic species, with many local races, which is now found in mountainous regions from Tibet right across to Transcaspia, but there were once lowland races which have been killed out. This is a large sheep; the adult stands nearly 3ft. at the shoulder and the rams have strongly wrinkled horns curled in typical ammon shape at the sides of the head. As in other members of its family, its coat has seasonal changes of colour, from reddish in summer, with whitish underparts, to greyish brown in winter. All forms have been heavily hunted and it is generally rare over its wide range.

The other main ancestor is the Mouflon, now found in two groups, the one in Sardinia and Corsica, the other in Asia Minor. It stands a little over

THOUGH FIRST PRACTISED by the Phoenicians, terrace-working had been forgotten for some 3,000 years. The lower half of this hillside west of Jerusalem has been terraced and the rest protected by tree-planting (p. 36).

EUCALYPTS PLANTED along hundreds of miles of roads give valuable shade and shelter, especially in the open wind-swept plains between Beersheba and Askelon. Sheep graze in the middle distance (p. 37).

EN GEDI, alongside the Dead Sea, has a desert climate. The lush crops of maize and alfalfa, for the herd of Friesian cattle, are the result of irrigating with water from the spring that David once used (pp. 24, 37).

THE BARLEY HARVEST in the northern Negev is over by mid-April and the long stubbles are then grazed by domestic stock. A Bedouin woman, her loose clothes blown by the constant wind, follows her fat-tailed sheep (p. 49).

2 ft. at the shoulder and is the smallest wild sheep; in summer it is dark reddish brown and in winter the adult rams have white or cream side-patches.

The earliest known evidence of domestic sheep comes from the famous Belt cave in northern Iran which is quite close to the hills where the Urial is found; this is around the time of the New Stone Age pottery of about 5000 B.C. Within a few centuries the sheep were being herded, probably with the aid of dogs, and breeding under control had begun. Turkestan is suggested as a possible starting-point. By 2000 B.C. five breeds had reached Mesopotamia, differing in horn type, coat and tail and also in size. About this time also the wool sheep with the coiled horns reached Egypt and began to replace earlier types. Thus Abram would have known several different breeds before he went to Canaan and they should have been familiar to the Hebrews in captivity. From then on sheep spread rapidly and widely, their movements – always organized by man – presenting a complex puzzle for the archaeologists to work out. More and more intermingling took place until few breeds could be said to have a single origin.

Perhaps the greatest difficulty is that most breeds now differ so widely from any living wild form, which is the main reason for regarding them as descended from a lost wild stock. These differences began to appear early and the most obvious are:

1. *WOOL.* Contrary to what is often reported wool is present in wild sheep as an undercoat and it is most apparent in winter, when it may cover the stiffer hairs; this is a factor in the colour changes mentioned above. The valuable felting and weaving properties of wool, in which it is far superior to hair, were quickly recognized and strains were bred to yield good wool in large amounts. Skill in the animal breeding field developed early in man's history. Breeds of sheep are still found in which stiff hairs make up the greater part of the coat, especially in the tropics.

2. *TAIL.* A number of changes have taken place in the tail and some breeds now have tails with two or three times as many vertebrae as any wild species, a character which is considered a disadvantage among Western sheep breeders. In others the tail has become an organ for storing reserves of fat, serving as the hump in camels. This strange feature had developed long before Abram went to Canaan and it is found in Egyptian mummies of c. 2000 B.C. This was a characteristic of at least one breed kept in Palestine, and the Heb. *'alyah* (tr. 'rump' AV, and 'fat tail' RV and RSV), refers to it.

3. *COLOUR.* Western man is so used to seeing white sheep that any other colour seems odd or an unfortunate throw-back. The first sheep were

D

probably brown, like their wild ancestors, but early remains can tell us nothing about colour and we must depend on pictures and descriptions. Before 2000 B.C. there were white, brown and black forms in Egypt, possibly much earlier than that. It is traditional to regard Biblical sheep as white, and while this was perhaps mainly true, it is not entirely supported by the text. The well-known promise of Isa. 1:18, 'They shall be as wool', was made late in Israel's history, while the phrase 'white wool' of Ezek. 27:18 is in a context suggesting wealth, and it cannot be assumed from either that wool was always white. It is obvious from Gen. 30:32, ff., that both sheep and goats were in various colours, presumably including white, but the term spotted is also shown to mean white spots on dark animals. It is often taken for granted that animals for Hebrew sacrifices had to be white, without spot, yet Heb. *tamim* (tr. 'without spot' AV in Num. 28:3, etc.), is elsewhere rendered 'without blemish' and is so throughout RV and RSV. This seems to refer to imperfections generally and not necessarily, or perhaps not at all, to colour markings. The prohibition of mutilated animals may confirm this.

From being largely an animal of the mountain pastures the sheep has now developed into a series of breeds able to thrive on almost any type of ground from the Romney marshes of Kent to the bleak uplands of the Falkland Islands or the dry steppes of Australia, but these are modern developments. The Hebrew sheep were fairly demanding and their need for pasture is suggested by passages such as I Chron. 4:39–40: 'to seek pasture for their flocks, and found fat pastures and good, and the land was wide and quiet and peaceable'. The erratic winter rains in the south of Palestine made the grass grow in patches and shepherds, with local knowledge and long experience, led their flocks to take advantage of this. David, writing as a shepherd himself, could say in Ps. 23:2, 'He maketh me to lie down in green pastures.' Most sheep in Palestine today seem to be of the Awassi fat-tailed breed, obtained by improving and selecting from local sheep. This thrives on the dry stubbles left after barley has been harvested in April; when this has been eaten off the Bedouin wander around the edge of the desert to find pasture, and they may be compelled to take their flocks north into the populated areas to graze on odd patches of fallow and the grass verges of roads. The same breed lives in greener country on the central plains where irrigation provides good grazing all the year round.

It is generally agreed that sheep were first domesticated for their meat and fat, the latter soon becoming much valued. As a ruminant the sheep was clean meat and it became important in the Hebrew diet, though as time went on this was largely in connexion with its use in sacrifices, and otherwise sheep were killed only on special occasions. Even so, it was their most common meat. The idea of cattle as wealth was already developing and it seems likely that the livestock could have been run much more efficiently, e.g., by culling all excess males by the time they have reached full size, as is done in the West today. This attitude to cattle is still prevalent in the Middle East and Africa, and it results in much loss of potential food. The large numbers of rams such as are listed among the presents brought by the Arabians – '7,700 rams and 7,700 he-goats' (II Chron. 17:11) – would be unlikely today when adult rams would be retained in the ratio of not more than about one to twenty ewes for breeding purposes. These rams were used for wool production, but the same volume could have come from flocks with a quicker turnover.

Wool became a commodity of great value and for a long time it was the most useful and easily available fibre. Weaving had begun with various plant fibres and then possibly wool shed by wild animals or taken from those killed in the hunting-field. Linen, made from flax, was still a luxury; cotton was known in the ancient civilizations but was always scarce, while silk cost something like its weight in gold. Wool production thus became important, especially in the colder climates, and several passages show that sheep-shearing was regarded as a festival, as it is today in the great wool areas of Australia. The first biblical mention of shearing is in Gen. 31:19, when Jacob took the opportunity of slipping away with his wives and cattle as his uncle Laban was busy supervising the work. Centuries later, when David was a fugitive in the north of Israel, the shearing feast which his men visited on Carmel was obviously on a grand scale. Another sheep-shearing that led to trouble was organized by Absalom (II Sam. 13:23).

The shearing-house of II Kings 10:12, 14 (AV) is an unlikely rendering, for the impression generally given is that sheep were shorn out-of-doors. Other suggested tr. are 'binding-house of the shepherds' or 'marking-house', which could hardly refer to marking sheep as we know it today.

Selective breeding of sheep had produced types for a variety of purposes long before the Israelites entered Canaan, and their wool was of different grades, though we can find no specific reference to this. A great wool trade was built up and part of the annual tribute paid by Mesha King of Moab, described as a sheep-master, was the wool of 100,000 rams (II Kings 3:4). Modern fleeces weigh anything from 3 lb. to over 30, according to breed and living conditions. These Moabite sheep would probably not have averaged more than 2 or 3 lb.; even so, this amounts to about 100 tons of raw wool a year! Among the Mosaic rules designed to teach the need for national separation was the ban on using a mixture of linen and wool (Lev. 19:19). In contrast to many of these laws it is hard to see any practical purpose in it.

The use of animal skins for clothing was general long before the goat was domesticated, and then increased greatly: skins taken from animals killed under control were obviously of better quality than those trapped or taken in the hunt. These skins were no doubt used for clothing after woven material came into general use but, as discussed above, they are only mentioned, with goatskins, as being worn by humble folk. However, there was one special use for rams' skins dyed or tanned red; they were sewn together to form the inner covering for the Tabernacle and this is mentioned a number of times, beginning with Exod 25:5, where they were among the items in the freewill offerings requested by Moses. Only one other verse calls for comment. The skin of any burnt offering, which could be sheep or goat, was to be the property of the officiating priest (Lev. 7:8).

It is suggested by some experts that the milk of the sheep was a more important part of the Hebrew diet than its meat and that it was rated more valuable than the fleece. This could be so, for milk would be yielded over a long period, but there is little direct biblical evidence for this. Ewe's milk, which is certainly rich, is mentioned specifically only once in Deut. 32:14: 'Butter of kine and milk of sheep.' This milk is especially good for sour curds but goat's milk makes better butter. The Awassi breed is now widely used for cheese production, for which it is kept in the most modern conditions, with machine milking.

The first mention of horn is in Gen. 22:13: 'a ram caught by his horns'. Then the word is used most often in figurative passages or for ornamental features but it also refers several times to the actual horns used for two separate purposes. First as a container, especially for oil, e.g., 'Fill thine horn with oil' (I Sam. 16:1). Second, as a musical instrument; Heb. *qeren* (horn) is sometimes used, e.g., Josh. 6:5, 'a long blast with the ram's horn'. The previous verse has 'The priests shall bear seven trumpets (*shophar*) of ram's horns' and it seems that the trumpet, used some seventy times, is often actually of horn. However, as early as Num. 10:2, referring to the start of the Exodus, trumpets were being made of metal and this development continued.

Apart from the above no direct mention can be found of tools, weapons, etc., made from bones and horns but archaeological material is rich in such objects, and it is obvious that until metals became freely available bone was important for making a range of domestic articles such as needles and scrapers, and also for harpoon and lance heads. Adult sheep and goats were probably the most important source but even birds' bones were used for special purposes; e.g., the hollow shank bones of cranes and other long-legged birds were made into cases for needles and pins.

No direct biblical reference can be found to sheep being valued for their manure, though this was recognized by some of the ancient peoples and in Egypt they were used for treading in seed as early as about 2500 B.C.

The wealth of Heb. names listed below emphasizes the sheep's central place in the economy. The Israelites were skilled shepherds and probably had several breeds suited to the different regions though only one of the names seems to confirm this. The need to go in search of grazing often took the shepherds and their flocks far from their villages and the presence of wild animals meant that protective folds had to be built in which the sheep could be penned safely at night, e.g., 'keeping watch over their flock by night' (Luke 2:8). The type of structure varied with the terrain; sometimes, especially in the hill country, natural caves could be adapted, e.g., 'to the sheepcotes by the way where was a cave' (I Sam. 24:3). In other parts boulders were built into rough walls and topped with thorny branches. Three, perhaps four, different words describe these folds, e.g., 'Build you ... folds for your sheep' (Num. 32:24). Our Lord's graphic metaphorical use of the fold and the shepherd in John 10 shows that the general method of management had not changed, and this still continues in a few country parts of the Middle East, where the sheep follow the shepherd, in contrast to Western lands, where they are driven in front of him.

Gen. 30:32–43 is an interesting passage which refers to a false theory, still widely believed even in the West, that things eaten or seen by the mother before or at birth may affect the colour, shape, etc., of the young. In this incident Jacob deliberately put a striped white pattern in front of lambing ewes, believing that this would increase the ratio of marked animals, which would be his, in lieu of wages. vv. 41, 42 explain that he studied the flock and separated the vigorous from the feeble, and the inference is that he unconsciously understood the flock genetics and mated accordingly, as he should have done after serving as flock-master for nearly twenty years. Then he wrongly attributed his success – a mistake sometimes made even today by competent scientists!

The gestation period of the sheep is about twenty-two weeks; one or two lambs are born at a time and some modern breeds average two per birth. The difficulties of breeding stock were known to the biblical writers. Job, speaking of successful men, noted that 'their bull gendereth and faileth not; their cow calveth and casteth not her calf' (Job 21:10), – i.e., the bull was fertile and the cow did not suffer from contagious abortion or other troubles that resulted in still births.

The shepherd in the parable of the lost sheep (Luke 15:4) was typical in recognizing his responsibility for a single sheep. The sheep knew his voice and he knew each by name (John 10:3, 4). It is also likely that the parable of the ewe lamb told by Nathan in II Sam. 12 was taken straight from life. It has always been the custom of shepherds in any country to hand-rear orphan lambs. So much so that there has been a special name for it in English since the Middle Ages – a cade lamb.

The sheep's Heb. names are too many for a complete analysis to be given but they are listed, with their most important settings and uses.

'attud, which is twice tr. 'ram' (AV), should be 'he-goat', as in RV and RSV.

'ayil, properly rendered 'ram' in all VSS, is the main word used for the ram of the many different sacrifices. A few occurrences are symbolic and a few literal, but the great majority are sacrificial. Four of the five mentions of the fat-tail refer to this, the other being to *keseb,* but it is likely that this is a general word for rams of all breeds.

'immerin is an Aram. pl. word used, in Ezra only, for the burnt offering at the dedication of the rebuilt temple.

kebes, 'lamb', occurs more than 100 times but is never used literally; with only five exceptions it refers to the great range of sacrifices. From this comes *kabsah,* 'ewe lamb', specified for a few sacrifices – cleansing of the leper, the Nazarite vow and sealing the Covenant. This is the ewe lamb of the parable that Nathan told David.

keseb is a transposition of *kebes* and is mostly used of sacrificial lambs but it includes the lambs bred by Jacob (Gen. 30:32).

kar, tr. 'ram' and 'lamb', is a word that probably refers to a breed clearly recognized as separate. It comes first in the Song of Moses (Deut. 32:14) contrasted with the general word *tson* 'flock' and *'ayil* 'ram'. Later it is applied solely to sheep imported from nearby lands in the dry steppe region; e.g., Moab (II Kings 3:4) and Edom (Isa. 34:6), and also from Babylon, Arabia and Bashan. The Aram. form is *dekar,* used three times in Ezra 6 and 7 for the rams given by Darius for the rededication of the temple. Both forms also denote battering rams, e.g., Ezek. 4:2, which is identical to the usage in English.

rachel is simply a ewe, for breeding, e.g., Gen. 31:38.

The collective words *tson* and *seh* are mentioned briefly under goat, for they can refer to either animal or both. Sometimes the kind is specified by attaching *'ez* 'goat' or *kebes.* These general words are, in fact, used in several key verses. The Passover lamb of Exodus 12 and 'a lamb to the slaughter' (Isa. 53:7) are both *seh,* one taken out of the flock. *tson* is found more than any other word and tr. more or less equally sheep (pl.) and flock, referring more often to sheep than to goats. This is the word in Gen. 4, 'Abel was a keeper of sheep' (v. 2), 'he also brought of the firstlings of his flock' (v. 4). It comes mostly in literal passages and is the main one used in the Prophets. As a sacrifice it is only as one out of the flock, e.g., 'A ram without blemish out of the flocks' (Lev. 5:15). The most familiar passage where it is found is 'All we like sheep have gone astray' (Isa. 53:6).

'eder is a collective word tr. 'flock' or 'herd', frequently qualified by sheep or goat.

taleh, with pl. *tela'im*, refers to young lambs, probably not yet weaned, e.g., 'He shall gather the lambs with his arm' (Isa. 40:11).

One other word – *'ul* – meaning gravid, is used, e.g., 'Ewes great with young' (Ps. 78:71). In fact the word ewe is assumed from the context; elsewhere the word is used to describe camels and cows.

In the NT four Gr. words are found far more often than those referring to any other animal – over seventy in all. *probaton* is tr. 'sheep', mostly in figurative passages. *amnos*, found only four times, refers only to Jesus Christ, the Lamb of God (John 1:29). *arnion* is used once in St. John and twenty-eight times in Revelation. *arnos* is found only in Luke 10:3 'as lambs among wolves'.

The English words retain the meanings that they had in the earlier VSS. The male and female are the ram and ewe, while the young up to nearly a year is the lamb. A farming community has a range of other names to signify ages and types, in addition to the breeds, and it is quite possible that some of the Heb. names are comparable; at this distance we cannot know.

Although alternatives were often allowed, when the offering was graded according to the means of the person, the sheep became preeminent in the elaborate series of sacrifices ordained in the Mosaic law. Detailed comment on these rituals, which occupy many chapters of the Pentateuch, and their deep typical significance, is beyond the scope of this book; they are dealt with fully in many commentaries and a good summary is provided in the article 'Sacrifice and Offering' in the NBD. Large numbers of beasts were involved, especially on some great days, and these were killed, usually by the worshipper who brought them, in the approved manner. In a few rare cases, namely some of the sin offerings, the whole was burnt; in the burnt offerings all was burnt except the skin, which was given to the priest. In all others there was a token burning of blood and certain portions of fat, after which the meat was eaten by the priests only, by the priests and their families or by priests and worshippers together. For many people, presumably, these were the only occasions on which meat was eaten in any quantity.

Above all the sheep has deep metaphorical significance throughout the Scriptures. In the early books it is found largely, though not exclusively, in literal and sacrificial contexts but from the Psalms onwards it is almost entirely figurative; of over seventy mentions in the NT the only two wholly literal passages concern the sheep being sold in the Temple court (John 2:14, etc.). The sheep is consistently a picture of man – lost, helpless, easily led astray, essentially sociable, and unable to fend for himself or find his way back; this is typified by Isa. 53:6, 'All we like sheep have gone astray; we have turned every one to his own way'. The other alternative, of man restored, is stated in the whole of Psalm 23, beginning with 'The Lord is my shepherd' and written from David's early experiences as a shepherd. The NT unfolds the great paradox of John 1:29, 'Behold the Lamb of God which taketh away the sins of the world', and John 10:14 'I am the Good Shepherd' with its climax in Rev. 5:6, 'In the midst of the throne ... stood a Lamb as it had been slain.'

Cattle

In contrast to the English words for sheep and goat, which have scarcely changed in meaning since the Bible was first translated, much of the vocabulary for cattle in the AV has become obsolete and it seems best to define these terms. Cattle itself comes from an Old English word *catel*, meaning property; because livestock were the most important possession of the ordinary person they were equated with property and thus acquired the name cattle. A variant, 'chattels', continued to mean material property but is now only a legal term. Heb. *miqneh* will be seen to have a similar meaning. In technical language cattle are wild and domesticated bovines; popularly they are domestic bovines, and in this section the term is used in this sense.

The words ox and oxen appear more often than cattle, kine or bull, and are widely retained in RV and RSV, yet in England ox is now obsolete or archaic for the animal itself and is found mostly in combinations such as ox-tail, ox-cart, etc. This is a strange development, for in effect it leaves bull and cow as the male and female of an animal with no common name, the term cattle being a vague collective plural. Bull is largely confined to the adult male kept for breeding; bullock is widely used in the Bible for both bull and young bull, which was its original meaning, but today it is correctly applied only to castrated bulls being fattened for beef. Steer, which is an equally old word, has always had this latter meaning. Cow, found only six times in AV, is not usually given until after the first calf. Heifer is a cow before calving, and calf remains the young of the first year, often specified as bull-calf or heifer-calf. The obsolete term beeves occurs only in AV where it seven times tr. the very common Heb. *baqar*; it is the pl. of beef, which is also archaic for the animal, though it has been the name of the flesh since the language took shape. Kine, an old genitive pl. of cow, is also obsolete, though still used in RV. The standard group name for larger cattle remains a herd.

The ancestry of cattle is simpler than that of both sheep and goats, and all breeds are regarded as coming from a group of races of the now extinct Aurochs, the Wild Ox (see Chap. V). As with the other basic food animals it was first tamed in Neolithic times, though later than the goats and sheep, so no records can be found of its early beginnings. The suggested centre for the first attempts at domestication is SW. Asia. Bringing under control such massive and powerful beasts – the bull standing about 6 ft. at the shoulder – would be hard enough today, with all modern aids, yet these men did it before the age of metals. This is an achievement that defeats the imagination. We must assume that it happened after man had worked out a more or less settled form of agriculture, for these huge cattle would need to be both enclosed and fed. It would have been impossible to provide a large enough grazing area, especially in the time long before much was known of grassland management. It is true that there are now certain tribes of specialized cattle nomads, such as the Masai of Central Africa, but they came into being much later; their strange mode of life, feeding almost wholly on blood and milk, became possible only after the cattle were domesticated.

It seems likely that the meat was the prime object of bringing these wild cattle under control; a bull would weigh perhaps a ton and carry a lot of red meat. The use of cows for milking followed and then, presumably, their harnessing for draught purposes; sleds were being pulled well before 2500 B.C. in Babylonia and perhaps ploughs earlier still. The invention of the wheel gave them their simple cart and other transport followed. Their hides were used both before and after domestication. This general order seems logical but the speed of development cannot be guessed at. It seems impossible that the adult bulls could have been broken to the plough, so their use for draught purposes must have depended largely on the knowledge of the effect of castration in making them docile. We must assume that this was practised in Palestine, but none of the Heb. names for cattle can be rendered bullock in its present sense. The taming of the ox eventually transformed the pattern of farming as radically as the breaking of the horse improved transport some 2,000 years later.

By the beginning of the Bronze Age, which was long before the Patriarchs settled in Palestine, the ox had already become a basic part of the farming scene over much of Eurasia and in the Nile Valley. Zoologists recognize several different parent stocks which are thought to have contributed to the great complex of domestic cattle now found the world over. These are principally three – *longifrons* (long-headed and small in size), *primigenius* (the main type of Aurochs, or Wild Ox) and Zebu (with the typical hump on the neck). These probably came from geographical races tamed independently and later interbred almost indefinitely until their origins were obscured. Cattle have now become by far the most important animals, with a world population of perhaps 700 million. Some 200 million of these are the sacred cattle of India, which normally die of starvation or natural causes and are thus of no productive value. Many others are of poor quality, such as those kept in parts of Africa largely as 'wealth'.

Most cattle countries now have their own breeds carefully developed for local needs and able to thrive in particular climates and on sometimes difficult terrains. They are grouped according to the purposes for which they are used. In Britain, for example, for bulk milk production we have among others the Friesian; for high quality milk the Jersey; for beef the Hereford; and also dual purpose breeds such as the Shorthorn. Milk and meat remain their most valuable products all over the world, with hides, manure and other useful by-products. Special breeds have been used for draught purposes, such as for drawing the huge ox-wagons in South Africa, but the value of cattle for this work, even in under-developed countries, is steadily decreasing.

Breeds appear very early and can be identified by their horns and other features from the figurines and paintings which are now accurately dated. Several distinct types are known from around 4500 B.C. in Mesopotamia, where mosaics and seals of about 1,000 years later show cattle in a wide range of uses, and this is the period for the earliest Egyptian material. Painted temple reliefs and models have kept their colours and we know that Egyptian cattle included black, brown and parti-coloured forms among the four or more distinct breeds, one of them without horns. This wealth of illustration is partly due to the bull's importance in religion. The bull cult reached its peak in Minoan Crete about the time when the Israelites were in captivity in Egypt. The massive sculptures also show that the bull was prominent in ancient Mesopotamian religion. All this time Western Europe was still in its Stone Age and the more or less sudden appearance of several types some time later suggests that immigrant peoples brought them from farther east or south-east.

Unfortunately the evidence from Palestine is still incomplete, especially as regards the different breeds, but the biblical record makes it clear that cattle were kept widely and in large numbers. The excavations at Gezer show how cattle have changed over the centuries, with recognizably different types in each of the five main layers, from pre-Semitic to the break-up of the Kingdom. However, it is not easy to see how they were distributed through the country. Abram and Lot had large herds somewhere near the southern end of the Dead Sea, but that was before the destruction of cities which clearly made great changes in the area, and perhaps of local climate. Cattle need regular water and good pasture and one of the promises for obedience was 'I will send grass...for thy cattle' (Deut. 11:15). This need for grazing perhaps restricted their range to the lower hills of Judah and to the better-watered parts of the plains; they would have thrived in the moister rolling country of upper Galilee and above all in Gilead. The precise limits of this territory are not defined but it seems to refer to the wooded hills and pasture-lands on the east of Jordan. In Num. 32:1 it is 'a place for cattle' and in v. 4 'a land for cattle'. The booty taken when it was captured is listed in the previous chapter and it almost defeats the imagination – 675,000 sheep, 72,000 beeves and 61,000 asses. The land continued to be fertile when the tribe of Reuben occupied it, as reported in I Chron. 5:9, 'their cattle were multiplied in the land of Gilead'.

The present distribution of cattle is no safe guide for it is based on special

breeds and, in many cases, on highly artificial conditions, as at Yotvata
and En Gedi where milking herds are kept permanently under cover and
fed on irrigated crops. To the Hebrews and to many contemporary peoples
their cattle provided food, clothing and labour, and were next only to
sheep in use as sacrifices, though for this purpose they were beyond the
means of the ordinary folk. It is recorded that Abram brought back cattle
from Egypt and it seems likely that they had been part of the 'substance'
that he took from Haran (Gen. 12:5); this Heb. word *rekush* is often stated
to include cattle. When the Hebrews left on their exodus they took their
herds with them, but life must have been difficult for cattle on this march
and they were little used for sacrifice; this was mainly to conserve their
numbers but perhaps also because of the bull's place among the Egyptian
deities.

We are accustomed to calves being born at all seasons though we still
expect to see lambs in the spring. The marked seasonal pattern in Palestine
makes it likely that most domestic animals were born in the early spring to
make use of the grass that sprang up after the winter rains. Later in the year
conditions would be difficult for new-born stock. The gestation period of
cattle is around forty weeks and a single calf is usual.

No estimate of numbers kept is possible but they must have been fairly
large at some periods. The peace offerings made by Solomon after the
dedication of the Temple included 22,000 oxen; only token parts of the fat
were burnt, and, in effect, the meat was for a huge public feast of thanks-
giving, which went on for some days. The ordinary person would seldom
or never taste beef at home. The size of Solomon's herds is suggested by
the daily ration for his household, which included ten fat oxen and twenty
oxen out of the pasture; it must also imply that his household was very
large. Job is recorded as having 1,000 yoke, i.e., pairs of oxen, and Elisha
was in charge of twelve pairs when he was called (I Kings 19:19), showing
that he came from a wealthy family.

Oxen were used for pulling a simple plough, first made entirely of wood
and later fitted with metal points. Also for dragging a hardwood sled
round and round the threshing floor. Reference to this work is found in the
humane order of Deut. 25:4; 'Thou shalt not muzzle the ox when he
treadeth out the corn'. The word 'tread' here is usually translated 'thresh'.
Oxen were sometimes used as pack-animals and there is just one reference
to this, in I Chron. 12:40; 'They brought bread . . . on mules and on
oxen'.

After the invention of the wheel a simple cart was used, drawn by a pair
of oxen and tr. either wagon or cart in AV. A clay model of a covered
wagon found in Mesopotamia is dated *c.* 2500 B.C. Spoked wheels were
invented about the time of Hammurabi *c.* 1750 B.C. and several types of
wagon are illustrated in Egyptian or Assyrian art. The first biblical mention
is in Gen. 45:19, where the pharaoh sent wagons to fetch the aged Jacob

down to Egypt; these might possibly have been drawn by horses. Otherwise, the carts and wagons were always manned by pairs of oxen, and the
chariots, for which there are some five Heb. words, by horses. The ox-
wagon is first mentioned specifically in Num. 7:3; 'They brought their
offering . . . six covered wagons and twelve oxen', which Moses allocated
to certain families of Levites for their work. Later the ox-cart features in
two incidents concerning the irregular transport of the Ark (I Sam. 6;
II Sam. 6). These were also drawn by pairs of oxen but were presumably
open carts of the type used for bringing in the harvest. They were made
of wood which in one case was used to burn the sacrifice (I Sam. 6:14).
Cattle still pull simple Arab ploughs, often yoked to a donkey or mule,
and around Jericho even a Friesian bullock may be seen used in this way.

The Westerners' butter and cheese are very different from the milk
products that the Hebrews knew and it is doubtful if more than one of the
ten AV references to butter is technically correct. The goatskin milk bottle
was probably never washed out and certainly never sterilized, so that as
soon as fresh milk was put in this was curdled by the bacteria already
there. In this form it was still regarded as milk. Shaken up for a while it
became thoroughly curdled and it seems that this was the butter of AV
and curds of RSV. What we would today call cream cheese was made by
salting the strained curds, shaping them into flat discs and drying, to give
them better keeping qualities.

When the art of butter-making was learnt it was found that it would
not keep in that warm climate, so it was heated to clarify it and stored in
bottles in the form of butterfat. The one mention of making butter is
more likely to refer to cheese, 'the churning of milk bringeth forth butter'
(Prov. 30:33). 'Butter of kine' is spoken of once (Deut. 32:14) and 'cheese
of kine' once (II Sam. 17:29). For the rest it must be assumed that the milk
of goats, sheep and cows was used as available. These milk products must
have been the ordinary Hebrew's basic source of animal protein for most of
the year, though literal references are too few to suggest quantities. One
mention of cheese in I Sam. 17:17, 18 is intriguing. David came from a
family employing a number of servants yet the food that he brought to the
battlefront consisted of ten loaves and some parched corn for his brothers,
but ten cheeses for their captain, which has always struck me as a little unfair!

Modern experience has shown that in the hotter parts of Palestine the
cattle need to be heat-resistant, and some old local breeds have been used
to introduce this factor into highly efficient types from temperate countries; this work makes it difficult to speak of the distribution of 'native'
breeds that have been there for many centuries. The humped Zebu, which
probably began in India, has been important in this respect. It was in
Mesopotamia by the fourth millennium B.C. and was widespread in Egypt
before Joseph reached there. It would therefore be expected that Abram

and Lot had this type on the hot plains of the Arabah; this may have been so, but the oldest evidence so far found in Palestine is for the post-exilic period.

Of some twenty-five mentions of dung only one clearly describes treating the ground (Luke 13:8) and the Gr. word *koprian* specifically refers to animal manure. One must presume that its fertilizing value had been learnt early by farmers as able as the Hebrews, but this is nowhere implied in OT. Dung was widely used as fuel in the less wooded parts, especially the droppings from such animals as camels whose fodder contained much indigestible fibre. The dung from cattle feeding in rough pastures would be similar and in the hot sun would soon be dry enough for use. This is referred to in Ezek. 4:12; 'thou shalt bake it with dung' (Heb. *gelel*).

The importance of cattle to the Israelites can perhaps be brought out best by a discussion of their many names. These are hard enough to classify in the original Hebrew; the wide range of tr. in the EV and the change in usage of words such as ox and bullock make distinction even more difficult.

'abbir, 'mighty one', is tr. bull in a few poetical passages.

'alluph, 'chief one', is usually tr. 'duke', 'captain', etc. This is another nickname and is rendered ox in two contrasting passages (Ps. 144:14; Jer. 11:19).

baqar appears to be a collective or generic name for larger cattle, always adult; usually tr. 'herd' or 'oxen', sometimes defined by more precise words such as *'egel, 'eglah* and *par*. Perhaps 'cattle' is the nearest equivalent. The combination of *par ben baqar*, tr. 'bullock', merits comment for it is used for a series of special sacrifices – including the Consecration of the Priests, the entry of the Priest into the Holy Place, Pentecost, Feast of Trumpets and so on.

behemah is a common word rendered beast or cattle and discussed in App. B (beast). When tr. 'cattle' the stress is usually on the animal aspect, i.e., as producers of food, clothing and labour. Only one context is sacrificial (Lev. 1:2) where reference is to a general class from which suitable animals may be taken. It is found in a very few poetic passages but, like *miqneh*, has no figurative importance.

be'ir is tr. 'beasts' or 'cattle' and is normally a collective name for beasts of burden, e.g., 'Pharaoh said . . . lade your beasts' (Gen. 45:17). In Num. 20:4, 'this wilderness that we and our cattle should die there' it probably has a wider meaning, including other animals.

'egel (masc.) and *'eglah* (fem.) are from a root meaning 'to roll', and can probably be regarded as nicknames for frisky young beasts. With few exceptions these are correctly tr. calf and heifer. *'egel* is found widely in literal and figurative passages, more than half of which refer to heathen calf-worship, including Aaron's calf. It also has a range of other uses,

including two of the burnt offerings. 'eglah is a sacrificial animal in all literal passages but is also found in several figurative verses, in one of which (Hos. 10:11) it is a heifer trained for threshing, though normally, without qualification, it is a heifer not yet broken to the yoke.

'eleph is from a root 'training', i.e. breaking in, and it is used infrequently. In three literal passages it is tr. 'the increase of thy kine' (Deut. 7:13, etc.). In two poetic verses it is tr. oxen, e.g., 'all sheep and oxen' (Ps. 8:7).

meri, meaning 'well-fed', is tr. 'fatling', 'fat beast', etc. Except for one prophetic passage (Isa. 11:6) this always refers to animals for sacrifice. The stall-fed cattle which provided the luxury food of I Kings 4:23 are described as fat, fed or stalled, i.e., penned for special feeding, as is done today. cf. 'ye shall . . . grow up as calves of the stall' (Mal. 4:2).

miqneh is close to English cattle and chattels; it appears never to be used for sacrificial animals but emphasizes the wealth aspect of cattle. Its first two mentions are typical. 'The father of such as dwell in tents and . . . have cattle' (Gen. 4:20); 'And Abram was very rich in cattle' (Gen. 13:2). The few occurrences of this word in the Prophets are consistent with this, e.g., 'the nations which have gotten cattle and goods' (Ezek. 38:12).

The two basic words for bull and ox are hard to differentiate but, as will be explained, their usage scarcely overlaps. par is normally tr. 'bull' and 'bullock', and it is rarely used apart from sacrifice. parah is the female, tr. 'heifer' and 'kine', principally in three contexts. It is the heifer of Num. 19, introduced as 'red' in v. 2, that was used for the elaborate ceremony of Levitical purification. Tr. kine it features in Joseph's prophecy of famine in Gen. 41. It also refers to the pair of oxen in the incident of I Sam. 6, whereas for the oxen drawing the cart with the Ark in II Sam. 6 the more general baqar is used. An interesting exception is found in Hos. 4: 16, RSV 'a stubborn heifer'. It seems unlikely that Hosea, with a farming background, would use two different words for heifer unless he recognized them as distinct (see 'eglah above). It is tempting to regard them as two breeds, but it could refer to age classes.

shor, tr. 'bullock' and 'ox', occasionally female, is the basic word for the single head of cattle. Its Aram. derivative tor is found in Ezra and Daniel only, and this is the root giving Gr. tauros, and English steer. When tr. ox, shor is found in a wide range of contexts, almost entirely literal. Only when tr. bullock is it used for sacrifice, which is a tiny fraction of the total.

It seems that one or two of these names may refer to breeds or colour varieties; e.g., Lev. 22:27 speaks of a bull (shor) being born, while v. 23 contains a ruling that a bull (shor) that is deformed in any way was acceptable only as a free-will offering. It is clear from many verses that shor applied to an adult animal, so that is definitely not an age-group.

The six Gr. words are used so seldom that they can be listed in less detail. *damalis* is the equivalent of the red heifer (Heb. 9:13). *thremma* (John 4:12), 'Jacob . . . and his cattle'. This means a beast that has been specially fed, and two others are similar. *moschos* is the fatted calf of Luke 15 and the calf of sacrifice of Heb. 9:12, 19.

sitistos (Matt. 22:4), is tr. 'fatling' and is contrasted with oxen – *tauros. bous,* always tr. 'ox', is the common word for bull in Greek literature. It is twice used for sacrificial animals (John 2:14, 15) and four of the five other passages concern the welfare of cattle. Watering cattle was permitted on the Sabbath (Luke 13:15). An ox could be rescued from a pit on the Sabbath (Luke 14:5). The same is also said of a sheep (Matt. 12:11). St. Paul twice quoted the Mosaic injunction in Deut. 25:4 not to muzzle the ox treading out corn (I Cor. 9:9; I Tim. 5:18).

With so many authentic comments on kindness to animals perhaps it is not surprising that notes have been added to ancient MSS in similar vein. One such concerns our Lord's care for a homeless cat. Another, which is certainly in keeping with the Gospel injunctions quoted above, is said to be found in a hand-written Coptic Bible in the Paris Museum. This describes the conversation between our Lord and a man who was ill-treating his mule.

Several other humane rules are also in the Mosaic law. The ox was to be included in the Sabbath rest (Exod. 23:12 and Deut. 5:14). A straying ox should be taken to safety if it belonged to an enemy (Exod. 23:4) or a brother (Deut. 22:1). A fallen ox should be helped to its feet again (Deut. 22:4). The ban on oxen and asses ploughing together (Deut. 22:10) is discussed under 'ass'. While most of these precepts have underlying moral teaching it is also true that they set a humane standard for the treatment of animals that was seldom seen elsewhere for several thousands of years and is still far from generally accepted. The comment in Isa. 1:3, 'The ox knoweth his owner' suggests a good relationship between them.

The Mosaic law also contained other rules about cattle (Exod. 21 and 22) which are ethical rather than humane, and deal with such problems as the compensation or penalty when an ox gored a person. It is interesting that the principle applied is recognized today with domestic animals – that the offence is more serious when the animal has shown itself to be dangerous through earlier incidents. Rules were also made to cover cattle theft and injury to cattle which fell into uncovered wells.

IV

Beasts

of

Burden

Camel, donkey, horse and mule; their history and uses.

ALTHOUGH THE WORKING ANIMALS CAME ON THE SCENE LATER THAN those enlisted by man to provide meat, milk and clothing, their addition to the labour force was a huge leap forward. A community was no longer dependent on its human man-power – for tilling the ground, for moving house, for hunting, and for going to war. The ox was a great multi-purpose beast – and still remains a working animal in some countries – but it has been dealt with elsewhere, for its basic use has nearly always been to produce food. This chapter deals with the camel, ass and horse, possibly enlisted in that order, though it will be shown that the camel's history is complicated and in some dispute. These all began their life in the service of man in lands around the E. Mediterranean. The two latter have spread to most parts of the world, and even the camel has become established in dry districts of Italy and Spain, and in some numbers in the deserts of N. Australia. Other kinds have also been broken in, but none has proved so generally useful as the horse. Yaks work in the high Himalayas, and llamas not quite so high in the Andes. The Water Buffalo of Asian jungles has spread as far west as Italy but is worth keeping only in wet areas. From India to Indonesia the zebu is as dual-purpose as the ox, and has been widely used for cross-breeding with it in warm countries. Times are changing rapidly and it seems that some of these may go on quietly in their homelands while the horse and donkey – at least as working animals in the Western world – are progressively pushed out by machines.

Camel

Whatever other problems it may raise, at least there is no difficulty about its identification. The principal Heb. name, in fact, is the root from which

A FEASTING PRINCE (*above*) receives war booty — sheep, oxen and one goat (*centre*) and onagers (*below*). From a mosaic standard in a royal tomb at Ur, *c*. 2500 B.C. (pp. 44, 48, 56, 94).

THIS WALL-PAINTING in a tomb at Thebes (18th Dyn., which is the period of Israel in Egypt) shows the type of oxen kept in mid-2nd Mill. B.C. (p. 58).

PAIR OF HORSES (*above*) pulling war chariot. (*below*) Pair of mules harnessed to a cart. From a coloured painting on the wall of unnamed tomb of 18th Dyn. Egypt (1570–1303 B.C.). The war chariot had been introduced to Egypt a little earlier by the Hyksos (pp. 76, 79).

THEIR TWO HUMPS show these to be Bactrian Camels; they were brought from the lands of Musri and Gilzami, beyond Lake Urmia in northern Persia, as part of the booty taken by Shalmaneser III. From the obelisk at Nimrud (841 B.C.) (p. 65).

the Gr., Latin and English names have come almost unchanged – *gamal* – *kamēlos* – *camelus* – *camel*. Another Heb. word *beker* (masc.) *bikrah* (fem.) is tr. 'dromedary' AV and RV, 'young camel' RSV. (Isa. 60:6 and Jer. 2:23 only). Heb. *kirkaroth* (f.pl.) (Isa. 66:20 only) is tr. 'swift beast' AV and RV, 'dromedary' RSV. Both of these probably refer to dromedary in the true sense, i.e. a thoroughbred camel used for riding and racing: this is taller and longer in the leg than the freight camel. This also comes from a Gr. word *dromos*, 'runner', through Latin, and this is seen in English hippodrome, a place for horse-racing. More popularly dromedary is used for the One-humped, or Arabian, Camel to distinguish it from the Two-humped or Bactrian Camel.[1]

Camels are properly referred to as bulls, cows and calves. Where *gamal* is found there is no distinction between sexes, except once where 'milch' qualifies it. Fossil records show that the family to which camels belong – *Camelidae* – was once found in many countries. Now only two groups are left – the llamas in the New World, consisting of two domesticated forms, the llama and alpaca, derived from the wild huanaco, and another wild species, the vicugna. These all live on the slopes of the Andes Mountains, mostly between 13,000 and 16,000 ft. The true camels live in the Old World, and both have become familiar by being kept in Zoos the world over.

Although the one is widely known as the Bactrian camel, this is not perhaps very well named, for Bactria was an ancient kingdom near the Oxus River in SW. Asia, whereas this camel is more typical of the steppes and plateaux of Central and NE. Asia, though it has been used as a beast of burden right across Asia to the Crimea. The one-humped camel, the only one that concerns us, is correctly associated with Arabia, which has always been its main centre; it has become the camel of the hot deserts, in contrast to the other, which is more at home in the extreme climate of the Gobi Desert, with hot summers and bitter cold winters. It is always assumed that only Arabian camels have been used in Bible lands; however there are records that Shalmaneser II of Assyria (*c.* 850 B.C.) received Bactrian camels as tribute from several sources.

Until recently it has been claimed that these two camels were distinct species unable to interbreed, but it is now known that crosses between bull Arabian and cow Bactrian camels are made regularly, especially in Turkey. This does not prove them to be one species; only that they are not far apart. More important, underneath the humps, which are only soft tissue, the two are more alike in skeleton than two contrasting breeds of horses, say a heavy draught horse and a thoroughbred, and many authorities now regard them as geographical races of the same animal. Their breeding habits are rather different now, largely because the Bactrian

---

[1] Esther 8:10 AV includes dromedaries and mules through a mis-reading of the Heb.; the RSV is probably better.

E

lives in a much harsher winter. The Arabian camel is usually a uniform pale brown and the other several shades darker, especially in winter when its coat is thicker and longer. Like most domestic animals, camels show some colour variation but these seem confined to albino and black forms.

The fact that experts are still uncertain whether they form one or two species complicates their history. It is often claimed that all wild forebears disappeared long ago; certainly there has been little firm evidence of wild Arabian camels in historic times, and the reports of wild Bactrian camels, from the Lop Nor and Tarim Basin, are accepted with caution for it is hard to know whether they are truly wild or perhaps domestic camels which had escaped and become established in suitable country: this certainly happens, but were there still wild herds for them to join? Many centuries of domestication have brought no major skeletal changes in camels, which means that the argument about these 'wild' animals from SW. China cannot be settled by examining their bones; nor can we use this method to classify material from 'digs' with any certainty as wild or domestic, as we can do with such beasts as cattle, and so find evidence for early taming on the one hand or for late survival of the wild form on the other.

The former presence of wild camels in Palestine is confirmed by finds in Pleistocene deposits up to one million years old. Its bones have also been noted in various other beds dated perhaps 4000 or 5000 B.C., but after that there is a blank. Strabo and others write of wild dromedaries in Arabia about the beginning of the Christian era, but these reports are not confirmed, and evidence as to when it was first brought into the service of man and later introduced into Palestine, is far from complete.

The Bible first mentions the camel in Gen. 12:16, where the presents are listed which the pharaoh gave to Abram. This is generally reckoned to be a later scribe's addition, for it seems unlikely that there were any camels in Egypt then. For many centuries the Egyptian camel is shrouded with mystery. There is not even an Egyptian word for it, nor is it illustrated in the very extensive galleries of animal life. Yet it is impossible that camels were completely unknown then, for there is firm evidence of domestication, in the form of a I Dynasty limestone carving of a loaded camel, found some sixty miles south of Cairo and dated before 3000 B.C.; there are also some drawings from Upper Egypt dated around 3000 B.C. Then there is a gap until the IV Dynasty and nothing more until the XIX, about 1300 B.C. Surprisingly enough, it is not until the reign of Ptolemy Philadelphus (285–248 B.C.), and the early part of the Roman period that camels developed into the important desert transport animals they were to be for the next 2,000 years or so. All this certainly makes it rather unlikely that Abram would have been given some camels, but why these long gaps in its history? Various theories have been suggested, of which the most probable is that the camel was not only unclean for food, as it was to the Hebrews, but also completely *tabu*.

Less than a century after the return from Egypt, Abraham sent his servant to Mesopotamia to find Rebekah (Gen. 24), and in this narrative the camel is not just an optional extra but an integral part of it; even so, some critics do not accept it on the grounds that camels were not yet available. Zeuner, who is a great authority in this field, regards this as a true account. Plenty of remains have been unearthed from town sites of about a century later, showing that they had been taken into use by the urban communities; by the sixteenth century B.C. at the latest camels were widely distributed, and it seems that they were in use for trans-desert work, i.e. between Palestine and Mesopotamia, well before that. The spread of the camel may be partly connected with the drying up of areas in Palestine, and even more in adjacent lands, following soil destruction caused by the unwise farming of marginal land. Camels are intractable animals and it may be that many people were reluctant to take them on; however, they could tackle journeys that had become too difficult for asses and they could carry much bigger loads, so they were now worth the trouble involved in managing them.

The main centre of the camel trade continued to be farther south east, in Arabia, whence came the Midianites whose camels were without number (Judg. 6:5); this was around 1100 B.C. David appointed an Ishmaelite to be his camel master (I Chron. 27:30). The Queen of Sheba, whose baggage was carried on camels, came from SW. Arabia about 150 years later (I Kings 10:2). By this time camels were commonplace and they appear throughout the historical books as part of the setting, serving as beasts of burden and a sign of wealth. If the numbers owned by Job seem excessive – 3,000 camels before his disasters and twice as many after them – it must be remembered that vast areas were occupied, not yet seriously degraded. Whole tribes owned many more than that, especially to the south and east of Palestine. I Chron. 5:21 records that 50,000 camels were taken from the Hagarites during the wars to possess Canaan; some confirmation of the truth of this claim is found in the boast of the Beni Sakk'r tribe, living in that area a century ago, to own 100,000 camels.

Actual evidence of camels in S. Arabia dates only from about the eighth century B.C., simply because so little work has been possible there, and Central Arabia is still a closed book. If the camel had had its origins in lands where records were kept in writing and art the story might be much more complete.[1]

Although a camel's performance has often been exaggerated, its ability to live for days off its hump allowed men to undertake journeys that were previously impossible and its use gave rise to the desert nomadism that is

[1] For further discussion of the camel in the Patriarchal period and more technical references, see NBD p. 181 F.

still practised in the Middle East and N. Africa. A cynic has described the camel as a horse designed by a committee, yet its apparently ill-assorted features combine to make it perfectly fitted, in anatomy and physiology, for a working life around the desert edge and for long journeys across it. The broad nostrils close to slits to filter out the sand that is always being blown around; the deeply sunk eyes are further protected by long and copious lashes. In most places and for most of the year camels must browse rather than graze when they are turned loose to search for food; this is often before they are fully adult and able to work. They make light of shrubs that seem to consist mostly of dry twigs and sharp thorns, to which the mouth and tongue are apparently insensitive, yet the very mobile lips can be used with great accuracy to pick leaves. The camel chews the cud, using this method of digestion that gets the most out of the poor food, but the fibre cannot be broken down and this goes through in the droppings, which are often collected, dried in the hot desert air and used as fuel to cook the evening meal. Camels do better in spring when the desert is often carpeted with grasses and flowering plants, and after the April barley harvest in the N. Negev they are hobbled, often with a young calf at heel, and allowed to graze off the nutritious stubble. Working animals need plenty of food; a common sight in parts of Jordan and N. Israel to-day is a camel, often led by the owner riding on a donkey, returning from work in the fields, loaded high with foliage and other green stuff for the evening meal.

On ordinary trips a camel can carry about 400 lb. and its rider. For such stretches as the Sinai Desert only about half that would be allowed. The owners take tremendous care of their beasts and on all journeys prefer to feed and water them properly every day, as is pictured in Gen. 24:19,20 but if need be the camel draws on its hump. This is a storage organ where fat is laid down in spongy tissue for use as a reserve. After a really exhausting journey a camel may have so drawn on these reserves that the hump becomes flabby. Camels can easily go three or four days without drinking and there are records of loaded camels passing a week without water; beyond this there will be casualties. An average of up to twenty-eight miles per day can be maintained without difficulty by freight camels. A fast dromedary, carrying only its rider, is on record as covering nearly 100 miles in thirteen hours, but this speed could not be kept up for long.

The camel has the rare ability to vary its body temperature; from an early morning reading of 93°F (34°C) it can rise to a maximum of 105°F (40·7°C) in the afternoon. Loss of water by sweating is thus avoided and the body temperature drops naturally in the cool of the night. More than this, the camel can, if need be, lose up to one third of its body water without danger whereas a man cannot survive the loss of more than one eighth.

The camel is the only animal that chews the cud but is not cloven-hoofed. The feet are unique, for the toes end in broad nails rather than hoofs and the weight is carried on broad cushions which are equally effective on sand, gravel, or rock, any of which may form the ground surface in the desert.

Although frost is rare in the desert, the winter nights are cold enough, often with strong winds, and the camel grows a thick protective coat which is shed in great patches before the end of April, leaving thinner summer hair underneath but looking very tatty during the moult. This hair is sometimes gathered in lumps but often the camel is shorn once a year so that the fibre can be woven into the rough cloth from which John the Baptist's garments were made – the cheapest material that was available. It is likely that this was also used for making heavy tents. Such rustic homespun should not be confused with the expensive and fashionable 'camel hair' coats of the twentieth century, which are made from the fine under-hair of the Bactrian camel. The coarse hair has long been used for making a range of goods, the first recorded being a cord, dated III or IV Dynasty (about 2500 B.C.). Found in the Fayum, west of Cairo, its purpose is unknown but it is further proof of the camel's presence in or near Egypt at that time.

Camel meat was regularly eaten by other peoples – and still is today – but it was little disadvantage to the Hebrews that it was forbidden under the Mosaic law, for most lived in parts of Palestine not really suitable for camels; better meat was provided by the more easily-managed domestic stock, or by hunting wild game. Camel's milk is rich but not very sweet, and is small in quantity; a cow may yield two gallons a day at first, but this soon drops to under half a gallon. It is drunk in various forms, and butter and cheese are made from it. It is not clear whether the Hebrews used this milk; there is no direct reference to it and no suggestion that the thirty milch camels and their colts in the present prepared for Esau were for milking. However, in more recent times the Jews in Palestine have been drinking it, while still avoiding the meat. A cow normally has a single calf every second spring, after a gestation period of nearly eleven months, and many stay in milk for nearly two years if milked regularly. Camel hides were dressed into leather and used for many purposes.

Though camels were accepted by the townsfolk and regularly used for carrying goods into and between towns and cities, they were of major importance only in and around the desert, for which they were precisely fitted. In theory they are fully domesticated, yet they have remained intractable and bad-tempered and seldom seem to obey orders without objecting. They are controlled not by a bit but by a halter which, in a train of camels, is fastened to the tail of the preceding one. A carefully chosen camel heads the caravan. They kneel down for loading and unloading, resting on the strange hard pads that form at all points in contact with the ground (Gen. 24:11). The males are actually dangerous at some seasons. It is hardly surprising that when conditions allowed them to keep other livestock these would always be preferred by the Hebrews. In addition, camels need rather large areas for pasturage. It seems that by NT times camels had become of little importance to the Jews themselves, who were increasingly town-dwellers, though they were still widely used by the natives of the drier lands to the east and south, from which they no doubt brought regular loads of merchandise for sale and barter; so they were still a familiar sight to our Lord and his disciples.

With the possible exception of two of the seven references in the prophetic books, all fifty-seven mentions of camel in the OT are wholly literal and it has no figurative meaning. It is listed twice as forbidden meat; in all other passages it refers to possessions or the transport of riders or goods and in only two cases the word is singular.

There is one possible reference to camels being used for draught purposes, but this generally had little scope in the desert. This is in Isa. 21:7, where the AV seems closer to the Heb. with 'chariot of camels', while RSV has 'riders of camels'. Camels were harnessed to a capstan for pumping, grinding grain, etc., and they have been used for ploughing since early Christian times, and possibly long before that; sometimes a camel is paired incongruously with a donkey for this work. More recently they have been used, especially in India, to pull carts and other wheeled vehicles, often with the driver seated high up to see over the hump and head.

The camel is mentioned only six times in the NT, the only two literal references being to John the Baptist's clothes. The proverb in Matt. 23:24 is discussed under 'gnat' (see p. 229). The use of camel in contrast to gnat is typical Eastern hyperbole, which is also the figure of speech in the other proverb used by our Lord (Matt. 19:24), 'It is easier for a camel to go through the eye of a needle than for a rich man to enter into the kingdom of God.' Some commentators have seen a more detailed picture in this, stating that this name is sometimes given to a small emergency gate, alongside or in one of the main city gates, through which travellers were perhaps allowed to enter after the large gate was shut for the night. The comparison is a good one, for it suggests that the camel could go in only after shedding its harness and ornamental trappings (Judg. 8:21, 26; Gen. 31:34) and all the loads that made it valuable, emphasizing the need for humility. This is an attractive interpretation but the evidence for it is rather slender.

Ass or Donkey

The English word ass is very old indeed and probably came to us from ancient languages like Sumerian and Armenian, through Latin, and it may be a diminutive, which is a sign of popularity. This is also seen in the wealth of nicknames such as cuddy, dicky, neddy and, latest of all, moke. Now the word ass is almost obsolete other than for biblical and figurative use, and in some zoological names. Except when we refer to a he-ass or she-ass, or perhaps a jack-ass and jenny-ass, for the stallion and mare, we use only donkey for the domesticated form. This word was not known before about the end of the eighteenth century and its origin is uncertain; it once rhymed with monkey and may be derived from the word 'dun', meaning dingy brown. Colts and foals are mentioned in both OT and NT. Colt is the young of any member of the horse tribe; in the Bible it is used for young ass only, except in Gen. 32:15, 'camels with their colts'. Foal, from the Gr. *pōlos*, which is used in all the Gospel references to our Lord's entry into Jerusalem, is almost the same as colt.

The donkey is descended from the Nubian Wild Ass, *Equus asinus*, which once existed in several races, from Somalia in the east through the Libyan Desert to Morocco in the west. The Atlas Mountains race, known from rock paintings and Roman mosaics, disappeared before the end of the Roman period. The Nubian form, which also lived between the Nile and the Red Sea, may also be extinct. Only the Somalian race is left, in small numbers and carefully protected. Evidence from Ancient Egypt suggests that though the ass may have been first used in Libya its main development was in the Nile Valley, and the Nubian race is probably the chief ancestor. As in other animals also, domestication may have taken place in different parts of the range, perhaps concurrently, with later mixing of the stock. This work began in one of the pre-dynastic cultures of Egypt; a war chariot drawn by four asses has been dated at the start of third millennium B.C., i.e., very early in the Dynastic period. The 'asses' which drew wheeled vehicles in Ancient Mesopotamia *c*. 3000 B.C. are now known to have been tamed onagers (See *ill. f.p.* 64). Asses are shown on the Nadga palette as being sent as tribute from Libya and are illustrated on a panel, dated *c*. 2650 B.C., together with cattle and goats.

The wild colour was brownish-grey, paler beneath. Donkeys are mostly brown or grey, with some albinos, black, piebald and skewbald. A few, including albinos, lack the stripe over the shoulders but almost all have both this and the clearly marked line along the back. The widespread legend that the cross formed by these two lines dates from our Lord's entry into Jerusalem is pure fancy: it is inherited from the wild ass. Different breeds were recognizable as long ago as 1800 B.C. in Mesopotamia. Today some are as large as a thoroughbred horse while others stand less than 36 in. at the shoulder. Asses are longer-lived than horses, usually passing twenty-five years and sometimes going to over forty. The gestation period is about nine months. Unlike horses, their habit is to sleep standing. Perhaps their strangest feature is their braying, an unearthly noise made at odd intervals and for little obvious reason, the result of muscular contractions of the body.

The real secret of the donkey's success is that it is both sure-footed and able to manage on poor forage, the result of having its original home in semi-desert mountain country, and it has always been useful in Mediterranean countries. While asses cannot work efficiently on quite such rough fodder as will satisfy a camel, they are content with coarse herbage, including thistles. In contrast the horse came from the grassy plains, where it was used to richer foods and easier going, and this is still largely true. The horse therefore never fully replaced the ass in hill country or around the desert edge, and for many centuries the ass has been the basic transport of poorer folk, both settled and nomadic. Although customs have since changed, the early pattern was for asses to carry only loads; the Hebrews were one of the few peoples who rode asses – mostly the women and children, while the men walked. In this way an average of twenty miles a day could be maintained. In the twentieth century it is usually the men who ride!

Except for a mention in the law about contagion (Lev. 15:9), where a different Heb. word is found, it so happens that saddling in the Bible always refers to asses. Heb. *chabash* means 'to bind up' or 'gird' and is used in other contexts as often as for saddling. The process was unlike saddling a horse with a leather seat. Several layers of thick cloth on the ass's back made a foundation on which a large flat straw pad was placed and bound, and the whole was then covered with a bright cloth or carpet. The same word is used of saddling pack and riding asses but of the thirteen mentions only one refers to goods being carried. 'Two asses saddled and on them 200 loaves of bread,' etc. (II Sam. 16:1). Arabs in Palestine still ride on donkeys but with the minimum of saddlery and usually sitting right over the hind legs. It seems that bits were not used for asses but they were controlled with a bridle which was often ornate.

The ass first appears in the biblical record in Gen. 12:16, among the presents that the pharaoh gave Abram, but this can hardly have been his first meeting with it. The spread from Egypt into Asia may have been slow but there are Early Bronze Age (before 2500 B.C.) traces of it at Tell Duweir and Jericho. Soon afterwards it had spread over most of Palestine and Syria. There is still no evidence about when and by what route the ass reached Mesopotamia but it was well before 1800 B.C., for this is the date of some tablets found at Chagar Bazar that list three different breeds of ass and their rations. It is important to establish this fact, for it was only shortly before this that Abram began his journey from Ur to Canaan. The first part would have been up the Euphrates or Tigris valley to Haran, in the watershed between them; this would be through developed country for most or all of the way, and would not be difficult. The second stage, made after a break of some years, involved traversing the Syrian desert, and this could hardly be done without transport animals. Until camels came into more general service nearly a century later, pack donkeys were used for such journeys.

The OT gives no real evidence of the ass pulling any wheeled vehicle. 'Chariot of asses' (Isa. 21:7, AV) is tr. 'troop of asses' (RV) and 'rider on asses' (RSV); – one of the latter seems more likely. However, the ass had a variety of other uses, including grinding corn by turning the millstone of Matt. 18:6, and pulling simple wooden ploughs. This last was more than a single beast could manage easily in the hard stony soils, often on slopes, and it was – and still is – usual to harness an ox and an ass together, largely because the farmer probably had only one ass. This was early forbidden by Mosaic law (Deut. 22:10) primarily, perhaps, to teach that intermarriage with other nations was wrong, but it was also humane, for these two animals have different actions and do not pull comfortably together.

Like all members of the horse family the ass was unclean under the food laws, since it has single hoofs and is not a ruminant. It was thus a measure of the Samaritans' desperation that an ass's head was sold for 80 shekels (32 oz.) of silver when Ben Hadad besieged the city. However, the Greeks ate it: this is mentioned by Xenophon and Pliny, who also noted the value of ass's milk.

The two Heb. words for ass cannot easily be differentiated in their uses: *athon*, meaning 'strength' or 'endurance' is found mostly in two incidents – of Balaam (Num. 22) and Saul's father's asses (I Sam. 9 and 10): *chamor*, meaning 'of reddish colour', is more generally used.

Heb. *ayir* meaning 'restless' is tr. ass, colt, young ass, etc. This is the beast on which the sons of the Judges rode. Standing alone it refers to the donkey, but in one figurative verse it is joined to *pere*; 'though man be born like a wild ass's colt' (Job 11:12). This is the word used in Zech. 9:9 for 'a colt, the foal of an ass'.

Throughout the OT the ass is portrayed as one of the basic possessions of the ordinary Hebrew and out of 138 occurrences only some twelve are other than wholly literal. In most cases the word is sing. and the clear impression is that the average householder had just one, e.g., 'they drive away the ass of the fatherless' (Job 24:3). Large numbers seem to be mentioned only in two contexts – among the booty captured in war and those brought by the returning exiles (Ezra 2:67), where 6,720 asses are shared between 42,360 people.

There are many detailed instructions about the treatment of asses (e.g., Exod. 21:33 concerning the responsibility of a man who digs a pit into which an animal falls). These all emphasize its value to the poor owner. There are at least two injunctions about the safety of asses and two more about oxen and asses (Exod. 23:4, 5, 12; Deut. 22:4). No doubt this was largely because the peasants depended on their asses for a living, but there is also a humane content quite foreign to the general sentiment in most Arab lands today, where few animals get much consideration. The ass finds less mention in the NT – only nine times – but its status seems little changed and our Lord makes two comments about the kind treatment of livestock, including asses (Luke 13:15; 14:5), adding further to the instructions in the Mosaic Law.

For four centuries 'ass' has been quite unjustly a metaphor for stupidity but there is no hint of this in either OT or NT, even in the two proverbial passages: 'a whip for the horse, the bridle for the ass' (Prov. 26:3) and 'the ass (knows) its master's crib' (Isa. 1:3), both of which are complementary.

It would be misleading to say that the ass was merely the invaluable possession of the peasant; far from being an animal on which it was undignified for wealthy folk to ride, it is specially noted that sons of the current Judge of Israel did just this (Judg. 10:3, 4; 12:13, 14) and there are other examples, e.g., II Kings 4:22. Later this role was in part taken over by the mule.

There is some evidence that in Palestine and surrounding lands it was correct for the king or other ruler himself to use an ass in peacetime, perhaps because, as will be shown in the next section, the horse was consistently and closely associated with war. The prophecy of Zech. 9:9, 'Thy King cometh unto thee ... lowly and riding upon an ass', is fully consonant with this, and this is repeated precisely when our Lord enters Jerusalem in fulfilment of it. (It is interesting that the war-horse is mentioned two vv. later as being cut off.) The use of asses on such ceremonial occasions has continued in some Muslim countries; for instance, until recently the family of the Sultan of Zanzibar rode a special breed of asses in processions.

Horse

Only one Heb. word *sus* (masc.) and *susah* (fem.) is used as a general word for the horse itself, in particular for one used to pull a chariot. Heb. *parash* is nearly always rendered 'horseman' in all EV, but this is now taken to mean a cavalry or riding horse, often perhaps with its rider, i.e., a mounted horse. Male and female are seldom named. Wycliffe used stallion in his tr. but it can be found now only in RSV, three times for horse and once for bull (Jer. 50:11). RSV also seems the only VS to use mare, another early word; this is found in Cant. 1:9, where AV has 'company of horses' and RV 'steed'. The young, which are usually born singly, are called colts or foals, but in the Scriptures these are not mentioned. The word horse itself is very old, being found in Chaucer, and the only English word ever to be used for this grand animal, other than a few nicknames.

The horse was the strongest[1] transport animal to be truly domesticated and, apart perhaps from the llamas of S. America, it was the last to arrive. When its value was fully recognized it spread rapidly over Eurasia and N. Africa; it was taken to the Americas and Australia by the first colonists, escaping and becoming feral in suitable areas; when the prairies were still only partly colonized these 'wild' horses probably numbered millions and they were often regarded as native. Almost everywhere it went the horse became the most important beast of burden, and a close associate of man, next only to the dog. After over 3,500 years and many changes of role the horse ceased to be used as a fighting animal soon after the end of World

[1] Elephants are, of course, much stronger but they are caught and trained individually.

War I, and in most developed countries mechanical transport has now taken over most of its draught work. Figures are hard to come by, but in Western countries the horse is more popular than ever for leisure activities, and perhaps as numerous as it ever was. This close association with man may be the basic reason for the prejudice against horseflesh in most English-speaking lands, and some others, though it is widely used elsewhere. Like the ass, the horse was forbidden meat to the Hebrews.

The early history of the horse is hard to sort out, though after it really became established it is well documented on tablets, monuments, etc., Zeuner is again the leading modern authority and he has brought together all relevant evidence, so the following paragraphs owe much to his research. All members of the horse tribe have a general shape too well known to need description. They belong to the so-called Odd-toed Hoofed Mammals! In the horse this development has gone to the limit, for the central toe alone does all the work and only minute traces of the others are left. Horses tend to be grazers rather than browsers and they have simple stomachs, not the complex ones of those that chew the cud. All the various species live – or have lived – in herds, sometimes numbering thousands. Horses were once found in four fairly distinct geographical groups.

1. The clearly striped Zebras of the open plains and grass woodlands of E. and S. Africa. Odd specimens have been tamed but no species or race has been fully domesticated.
2. The true Asses of N. Africa from which the donkey has been derived.
3. The 'Half-asses' known as Onager, Hemione, etc., from the dry lands running east from Palestine to the Gobi Desert; this is the Wild Ass of the Bible and it was at least partly domesticated in the ancient Mesopotamian civilization.
4. The true Horses, from the grassy lowlands of Eurasia, north of the main mountain ranges.

All of these groups were divided into various species or races, and the only ones to survive into the twentieth century in any quantity are the Zebras. The half-striped Quagga from the Cape had gone before this century began, and two forms are now very scarce, but the others are still plentiful. The Asses and Half-Asses have almost vanished, and this is true also of the Wild Horses. Only the eastern form, Przewalski's, survives precariously in Mongolia under careful protection, and in some zoo parks where every effort is being made to build up the tiny herds. It is a small horse, standing only 10 hands, i.e., 40 in., and it is reddish brown, the hair becoming longer and paler in winter. The mane is dark brown, short and erect, not long and falling to one side as in most domesticated breeds. All races, wild and tame, have long hair on the whole of the tail, in contrast to the asses and zebras in which only the end hairs are long, giving the tufted effect.

The Western race was known as the Tarpan, of which the last known specimen died in 1851 in the Ukraine. It was small and grey brown, with an upright mane, and it is reckoned to be the chief ancestor of the many and varied modern breeds.[1] The plains of Turkestan are considered a likely starting-point for domestication, though not the only one, and it seems certain that the process began later than with sheep, goat, ox and ass. Oxen had been pulling ploughs and wheeled carts, perhaps actually carrying goods on their backs. The fertile patches of plains country were becoming exhausted and dried out, a common problem after a few centuries of primitive agriculture, and the need for faster draught animals might have prompted farmers to catch and break in these immensely strong wild horses. As is discussed elsewhere, modern man is left gasping that such feats were successful, for with all his resources he has achieved nothing comparable.[2]

Just where it began, and what folk tackled this Herculean task we do not know, for evidence prior to 2000 B.C. is either non-existent or unreliable, and the battle had been won by then. The great Sumerian culture flourished through the third millennium B.C. in S. Mesopotamia; the horse has not been identified in their copious records and finds regular mention only from about 1800 B.C. However, we know that it had reached Troy by then and was in the Caucasus and Asia Minor perhaps two centuries earlier. Its tremendous potential still had not been recognized and Hammurabi's law (c. 1750 B.C.) does not list it, but within the next fifty years or so it spread swiftly to the south-west, to Palestine and Egypt, where it arrived in or just before the Hyksos era not many decades before Joseph came to power. All this resulted from its use in war-chariots. It may have been first tamed for more peaceful purposes, but when the first horse was harnessed to a war-chariot it quickly added a new dimension to invading armies, a change comparable to the arrival of tanks in World War I.

The first Biblical mention is in Gen. 47:17. Several years of famine had used up all the Egyptians' money, so Joseph gave them bread in exchange for horses. The horse was still mainly a draught animal, above all being used in war chariots, and the first clear evidence of one being ridden is a figurine of the XVIII Dynasty (c. 1580 B.C.). An individual rider is mentioned first in I Kings 20:20, 'Ben Hadad King of Syria escaped on a horse with the horsemen', but much earlier Gen. 50:9 records that both

[1] Recent research has questioned the existence of a western race of wild horses and some zoologists now consider the tarpan a primitive domesticated form.

[2] Moving huge white rhinos that have been 'darted' with some new drug is useful enough, but this is only a triumph of technology; the next day the rhino is as wild as ever – in another reserve.

horsemen and chariots accompanied the great cortège that took Jacob's body for burial in Canaan, and the army used both cavalry and chariots to pursue the escaping Hebrews, who must have seemed an easy prey as they struggled on with their flocks and herds and all their impedimenta. It is very unlikely that they had horses in the land of Goshen or took any with them into the desert. Egypt was later an important source of supply, some of which were marketed through Solomon's agency when he controlled the two main routes, parallel to the coast, along which horses could be taken safely. (I Kings 10:28, 9; but see page 78.)

God specifically forbad any amassing of horses by the Hebrews (Deut. 17:16) and in the light of history the context of this ban is notable – it follows immediately on the statement that the people would one day demand a king. Some two centuries later (I Sam. 8:11) they did indeed make this demand, whereupon Samuel warned them plainly that this ban on horses would be ignored and that they would suffer. It seems that God's command was obeyed through the whole of Saul's reign and most of David's; all this time horses and horsemen were conspicuous units in the enemy armies. From the material point of view this ban would have been little handicap in their occupation of Palestine for they were pastoralists, and their limited ploughing was better done with the ox or ass. The only areas where chariot warfare was profitable were the plains of the coast and Esdraelon, and the strange position was later reached where the invading Hebrews took over the hill ground and left the native tribes holding the plains. Even so, when Joshua obeyed God's instructions for dealing with cavalry (Jos. 11) he defeated the King of Hazor on the plains of Upper Galilee. 150 years later the mounted troops of Jabin, King of Canaan, finally came to grief in the swamps alongside the flooded Kishon river (Judg. 5). Judg. 1:19 states the position clearly: 'Judah drove out the inhabitants of the mountains; but could not drive out the inhabitants of the valley, because they had chariots of iron.' The Hebrews always made good infantrymen, which later prompted the Syrian complaint that 'their gods were gods of the hills' (I Kings 20:23).

Eventually Samuel's forecast came true and II Sam. 8:4 points out that David kept enough horses for a hundred chariots, having killed the rest. This disobedience led to personal trouble for David, for these horses were now available for two of his insurgent sons. Absalom plotted against him and II Sam. 15:1 records that he 'prepared him chariots and horses, and fifty men to run before him'. This plot was finally defeated, after causing David much grief, and then, twelve years later, with David almost on his deathbed, a younger son Adonijah exactly followed Absalom's example (I Kings 1:5).

Solomon made no pretence at obedience but kept up with the kings around, though his horses were for use with chariots and not as cavalry,

and within a year of succeeding to the throne he had built stabling for
4,000 horses in several cities, though not at Megiddo as is often claimed.[1]
The extensive stabling there probably dates from Ahab's time.

Solomon imported horses from Egypt, with which he had profitable
trading arrangements through a marriage with a daughter of the pharaoh,
and paid 150 shekels (60 oz.) of silver per horse.[2] He also received horses
and mules in annual tribute from various countries around (I Kings 10:25).
From then on both Judah and Israel regarded horses and chariots as an
integral part of their armed forces.

Early in its history the horse sometimes had sacred associations and,
subsequently, featured in Greek mythology; the only Biblical reference is
in II Kings 23:11, where Josiah in his sweeping reforms removed horses
that earlier kings had dedicated to the sun.

In all the many biblical passages there is almost nothing to be learnt
about the horse's biology or habits or even its management. Psa. 32:9 lists
it, with the mule, as 'without understanding, which must be curbed with
bit and bridle else it will not keep with you.' RSV here corrects the obvious
error AV which has 'lest they come near unto thee'. The invention of the
bit was a major triumph, for it gave a degree of control possible by no
other method; at first they probably used a leather thong, then wood and
bone, and finally metal. Bronze bits found at Gezer are dated 1400–1000
B.C. The same principle is still used, and the actual design of some head harness seen widely today is little different from that seen in Assyrian carvings.
Three Heb. words and one Gr. are used to describe the various items tr.
bridle, bit, curb, etc. These are found only in figurative or proverbial
passages, e.g., 'we put bits in horses' mouths' (James 3:3). Bells decorating
the harness are mentioned in Zech 14:20.[3] Saddles, as we know them, and
stirrups came much later. Horseshoes were not thought of until at least
the second century B.C., and were not in general use until long after that;
horses are still ridden unshod in some parts of the world.

The horse described in some detail in Job 39:19–25 is the war-horse,
strong and fearless in battle; the passage tells us little else. I Kings 18:5,
set in the drought foretold by Elijah, includes an interesting comment, 'Perhaps we may find grass to save the horses and mules alive'. There would
have been many more asses than horses and mules, but they were mostly
in ones and twos and could manage on poorer forage. Only the king would

---

[1] 4,000 is the figure in II Chron. 9:25; the corresponding passage in I Kings 4:26 reads 40,000
which is regarded as a scribal error.

[2] Some authorities, including Albright, follow the LXX reading and read Cilicia instead of
Egypt. There is some evidence that horses from Cilicia were among the best obtainable at that
time, and it is suggested that horses were not bred in numbers in Egypt before the Hellenistic
period.

[3] 'Reins' is an archaic word found in both AV and RV and it comes from the same root as
'renal', referring to the kidneys. These were once thought to be the centre of certain emotions,
e.g., 'try my reins and my heart.' (Ps. 26:2). In literal passages, all of which are sacrificial, the
Heb. word is tr. 'kidneys'.

be likely to own the others, and finding food under such conditions was a big problem.

The horse's place in the Scriptures contrasts markedly with the ass. Of some 140 mentions only about fifty are wholly literal. Horsemen appear fifty-five times, two thirds of which are literal. The others, with all the NT instances except the horsemen that accompanied Paul in Acts 23, are figurative or symbolic. In a tiny minority of cases a single horse is mentioned; notably in I Kings 10:29 quoting the price of a horse, and in nine quasi-proverbial expressions in Job, the Psalms and Proverbs. For the rest the word is pl.; and horsemen never come singly. Horses and horsemen are uniformly in a setting of power and war, and the one solitary case of truly peaceful use is in a figurative passage: speaking of threshing corn the prophet says 'he will not bruise it with the horsemen' (Isa. 28:28). Throughout the OT horses were a monopoly of kings and nobles in both Palestine and surrounding lands, a symbol of human power. An apparent exception is in Neh. 7:66, but these horses brought by the returning exiles were part of a donation organized for them by King Cyrus.

This confirms its consistent metaphorical importance. Some of the prophetic passages of Zechariah and the Revelation are highly symbolic and beyond the scope of comment here, but the true significance of the horse is aptly summed up in two typical vv., 'The war horse is a vain hope for victory' (Ps. 33:17, RSV), and 'I will not save them by bow, nor by sword, nor by battle, by horses, nor by horsemen' (Hos. 1:7).

Mule

The Heb. *pered* (masc.) and *pirdah* (fem.) is properly tr. 'mule'. The other words are wrongly so rendered in AV which are corrected in more modern VSS. They are Gen. 36:24 where mules should read 'hot springs'; and Esther 8:10, 14, which should read 'steed'.

The mule is the result of crossing a donkey stallion with a horse mare; the reverse cross is seldom made. The English word mule is old, coming from the Latin, and although first and mainly used for this animal it is also applied to various other odd combinations, including weaving machines and coins. Like most hybrids between distinct species the mule is sterile; a few rare reports to the contrary are not generally accepted.

Such a hybrid could not be produced in the wild, for the two parents lived in different continents and different habitats. The mule has turned out to be a useful animal, for it combines some of the strength and size of the horse with the patience and sure-footedness of the ass. To this is added what is known as 'hybrid vigour', a phenomenon used widely today by plant- and animal-breeders. In biblical times the mule was used mostly for riding; Naaman's request for 'two mules' burdens of earth' (II Kings 5:17), implies that they were also regular pack animals. As such, they did great service in two World Wars in the hilly country of the Mediterranean, where they can be seen at work every day now, bringing home huge loads of firewood and forage.

The breeding of mules was obviously included in the prohibition of Lev. 19:19 (RSV). 'You shall not let your cattle breed with a different kind.' Mules first appear in II Sam. 13:29 as mounts for David's sons. Obviously they were highly regarded as transport and their use seems largely confined to the nobility. Absalom was killed while riding on his mule.

Later, David instructed his servants to prepare his own mule for Solomon as he went to be declared king (I Kings 1:33). Mules were among the livestock taken back to Jerusalem by the returning exiles, given them by royal command.

Mules seem to have been imported from countries that specialized in producing them (I Kings 10:25), perhaps to evade the ban on breeding them, but it could have been that this work was left in the hands of specialists, for Ezek. 27:14 refers to Phoenicia importing mules from Armenia.

The mule's stubbornness is proverbial today, as it has been since the word was used metaphorically as early as A.D. 1470, but this is rather unfair, for its obstinacy, if it can be called that, may be partly due to the way it is treated. It is referred to in Psa. 32:9, where it is classed with the horse as without understanding and therefore in need of control by bit and bridle.

Route to:
I-Share Library

Request number:

Patron comment:

Patron Barcode:
Patron Name:Alyson Renee Chitwood
Enumeration:c.1 Year:
Title: All the animals of the Bible lands / by Ge
Author: Cansdale, George Soper

Item Barcode:
Call Number:220.8 C22
Request ID: 44348
Request date:2/13/2014 05:23 PM

Callslip Request   2/13/2014 6:36:40 PM

DESERT ORYX being chased in southern Arabia. These were taken alive and sent to the security of a reserve in Arizona, U.S.A., where they are now breeding. One of the very few pictures of this rare animal ever taken in the wild (p. 84).

A LION PULLING DOWN a Red Deer stag, clearly identifiable by its antlers. From the black basalt obelisk of Shalmaneser III of Assyria, Nimrud (841 B.C.) (p. 89).

PERSIAN WILD ASSES, closely related to the Onager that once lived in Palestine, have been introduced into the Hay Bar Nature Reserve in the southern Negev, about 30 miles north of Eilat (p. 94).

ALTHOUGH ONAGERS were no longer used as working animals they were still being caught alive in the time of Ashurbanipal (8th Cent. B.C.). They are clearly recognizable by the short ears and tufted tail (p. 95).

V

Beasts
of the
Chase

Tentative identification of the wild animals allowed as food. Wild ox, Desert oryx, Addax, Bubale, Mountain sheep, Wild goat, Deer and Gazelle; also the Wild ass, or Onager.

THE WILD HOOFED ANIMALS HAVE ALWAYS FASCINATED MAN THE hunter as providers of tasty meat, as well as clothing and a range of tools and useful objects. They are often illustrated in cave drawings, which sometimes showed how early man hunted them. It seems likely that the Hebrews' cattle, sheep and goats were mostly eaten as part of the many sacrifices which were offered regularly, and though there are accounts of calves, lambs or kids being killed just as meat, the inference is that these were usually special occasions, such as the arrival of an unexpected guest, rather than the rule. Wild game probably supplied quite a lot of meat eaten in the country areas, though we have no way of knowing how much. All the evidence suggests that only three animals were common enough to be important: the Fallow Deer in the more wooded places (this was lost quite early), the Gazelles more or less everywhere, and the Nubian Ibex in the dry hills of Judaea, trans-Jordan and the desert. The last two have survived, though their future was threatened when the trophy and sport aspects of hunting became more important than the meat. A change of attitude during the 1960s seems to have removed this danger, but there is little chance of bringing back the long-lost species of larger game that were still there when Abram arrived from Haran. The Onager is included here because it was hunted in Mesopotamia. Palestine itself was right on the edge of its range and, in any case, it was single-hoofed and did not chew the cud, so it was of no interest to the Hebrews as food.

The following table lists the clean mammals of Deut. 14:4, 5, and also the Aurochs, with their rendering in the main VSS. The first three are

domesticated animals already discussed in Chap III; the others are the
main subject of this chapter.

Heb.	AV	RV	RSV	Suggested identification
shor	ox	ox	ox	ox ⎫ domes-
keseb	sheep	sheep	sheep	sheep ⎬ ticated
'ez	goat	goat	goat	goat ⎭
'ayyal	hart	hart	hart	deer generally
tsebi	roebuck	gazelle	gazelle	gazelle
yachmur	fallow deer	roebuck	roebuck	doubtful; perhaps bubale
'aqqo	wild goat	wild goat	wild goat	Nubian ibex
dishon	pygarg	pygarg	ibex	addax (?)
te'o	wild ox	antelope	antelope	Arabian oryx
zemer	chamois	chamois	mountain sheep	mountain sheep
re'em	unicorn	wild ox	wild ox	aurochs

Wild Ox

The splendid animal that masquerades in AV as the Unicorn is quite
properly identified in RV and RSV as the Wild Ox or to give its more formal name, the Aurochs, *Bos primigenius*, ancestor of our domestic cattle.
This is the beast that the Hebrews knew as *re'em*.[1]

It is hard to see how this mythological unicorn, first appearing in literature about 400 B.C., but having much older roots, became involved: the
LXX had called it 'the one-horned' and the name unicorn, which had
come into Middle English straight from the Latin, was there for the translators to use, notwithstanding the statement in Deut. 33:17 about the
horns of a unicorn! This whole passage should be read in RSV to get the
real force of it, but there is no possibility of it referring to a one-horned
animal.

The last recorded specimen of aurochs died in A.D. 1627 in a Polish
park north of Warsaw, where a herd had been enclosed for at least a century – possibly even two centuries, for it had disappeared from W.
Europe generally by about 1400. It could perhaps have survived a little
longer elsewhere, such as in remote and less inhabited areas of SE. Europe
and SW. Asia. It is worth noting that the European Bison, or Wisent,
with which the aurochs has often been confused, managed to hold out
until the twentieth century in two areas – in Poland in the north and the
Caucasus in the south-east; man at last recognized his responsibility to
preserve these remnants and did so just in time.

[1] The AV rendering of 'wild bull' or 'wild ox' for *te'o* cannot be supported; this was almost
certainly the Arabian Oryx.

Adequate descriptions and several good pictures left by Continental naturalists tell us quite a lot about the aurochs.[1]

The bulls were enormous, over 6 ft. at the shoulder, with long, forward-pointing horns; the coat was very dark brown or black, with a white dorsal line, curly in winter and sleeker in summer. The smaller cows were usually brown; in this the aurochs differed from most modern breeds, in which the sexes are of the same colour. Many of the original characteristics survived, distributed among many breeds of domestic cattle; breeding experiments in the Berlin and Munich Zoos over the past forty years have recombined many of these features to produce a 're-constructed' aurochs which gives a good impression of its appearance and also, perhaps, of its temperament.

In prehistoric times, the aurochs was found in suitable parts of Europe, W. and Central Asia and even parts of NE. Africa. The information about the various geographical races, which varied in colour, size and horn shape, is patchy, and most descriptions are based on European material, including the magnificent cave drawings of Lascaux.[2] Towards the end, if not all the time, the aurochs was a woodland animal, and the destruction of forests in W. Europe was the main cause of its extinction there and, probably, everywhere.

In lands where civilization came early the aurochs was soon driven out. Thotmosis III of Egypt (c. 1500 B.C.) enjoyed hunting aurochs, and when he had news of a herd he would embark at Memphis, go as far as possible by water and then take to his chariot. One such hunt, when he claims to have killed seventy-five out of a herd of 176, is commemorated on a special hunting scarab. The last Egyptian evidence, in a scene where they are being hunted from chariots, is dated around 1190 B.C., in the reign of Rameses III, when they were still reported to be common in the Gezira, farther south in the Sudan. Assyrian kings also hunted the aurochs on horseback and rated it almost equal to the lion as a trophy, but it survived in the less accessible parts of Iraq until a few centuries ago and Bodenheimer[3] reports vague rumours of it from remote valleys in Kurdistan even into the present century.

It is hard to speak accurately of its status in Palestine, where there are plenty of remains from the Pleistocene period; it had certainly disappeared long before the start of the Christian era. The OT passages, discussed below, make it clear that the biblical writers knew it, yet it is not included among the animals whose flesh could be eaten, though technically it was 'clean'; nor is there any evidence that it lived in Palestine during their time. Perhaps its early loss there is not surprising, for Palestine is

---

[1] An article by R. Lydekker on pp. 621–4 of *Harmsworth's Natural History* (1910) gives a detailed account of the aurochs in the sixteenth and seventeenth centuries.

[2] See Windals, *The Lascaux Cave Paintings*, (London, 1948).

[3] *Animals and Man in Bible Lands* (1960), p. 103.

comparatively small, with only a limited area of forest where such a large animal could feel safe.

The aurochs is mentioned nine times in the OT in more-or-less figurative contexts, all of which fully endorse this tr. and also give some useful information about this massive beast, though the metaphorical uses are varied. 'The strength of a wild ox' (Num. 23:22 RV). It was not only the most powerful hoofed animal they knew but it was also the largest, apart from the hippopotamus and elephant. Deut. 33:17, discussed above, associates it with a domestic bull and in Isa. 34:6, 7 it is again grouped with 'lambs and goats' and 'young steers with the mighty bulls'. Job 39:10 contrasts the strong wild ox with the domestic oxen that pull the plough and thresh the grain. Its fierceness is the point in Ps. 22:21 (RSV) 'Save me . . . from the horns of the wild oxen'. On the other hand, in Ps. 29:6 Sirion is made to skip like a young wild ox, referring to the friskiness of calves, and in Ps. 92:10 (RSV) 'Thou has exalted my horn like that of the wild ox', the strength and grandeur of the aurochs with its huge horns is in mind.

Arabian or Desert Oryx

The Hebrew word te'o is found only twice and in the AV it appears as 'wild bull' or 'wild ox', while RV and RSV tr. 'antelope'. The former is wrong, for this name belongs to the aurochs, and the latter is preferred. However, antelope is a vague name, applicable to many species, and it seems likely that this is in fact a particular antelope – the Desert Oryx, *Oryx leucoryx*. This conclusion is based on information in the passages where it occurs and on our knowledge of the animals found in these deserts.

Its place in the list of clean animals shows it to be a wild ruminant, and Isa. 51:20 speaks of it being caught in a net. This method of taking even large game is mentioned several times in OT, and it was practised in Arab countries until the end of the last century. It is generally agreed that four types of antelope would once have been found in these and adjoining deserts – Gazelle, Addax, Bubale and Oryx. Of these the first is firmly identified with the roebuck of the OT. The Addax and the Bubale, which rarely, if at all, reached Palestine are thought to be identified with other names in the Heb. list, and it is therefore reasonable to equate te'o with the Desert Oryx, which was certainly a member of the Palestine fauna in earlier times.

This is the smallest of four species of oryx, and the only one outside Africa. Standing around 40 in. at the shoulder it has slender, nearly straight horns, those of the cow usually being rather longer. These horns can be used very dangerously, for they are needle-sharp and they point forward when the head is lowered. The whole body colour is ashy-white, with some fawn or yellow areas, but in some lights it looks white. Its smooth tail ends in a tuft. It is mostly a browser and for much of the year is dependent on the dry shrubs of the desert; after rain it seeks out patches of green growth and also digs up tubers, but is able to go for long periods without water. It feeds mostly at night, and by day lies up under a bush or other shade; it is said to dig a trench for itself if it can find no other shelter.

Until the beginning of the nineteenth century, it could still be seen in most suitable parts of the Middle East, including Palestine, Syria, Iraq, Sinai and Arabia. It was always a desirable trophy but the primitive hunting methods did not seriously reduce its numbers, for it could usually escape into the heart of the desert. When the Bedouins killed an oryx they used every scrap of it; the skin was turned into leather and the horns made pipes for shepherd-boys. The arrival of rifles soon changed the position tragically. By 1864 it had disappeared from much of its territory and was common only in parts of Arabia. Canon Tristram, an accurate observer, reported seeing one at extreme range in the Palestine desert, but his party did not collect one. The horns were still plentiful in the Damascus market.

By 1914 there were hardly any outside Arabia; in 1930 only two groups were left in the wild and a tiny handful in captivity. One of these small herds was in the north of Saudi Arabia, but this had been wiped out by the end of the 1950s, leaving only those in the *Rub al Khali*, the Empty Quarter. It is possible that a few lingered in S. Jordan until c.1950.

This catastrophic decline is due to modern weapons and transport – machine-guns used from special desert cars by men who hold no life dear. Against such the desert oryx has no protection. When it was realized that it had become one of the rarest of animals, world public opinion was stirred and 'Operation Oryx' took place, to transfer a handful to the Arizona desert, where they are now breeding. It may also have had some impact in Arabia, where numbers have now risen to a total of perhaps 200 head in several groups.

Addax

Among several quaint animal names found only in the AV is the Pygarg, from Heb. *dishon*; this is merely a transliteration of the Gr. word meaning 'white-rumped', by which Herodotus and Pliny had long ago described an antelope. Such a name could be given to a number of ruminants, including gazelles and deer, in which a white rump pattern is a common recognition feature. Its position in the food list, between two animals that are probably desert species, coupled with a long-standing tradition, suggests that this is the Addax, *Addax nasomaculatus*, a desert antelope classified between the oryx and hartebeests. It is often stated that this species was never found north of Egypt but Canon Tristram, working in the Arabah – the wide, low plain south of the Dead Sea – saw one and identified it clearly on his 1863–4 expedition. He also reported that it was well known to the Bedouin. The last specimen was killed by c.1900.

Both bull and cow have horns up to 36 in. long and in an obvious spiral which distinguishes them positively from the desert oryx, even at great range, where the slightly smaller size of the latter would not be noted. Both species have the same pale desert coat, but the addax becomes darker in winter and it also has a short black mane. It lives a similar life to the oryx. Its former range was probably from Senegal across the Sahara to Egypt and the edge of Palestine, but this has been reduced to a few small areas deep in the desert where only the hard terrain has saved it. It is still hunted remorselessly and unless some action is taken it cannot survive.

Bubale or Bubal Hartebeest

Heb. *yachmur* (Deut. 14:5), is perhaps the most difficult name in this list of clean animals. AV renders it 'fallow deer', which RV and RSV change to 'roedeer', neither of which is very likely, especially the latter. LXX has used Gr. *bubalos*, the same root from which buffalo comes, and Bubale is the transliteration of this. Unless there has been a switch of names this is the N. African race of *Alcelaphus buselaphus*, that was well-known to the ancients, especially in Egypt where it often featured in inscriptions and was also prepared as a mummy. Many authors wrote about it and it was much hunted for its venison. It is generally known today as Red Hartebeest.

The range certainly extended from Morocco to Egypt, and Canon Tristram (1867) reported that Arabs in southern Palestine knew it by its N. African name and claimed that they often took it as it came to drink at streams on the east side of the Dead Sea. Unfortunately, there seems to be no other evidence for its occurring so far north. Closely related forms are found in other parts of Africa, but this one disappeared from Egypt long ago and may even be totally extinct now.

On the facts so far the tr. bubale is not impossible, but a complication comes from its other mention (I Kings 4:23), where it is listed as a regular item in Solomon's daily provision. This suggests either an animal so common that it could be caught with little difficulty, or one suitable for keeping as a park animal, and therefore always available. In ancient Egypt quite a range of wild animals were kept like this. This makes bubale less probable and this identification is left open.

Mountain Sheep

One difficulty faced by the early translators of the English Bible was that they knew little about the animal life of the Holy Land and therefore translated in terms of what they knew. It is true that Crusaders had been going – and sometimes returning – but they were seldom interested in such matters, nor did they have much opportunity of studying them. So it came about that *zemer*, the leaper, last in the list of clean animals, was rendered 'chamois', until the RSV changed it to 'mountain sheep'. Considering their limited sources of information, chamois is quite near. It was well known from the high mountains of S. Europe and extended as far south east as Asia Minor. It is a most distinctive ruminant, the only representative of the goat-antelopes in Europe, and one whose remains are unmistakable, so that when the experts assure us that it never lived in or around Palestine we must take their word for it. In any case there is virtually no suitable habitat there, for these animals live between the tree line and the perma-nent snow.

The Nubian Ibex, or Mountain Goat, is identified with *ya'el* and *'aqqo*, so that the most likely candidate for *zemer* is mountain sheep, though this is an indefinite name. The word is found only in Deut. 14:5, so we have no background information other than that it is a ruminant, but if the above suggestion is correct, only two animals need be discussed:

1. Barbary Sheep (*Ammotragus lervia*), often called by its native names *Aoudad* or *Arui*, which is the only African sheep, though not closely re-lated to the true sheep. It is heavily built and stands nearly 40 in. high, with massive curved horns. Its long coat is tawny. It is at home in dry rocky hills and mountains from the Atlantic coast across the Sahara to the Red Sea, but there is no firm evidence that it ever extended farther north. A century ago Bedouins spoke of a mountain sheep from the hills around Petra, and there is a further unsupported record for early this century, but no specimen has ever been taken, and these reports cannot be taken as proved. It was well known in Egypt and among the animals which were mummified.

2. One or other form of Mouflon (*Ovis musimon*), which is found in several races, some in S. Europe and others in SW. Asia, mostly in the hills of Asia Minor; perhaps, earlier, in the hills of Palestine. This is much smaller than the *Aoudad*, standing only about 26 in. and dark reddish brown in colour, with white or yellow flank patches developing in winter. It is a true sheep and thought to be, in small part, an ancestor of the domesticated sheep.

This latter seems to be the more likely identification, but it is by no means certain.

Wild Goat

It is best first to point out the distinction between two closely related species which have often been confused. The true Wild Goat is *Capra aegagrus*, the main ancestor of the many breeds of domesticated goats found all over the world today. This wild goat once lived as far south as Palestine where its remains have been found in Stone Age deposits, but it had disappeared long before biblical times and it is most unlikely that the Hebrews knew it.[1]

---

[1] This complex problem is discussed fully in Zeuner, *A History of Domesticated Animals* 1963), Ch. 6.

The other is the Nubian Ibex, *Capra nubiana;* it is still found in Palestine and known as *Beden* to the Arabs, and it has never been domesticated in any way. Without doubt this is the wild goat of the Scriptures and it will now be described more fully, using its proper name of ibex to avoid further confusion.

Heb. *ye'elim*, always pl., occurs three times and in all EV it is tr. 'wild goat', except that RSV once has 'mountain goat'. The root means 'climber' and all passages associate it with mountains; e.g., 'The high hills are a refuge for the wild goats' (Ps. 104:18). It is significant that this word does not occur in the sing., for the Nubian ibex is a herd animal and usually lives in small family groups of up to ten. The incident in I Sam. 24:2 ff. gives useful confirmation by describing David and his men as being 'on the rocks of the wild goats'. This was at En Gedi, the oasis just above the west side of the Dead Sea. The name itself was significant – the Fountain of the Kid – and the ibex themselves are still there today, in a Wildlife Sanctuary made specially to protect them among the barren hills where they have always lived. In Job 39:1 the ibex is associated with the hind (deer) in a way suggesting that they belong to the same class of animals.

Heb. *'aqqo* is found in the food list of Deut. 14:5 and nowhere else. It is consistently rendered 'wild goat' and though many scholars have regarded the word as too uncertain to be worth attention, there is good reason to follow Canon Tristram when he suggests that this is a synonym for *ya'el*; otherwise the ibex would be omitted from the food list, which would be unlikely, for it was obviously common enough then to be worth hunting. It is quite usual for common animals to have alternative Heb. names, e.g., ass, wild ass, lion, etc.

The Nubian ibex is the same size as the better-known Alpine ibex, or Steinbok, of Switzerland and Italy, standing about 34 in. at the shoulder, but having rather more slender but more clearly ridged horns, sweeping back in a wide curve to a length of up to 50 in. in the buck, and much less in the doe. The general colour is grey, becoming browner in winter. Like most members of the goat family it both browses and grazes, but in the desert hills it would be dependent on dry shrubs for much of the year. The ibex has one or two at a birth, once a year. Its venison is considered far better than the rather dry meat of the gazelle and for this reason it has been suggested it was this that Jacob asked Esau to find for him. When an ibex is killed nothing is wasted; even the heavy horns are in great demand in the Jerusalem workshops for making knife handles and other souvenirs.

This species is confined to mountains east of the Nile, in Sinai and S. Arabia, with outlying groups in Israel and probably Jordan. Up to a century ago its numbers had not been dangerously reduced by hunting and it was still fairly common around En Gedi and the south end of the Dead Sea. In the line of hills in which Petra was built it could be seen in parties of eight or ten; there were a few in the dry hills east of Jerusalem and even

perhaps between Samaria and the Jordan. Since then its position north of
Sinai has seriously worsened, but its numbers are hard to assess, for it
lives in terrain which is hard physically and often near frontiers where
naturalists are not encouraged. It is recovering under the protection that it
receives in the Reserves and it should be safe.

The word doe is found only in Prov. 5:19; 'a lovely hind, a graceful
doe' (RV and RSV, AV has 'roe'). This is from Heb. *ya'alah*, the female of
the Nubian ibex or wild goat. Perhaps the word doe is acceptable, for it
is the correct term for the female of various species. However, there is an
Arabic phrase 'more beautiful than a wild goat', so there is no reason why
an accurate tr. should not be used.

Deer

To most English-speaking people any hoofed animal with branched antlers
is just a deer; size, colour and shape of antlers are all immaterial. It is
unlikely that the Hebrews were any more discriminating and although
two, perhaps three, kinds lived in Palestine we cannot expect them to be
named separately, and this simplifies our search for information.

Reasons are given elsewhere for rejecting the tr. 'roebuck' (AV); this
is without doubt the Gazelle. 'Roebuck' RV and RSV – from Heb. *yachmur*) is also incorrect, while the AV rendering of 'fallow deer' is doubtful.
We are thus left with the words that most authorities now agree stand for
deer, though this word does not seem to be found, other than in fallow
deer, in any common tr. Heb. *'ayyal* and its fem. forms *'ayyalah* and *'ayye-
leth* are normally tr. 'hart' and 'hind', which in popular usage is near
enough. The more technical meaning of hart is the male of several kinds of
deer, especially after the fifth year; hind is parallel to this and is applied to
a female deer (usually Red Deer) of the third year and upwards.

With a few exceptions this is how most VSS treat these words. RSV regards the text of Ps. 29:9 as needing revision and '(The voice of the Lord
maketh) the hinds to calve' becomes 'the oaks to whirl'. It also reconstructs
Prov. 7:22 which is now 'as a stag is caught fast'. Stag also replaces hart in
three vv. in Song of Solomon and is apparently not used in any other
VS. Stag is generally defined as an adult male of most species; however,
in the reindeer the male is a bull and in fallow deer a buck.

Having dealt with this confusion in English naming we can now look
at the three kinds of deer that once inhabited Palestine:

1. Red Deer (*Cervus elaphus*). This familiar species once had a wide distribution, for it lived in all suitable wooded parts of Europe and SW.
Asia, as well as in N. Africa. Destruction of forest greatly reduced its
range but in some parts, as for instance in Scotland, it changed its habits
and occupied an otherwise empty niche – the moorlands and mountains.
However, this is exceptional and it remains basically a forest animal,

being quick to find its way back into new forests such as those that have been established in East Anglia in the past fifty years.

Red deer were often preserved as royal game and with continuing protection, often in parks, they have survived even in industrialized lands. An adult stands between 4 and 5 ft. at the shoulder and may weigh up to 4 cwt. The spreading antlers, with ten or even more points, are shed and renewed annually, as in all deer. The hind has no antlers.

Suitable areas in Palestine must have been few and it disappeared early, perhaps even before the Hebrews arrived; there is no evidence on this point. It was pushed back continually to become extinct in the remoter parts of Iraq during the last century, and the nearest left now are probably those in the mountains of Anatolia, in Turkey. An Egyptian form of this deer is illustrated in temples, but it was killed out many centuries B.C.

2. Fallow Deer (*Dama dama*). This is much smaller, standing only about 3 ft. All deer are more or less spotted at birth but in this species they remain spotted at all ages, most noticeably so in the summer. The normal form is red brown; in captive herds the colour varies from almost white to nearly black. The antlers are palmate, i.e., flattened towards the ends, with short points. This deer has been so long a park animal, and introduced so widely, using different races, that its natural distribution is now almost impossible to map. Its decline in Palestine is hard to plot, but it hung on in small numbers until about a century ago, when Canon Tristram records seeing one in an open glade about ten miles west of the lake of Galilee, and a few were said to be living between Mount Tabor and the Jordan. The last in Palestine had been killed by 1922 and the nearest survivors are in Anatolia. A larger brighter species, *D. mesopotamica*, known variously as Persian, Mesopotamian or Giant Fallow Deer, once extended from Mesopotamia to Palestine, living in the hill forests, but is now found only in the Zagros Mountains of Persia.

3. Roe Deer (*Capreolus capreolus*) is the smallest of all, standing only about 28 in. with short, upright antlers quite unlike any other kind. The doe is heavier than the buck, and weighs up to 60 lb. In contrast to the other two deer it is solitary. It stays mostly in cover, coming out of the woods only to graze in nearby fields, and as a result of these secretive habits it exists almost unknown in many woodland areas, especially in Britain, so that recorded facts about it are scanty. It is also not surprising that although it was once probably the commonest and most widespread species, as it is throughout Europe now, it was rarely depicted in ancient art, whereas both red and fallow deer were often clearly illustrated. The last roe deer was seen on Mount Carmel early this century. Its nearest locality now is Kurdistan.

All deer make good eating when killed at the right season and in good

condition. Being hoofed ruminants they were clean meat to the Hebrews; more than that, they were once so common that their venison was
almost used as a standard, with gazelle; e.g., 'Even as the roebuck (gazelle)
and the hart (deer) is eaten' (Deut. 12:22). In contrast to most others
treated in this chapter, the first five mentions of deer are all in literal contexts and clearly imply that these were familiar animals and regularly
eaten. This was one of the meats supplied daily to Solomon's kitchen.

The conclusion seems to be that while *'ayyal* was probably used for deer
generally, both red and roe deer could largely be discounted, the former
because it had probably gone already, and the latter because it was small
and hard to come by. The Biblical hart and hind can therefore be regarded
as the fallow deer, and it is possible that Solomon had deer parks where
they were kept in readiness. Such animal husbandry had flourished at a
high standard many centuries earlier in Egypt. At least two towns were
called Aijalon, from this Heb. word. One stood at the entrance of a valley
leading up to Jerusalem from the coastal plain, then in the sort of wooded
country where deer would be plentiful.

Finally some reference must be made to the figurative aspect of deer in
the Scriptures. Hart and hind between them are found twenty-one times
and apart from the first five all are in poetic or figurative passages where
they have a range of meanings. Perhaps the most familiar verse is Isa. 35:6,
made so by being sung as an aria in the Messiah, 'Then shall the lame man
leap as an hart'. The same suggestion of swiftness and agility is found in II
Sam. 22:34, 'The Lord God . . . will make my feet like hind's feet', and
this is quoted again in Ps. 18:33 and Hab. 3:19. The three times repeated
'My beloved is like . . . a young stag' (Cant. 2:9, 17; 8:14 RSV) also
echoes this thought.

There are three references to the hinds bearing their young which are
comments on the nature of the hind rather than spiritual lessons. In Job
39:1 God asks 'Canst thou mark when the hinds do calve?', which may
suggest their careful choice of a secluded spot. Ps. 29 is the great poem
about the thunderstorm and v. 9, already mentioned above, is often taken
to mean that the hinds are so sensitive that the thunder may make them
calve prematurely. Jer. 14 opens by describing the sufferings caused by a
famine sent as a result of sin and disobedience, and even the animals suffer.
'The hind also calved in the field and forsook it, because there was no
grass.' The young of these grazing animals are normally dropped when
fresh grass is obtainable, to provide a good flow of milk and also suitable
food for the growing fawns. This is a case of animals suffering as a result
of human sin. Jeremiah speaks in the same strain in Lam. 1:6, 'Harts that
find no pasture'. Prov. 5:19 uses the hind as a picture of an ideal wife, 'Let
her be as the loving hind', though naturalists might feel that the simile
should not be pressed too far!

Another verse is made familiar by a hymn based on it, 'As pants the hart for cooling streams' (Ps. 42:1). Only those who have lived in Palestine for any period can realize the real value of water, and understand why it is so frequently a picture of God-given life in the OT, as it is here.

My attention has been drawn to some German game reports that may give this passage a different emphasis. In all VSS and Commentaries the word 'pant' is taken to mean 'yearn for', but AV marg. has 'bray' and the same Heb. word *arag* is found in Joel 1:20, 'The beasts of the field (*behema*) cry also unto Thee'. Reports suggest that in times of drought stags do indeed call loudly for water. A game supervisor, Mr. E. von Ahrensberg, noted that in a severe January frost all water was frozen solid and 'the stags called from all directions day and night,[1] as the game-keepers and hunters supposed because of thirst'. Stags are normally quite silent except in the autumn mating season. A similar call was heard from an enclosed stag which by accident was kept without water for eight days; the calling stopped when water was given.

Gazelle

After so many animals whose identification has to be argued from all the evidence available it is a relief to find that the tr. 'gazelle' for Heb. *tsebi* is not disputed, though this has been fully accepted only in RSV. The key is found in Acts 9:36; 'Tabitha, which means Dorcas or gazelle'. The good lady best known as the doer of good deeds and the inspiration of church sewing-parties took her name from this graceful member of the antelope tribe. AV has 'roe' and 'roebuck', which was about as near as the translators could get in size and general shape; the English word gazelle, derived from the Arabic through Spanish, did not appear until 1610. RV uses 'gazelle' for all literal passages but retains 'roe' for figurative uses, e.g., 'Deliver thyself as a roe from the hand of the hunter' (Prov. 6:5). This treatment is unfortunate and unnecessary, for roe has no greater poetic feeling than gazelle, a name always associated with grace. Perhaps the Heb. *'opher tsebiyyah*, found in Cant. 4:5 and 7:3, needs comment: 'young roes that are twins' (AV); 'fawns that are twins of a roe' (RV); 'fawns, twins of a gazelle' (RSV), which is correct. The word fawn is found in only one other passage and is acceptable though strictly fawn is used only for the young of certain species of deer.

Gazelles are small to medium-sized antelopes characteristic of dry grass woodland, steppe and desert as they extend, in about twelve species, from W. and Central Africa through SW. Asia, Persia and India to the Gobi Desert of Mongolia. The Springbuck of the Kalahari Desert in S. Africa is also a gazelle, with the scientific name of *Antidorcas*. Its Gr. name is also seen unchanged in *Gazella dorcas*, known as the Dorcas Gazelle: this was about the first to be described and it is still found in Palestine, mostly in the south. The Palestine Gazelle is much more common and widespread; it is

[1] F. Vanneyen, *Das Rotwild* (1957).

about the same size, standing a little over 24 in. at the shoulder. East of the Jordan its place is taken by the rather darker Arabian Gazelle, but perhaps they are only races of the same species. All gazelles have horns and, with only about one exception, they are carried by both sexes. There is much variation in size – from 6 to 30 in. – but they are all more or less lyre-shaped. All gazelles have the same general colour pattern – pale brown or sandy above, usually with a dark line along the flanks demarcating the almost white underparts. This has some camouflage value and at a distance gazelles are hard to spot, especially if there is some heat haze. Their speed is equally useful for self-defence, and this is referred to in all the four figurative passages outside the Song of Solomon.

For a long time gazelles must have been common enough in Palestine to provide a useful source of meat. This is clearly implied in Deut. 12:15, 22, where they are bracketed with deer (see above). Gazelles were taken in nets and other devices, e.g., 'He is as a roe escaped out of the snare' (Ecclus: 27:20). It would have been the most plentiful game around Beersheba, at the gateway to the Negev, when Esau was sent to hunt venison for his father, but it was not reckoned to be such good eating as Nubian ibex, and the time taken suggests that he might have tried for this latter. In Palestine gazelles are found in most regions, not only in and around the desert, which is true of few kinds of game. Canon Tristram, describing conditions in the mid-nineteenth century, found gazelles the only plentiful game animal, with small groups everywhere and, in the south, herds of up to a hundred. He also saw them on the Mount of Olives, on Mount Carmel and among the hills of Galilee. The spread of cultivation must have reduced their numbers, but gazelles generally are not worried much by lack of cover or the presence of man. In fact around the Plain of Esdraelon, where gazelles have made a good recovery, they can often be seen feeding while tractors work in the same field.

The rifle began to do what older hunting methods, using nets, bows and arrows, dogs and falcons had not done, for there was little cover in the desert and the gazelles took time to learn the range of a rifle, but even this only became really deadly when man used it from special cars able to cruise freely over the desert. In most Arab countries there is little or no control over such slaughter, though there is the promise of it in Jordan. The position in Israel worsened seriously in the 1950s and in a period of 5 years Army officers are said to have killed 1,000 gazelles in the Negev but there has been a big change in outlook. With general regulations and the establishment of reserves, stocks have already made a fine recovery and will, in time, be able to spread out and re-colonize former territories. With a little patience the visitor has a fair chance of seeing one or two in the desert, as we did near Eilat in 1962, though without the keen eyes of the Warden we would never have spotted them.

In a number of figurative passages the gazelle is coupled with the deer, e.g., 'He comes leaping upon the mountains, bounding over the hills. My beloved is like a gazelle or a young stag' (Cant. 2:8, 9, RSV). To Eastern folk the gazelle was the embodiment of many graces – swiftness, beauty and gentleness. Asahel, Joab's brother, was 'as swift of foot as a wild gazelle' (II Sam. 2:18, RSV). Some of David's army recruits from Gad were 'mighty warriors . . . as swift as gazelles upon the mountains' (I Chron. 12:8). Yet Isa. 13:14, referring presumably to its timidity, speaks of Babylon being like 'a hunted gazelle'; not long before it had been described as a roaring lion (5:29).

Two names are thought to mean gazelle. Zebaim (Ezra 2:57) is a place not yet identified. Zibia was the name of a woman from Beersheba (II Kings 12:1), an area where gazelles were once very plentiful.

Wild Ass

Two Heb. words are rendered 'wild ass'. *Pere'* is the main name while *'arod*, found only twice, seems to be an alternative, perhaps a nickname. There has been some confusion about its identity, for many writers reasonably assumed that it was the wild form from which the donkey has been domesticated, but this latter has a wholly African ancestry. The animal that Job and the Prophets knew was a native of SW. Asia whose correct name was Onager, *Equus hemionus*, and classed by zoologists as a 'half-ass'. It was found in Palestine, or at any rate around its borders, for well over 2,000 years more but had almost disappeared by the middle of the nineteenth century; a few lived on in SE. Jordan until early this century. This western race of onager was still fairly common in Iraq; now these have gone, too, and the species is represented only by some survivors in Persia, India and central Asia, where their status is hard to determine. The onager of Mesopotamia was probably smaller than any that are left and stood perhaps 45 in. at the withers; it was almost white, with pale fawn areas on the flanks and a black dorsal stripe and mane. The ears were shorter and narrower than in African asses.

The Persian Wild Ass is on the list of endangered animals and three pairs were recently introduced into the Hay Bar Nature Reserve in the Negev, where they are already breeding (*ill. f.p.* 81).

The original range, of the several geographical races, was from the borders of Europe and Palestine on the west and south through to India and Mongolia. It was a gregarious animal of the dry grassy plains and Job described its habitat precisely: 'the steppe for his home and the salt land for his dwelling' (Job 39:6, RSV). Its instinct was to escape by running to the open plains, which was dangerous enough when its enemies were horsemen armed with bows and arrows, even though many old writers commented on its great speed: it became disastrous when rifles arrived.

Onagers were also pursued by the heavy dogs developed in Mesopotamia for use against lions; these methods were still being practised in Syria about the beginning of the Christian era. Onagers were killed for their meat, which Xenophon reported to be of more delicate flavour than deer; it is single-hoofed and as such was forbidden food to the Hebrews.

For a long time the onager was thought to have been untamable, and this had resulted in some confusion about the draught animals used in Ancient Mesopotamia. Further scrutiny of the illustration from the royal cemetery at Ur (*c.* 2500 B.C.) has shown that the Sumerians used it for drawing four-wheeled chariots; the apparently tufted tail is obvious (in fact the tail is short-haired for much of its length), and the identification has been further confirmed by a study of the bones from Tell Asmar. Unfortunately there is no way of knowing whether they were ever fully domesticated, or just captured when young and trained, as elephants are. Writers tell of their being taken with lassos, presumably for use alive, and this is illustrated in a scene from the Palace of Ashurbanipal at Ninevah.

Onagers were bridled quite differently from horses, with nose-rings when not working and a strap tied around the muzzle when harnessed up. This suggests that their use for draught purposes was based on previous experience with oxen rather than in imitation of horses in nearby countries, where in any case, it is doubtful if horses were yet in use. The horse had arrived in Mesopotamia early in the second millennium B.C., so there was little point in carrying on with the onager. The horse was bigger and stronger, as well as much more amenable, and the horse-bit gave the driver, in his two-wheeled chariot, far more complete control than he ever had over the onager.

The wild ass features mostly in the poetical and prophetic books, where it is usually spoken of as wild and untamable. In Jer. 2:24 Jehovah calls Judah 'a wild ass used to the wilderness, that snuffeth up the wind at her pleasure'. In Gen. 16:12 Hagar is promised that her son Ishmael will be 'a wild ass of a man, his hand against every man' (RSV).

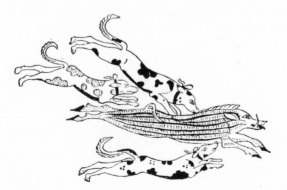

VI

Pig
Hippopotamus
and Elephant

Wild and domesticated swine, their history and reasons for being forbidden as food. Behemoth – the Hippo? Elephants as producers of ivory and as fighting machines.

PIGS ARE FOUND WILD ALMOST ALL OVER THE WORLD EXCEPT IN Australasia, though even there domestic pigs have escaped from farms and reverted to the wild state in suitable areas. In spite of this wide spread there are less than a dozen different kinds, of which half are the various species of true wild pig from which the domestic breeds are descended. These have a wide range throughout Europe, N. Africa, suitable parts of Asia and right down into the Malaysian islands. These pigs had to fall back as lands were developed and their haunts occupied, and the last British specimen died early in the seventeenth century, but they are still far from rare in the forests of most European countries – and even in small lands such as Palestine.

The main species, *Sus scrofa*, stretches right across into Asia, so Palestine is just about in the middle of its range. The Wild Boar is hardly an attractive beast; 4 ft. long, standing about 3 ft. at the shoulder, it is covered sparsely with long, stiff, bristly hairs, usually with an upstanding mane on the nape and neck, and often along the centre of the back too. The colour is dark grey to brown, sometimes almost black. Its four canine teeth grow continually and can become formidable weapons – and also trophies of the hunt. It is most at home in forests and marshes, which explains its early loss to Britain, and both of these habitats are mentioned in the only two vv. where the wild boar can be identified in the Scriptures, 'the boar from the forest ravages it' (Ps. 80:13, RSV); in the other (Ps. 68:30, RSV) the description 'the beasts that dwell among the reeds' is generally taken to be a euphemism for the same animal. Pigs are rightly described as

THE NUBIAN IBEX — the Wild Goat of the Bible — feeds largely by browsing trees and shrubs and is an animal of the rocky hills, especially around En Gedi (p. 88).

WILD BOARS are still widespread in the Middle East, now mostly found in marshes and dense thickets, such as those along parts of the Jordan valley (p. 97).

PART OF THE LION HUNT relief. (*top right*) Ashurbanipal in single combat with a lion. (*centre*) Riderless horse being attacked by a wounded lion. (*bottom left*) Flock of gazelles, with males, females and young (p. 109 top., p. 92).

omnivorous and they eat just about everything they find in, on or within their reach above the ground – roots and tubers, grubs and snakes, mice and young birds, as well as grapes and other fruit.

A century ago, long before the heavy immigration and the effective occupation of many parts of Palestine, wild boars were really plentiful. Then, as now, they were most common in the thickets along the Jordan, but Canon Tristram reported seeing them wherever water was within reasonable reach. One of the boar's favourite foods there is the tuber of the iris. Most of its refuges have now gone and its habitat has been greatly reduced, but it still survives and does some damage to farms in the Jordan Valley. It is unclean to both Jew and Muslim, though some individuals now are less scrupulous, and there is naturally less urge to hunt prey which will not be eaten and which causes ritual defilement. A few people, though not many, regard hunting as a sport and to them the boar is a worthy quarry.

Heb. *chazir* is used for both wild and domesticated forms; the context normally shows which is meant. The first two mentions are in the Mosaic food laws, which covers both, for they are equally unclean.

Although pigs are in the same group as the cattle and antelopes, known as even-toed hoofed animals, they differ radically from these 'clean' animals in having simple stomachs and not the complicated ones that enable ruminants to chew the cud. They differ in other major ways also, especially in their breeding pattern; a litter or farrow of anything up to a dozen piglets is born after a gestation period of under four months, while cattle bear one calf, rarely two, after more than nine months. This gave the pig tremendous potential when it became domesticated, as is described below. With very few exceptions wild piglets are born with a pattern of broken lines along the sides which disappear as they grow. This characteristic has been lost completely in all domestic forms but it is said to reappear sometimes if they escape and become truly feral. All forms are more or less gregarious and go about in herds or sounders; this feature probably made it rather easier to domesticate them in the first place.

As we turn to the domestic pig we find some problems in the English names. The word swine was already old when the Bible was first translated and the same root is seen in German *Schwein*. It has now become obsolete in ordinary language and is retained only in a few technical terms such as swine fever, which is a dangerous disease of the pig, and it is also used as a term of abuse. Long custom perhaps justifies its retention in most EV, but J. B. Phillips prefers pig. This word also is very old and began by meaning a young swine. The male is the boar and the female the sow, usually after they have become adult. In accordance with a strange convention the meat is given a name from the French – pork. Wild Boar is the generally accepted name for the wild ancestors of the pig; most other wild species are called hog, e.g., Wart-hog.

Pigs were brought into the service of man independently in several parts

G

of the world; those in Europe and W. Asia came from *Sus scrofa*, in its various geographical races, and the Chinese pig from the eastern species, S. *vittatus*. The position has been hopelessly confused by these pigs being taken around by man in his wanderings, so that most are of very mixed stock. For instance, in the Swiss Neolithic villages remains of two entirely different breeds have been found; one was the small Turbary pig, which had been brought from somewhere farther east, and the other had been derived from the local wild pig. This all happened in the days long before carved or written records and it is impossible to suggest what might have happened.[1]

Experts are agreed that domestication took place in the Neolithic period, of which the dates varied in different parts of the world, but it was after man began living in more or less permanent settlements. This was an absolute necessity, for the crops had to be protected by fencing while the pigs roamed the forest, controlled by swineherds, whose job was important. This was the work that the prodigal son (Luke 15) found for himself; his job was not so much to feed as to herd and protect them as they rooted around for seeds. Pigs stayed as omnivorous as their wild ancestors and took anything that was edible, whether of plant or animal origin. The pig's sensitive but muscular snout ends in a ring of gristle capable of root-ing through almost any soil in search of tubers, field-mice, etc.; or a field of root crops, given the opportunity. This digging had a most important side-effect found in none of the other livestock, for by turning over the soil to a depth of several inches the pigs destroyed shrubs and stopped re-growth of trees, allowing grass to come in. This gave pasturage for other animals; it also made it easier for the farmer to take over for his next en-closure. Pigs were certainly being kept in such 'villages' before or around 2500 B.C. in places as far apart as Greece, Switzerland and Hungary in the west; Egypt in the south; and Mesopotamia in the north-east. The Chinese pig was doing its bit some centuries before this.

Although it is sometimes suggested that the pig first made itself useful by scavenging, it soon proved of tremendous value to these early farmers; it notably helped prepare the land and deal with plagues of rodents, but it also converted all sorts of vegetable and animal matter, otherwise useless to man, into good meat and especially fat. In the autumn it lived largely on acorns and beech-mast, to which Chaucer gave the name 'pannage'; this later came to mean the jealously-guarded right of villagers to let their pigs search for this food on common land.

In some countries, especially Egypt, pigs also had to tread in the seed in the flooded fields. Compared to other livestock the pig had few by-prod-

---

[1] In the middle of the twentieth century we have had a good example of this mixing of breeds. The Ministry of Agriculture imported from Denmark some specially selected Land-race pigs of radically different shape, to breed with local bacon herds and so change the type. Things were less sophisticated in pre-historic times, but without the introduction of foreign types and the subsequent interbreeding the evidence would be much easier to sort out.

ucts; its bristles have always been of some use; and skins were sometimes made into a special type of leather, though they were usually left on the meat and eaten. Pig's bones are useless for making tools because they remain in an undeveloped state until long after the animal becomes adult – at about eighteen months. Tusks are made into ornaments, but one of the typical changes in the domestic form is that these become much smaller, and most carvings are made from wild tusks.

Modern pigs bear little likeness to their dark, shaggy forebears. Now they come in a range of colours – black, red and saddleback, though most are still white – and one even has curly hair. They vary in size and shape too, being bred precisely for the products they must supply. More and more they are having to spend their whole lives under cover in warm dry buildings where their food conversion factor is almost studied by computer! Today they have one basic use – to convert accurately compounded rations into human food more quickly and efficiently than any other animal. In China the pig has always been the main meat-producer, one reason for this being that it thrives in the small sties where it was kept in densely populated areas. As regards pigs there seems to be little new under the sun, especially when we learn that Julius Caesar enjoyed his smoked ham and full meat sausages!

It may at first seem strange that such a useful producer of nourishing food should have headed the list of Hebrew abominations and been totally forbidden; later the Muslims came to avoid it with a fanaticism that caused riots. The fact that even in Britain pork was long considered edible only when there was an 'r' in the month – from September to April – should have suggested that pork is not as other meats. Discoveries about human diseases have now thrown interesting light on this ancient ban, and we know that pork is completely safe only when it has been fully cooked. We also know that the pig is a potential victim of several complex parasites that have alternate hosts, one of which is man. The most important and dangerous of these is a tape-worm that causes trichinosis; it passes one stage in the muscles of the pig and can only progress to the next stage after being eaten by man or by some other suitable host. Various tissues are invaded, causing much pain, and death is likely if there is repeated infection. The contaminated pork cannot always be found by inspection and thorough heat treatment is the only way of making sure. In those early days firewood could be scarce and cooking inadequate, so prohibition was the safest policy. But trichinosis was not the only danger. The pig has always been a scavenger and, living around human settlements, it could easily pick up infected material, even after this had been buried, and be affected itself or just carry disease around. In such conditions the pig was better kept on the black list – but it has taken twentieth-century medicine to discover the soundness of that piece of Mosaic law!

Presumably the Muslims took over the ban from their neighbours, but they are not the only people to have observed it, for some strata of Ancient Egyptian society held the pig to be *tabu* while others enjoyed it. The pig in Egypt had a mixed history, for sometimes it was sacred and sometimes evil; at one stage it was believed that souls of the wicked migrated into pigs. These facts would have increased the horror with which the Hebrews viewed it, and all six OT references reflect its unclean nature. The first two state this plainly in the food laws. Where swine's flesh and blood are listed in Isa. 65:4 and 66:3, 17 the prophet assumed that some, at least, of the people he was addressing were keeping pigs and quite deliberately breaking God's law. The sixth mention is a proverb, 'like a gold ring in a swine's snout' (Prov. 11:22), no doubt referring to the custom of wearing a jewel in the nose (Isa. 3:21 RSV). It may also suggest that the custom of putting a larger ring in a pig's nose to limit its digging was already known; we have not found any evidence as to when this began.

The Gr. *choiros* occurs fourteen times in NT, with eleven in one incident, the healing of the two demoniacs which resulted in the loss of the Gadarene swine in the lake (Matt. 8:30 ff.). Pig-keeping was obviously more widespread now and it is assumed that the owners were Jews. The prodigal son went to a 'far', i.e., a foreign, country but he was still breaking the law in looking after pigs. The other mention of swine is in the proverb of Matt. 7:6, and while we still speak about casting pearls before swine, this has not quite the force that it had then.

Finally there is the only occurrence of sow (Gr. *hus*) in II Peter 2:22. Describing back-sliders Peter uses two forceful animal proverbs. 'The dog returning to its vomit' is quoted from Prov. 26:11, but the other is of unknown origin: 'the sow that is washed – only to wallow in the mire'. Analogies should not be pressed too far, for these two bits of behaviour are more or less instinctive! However, the lesson Peter wants to teach is clear enough, and we find without exception that the biblical pig is unclean from start to finish.

Hippopotamus

No EV seems to include this huge beast in the text, but it is RSV mg. for the animal so picturesquely described in Job 40, and many zoologists and Heb. scholars over the centuries have concluded that Job was indeed referring to the hippo. The fact that it is called *behemoth* merely shows that the translators were at a loss and therefore just transliterated the Heb. name. In its singular form *behemah* this is the word most often rendered 'beast' in all VSS. The pl. is usually 'beasts', with the sole exception of this passage, where the whole setting suggests that a particular species is meant. Some Heb. commentators consider this pl. form is used for intensive effect and support RSV mg. Bodenheimer, the eminent Jewish scholar, does not agree, but regards it as an expression for beasts generally. He gives no reason for his opinion even though he goes on to point out that the hippo was reliably reported from the Orontes river in Syria around 1500 B.C., and was in the lower Nile until the twelfth century A.D. He also notes that it was hunted by the use of harpoons with barbed hooks, which would fit in with v. 24, 'can one take him with hooks?'

It is obviously impossible to be dogmatic, but this tr. hippo is at least possible on two different grounds. Firstly there is ample evidence that it was well known in Biblical times, especially in Egypt, where the Romans later had to reduce its numbers drastically because of the damage it was doing to crops. As regards rivers of the E. Mediterranean we know that it had an extensive distribution in the early Stone Age; this was followed by a rather drier and cooler climate which did not suit the hippo so well. It must be pointed out that there is no evidence about date or setting for the story of Job, except that it must have been somewhere around the Fertile Crescent. Secondly, this whole passage, which is best read in RSV, is certainly very figurative, with few purely factual comments, yet several points are clear: that this animal is aquatic and powerful (vv. 21–23) 'in the covert of the reeds and in the marsh'; 'if the river is turbulent he is not frightened; he is confident though Jordan rushes against his mouth' (Jordan here can stand for any river); and that it is vegetarian: 'he eats grass like an ox' (v. 15). Observers of grazing hippos in Central Africa have sometimes likened them to giant mowing machines, cutting great swathes through the grass, which is their main food. Also in v. 20, 'the mountains yield food for him'. Hippos normally feed well away from water and can climb steep slopes.

The name Hippopotamus was just coming into use in the seventeenth century, and little was yet known about it. It comes straight from the Gr. for river-horse, which is not very accurate, for it is one of the even-toed hoofed animals and is nearest to the pigs. By the Mosaic classification, therefore, it divides the hoof but does not chew the cud; in fact, it goes half-way to doing this, having a complex three-chambered stomach for dealing with the large masses of coarse food that it must work over.

Ever since the few hippos disappeared from the E. Mediterranean rivers this has been a purely African animal. Its range is much reduced, and it is probably extinct in one or two more countries by now. In the National Parks around the great lakes it lives, literally, in tens of thousands, and is doing so well under protection that it now needs regular thinning out.

An interesting case, supported by very early material, can also be made for identifying *behemoth* with the elephant and this is stated well in the Epilogue of *The Natural History of the African Elephant* by Dr. Sylvia Sikes. Her argument is based on a paraphrase in which some of the passages certainly seem to fit the elephant better than the hippo. If this theory is correct it seems likely to refer to the Asiatic rather than the African elephant, whose nearest habitat was far away to the south. The former distribution of elephants is discussed below.

Elephant

The elephant does not appear in the Canonical books but finds several interesting mentions in the two books of Maccabees as part of the forces brought against the Jews first by Antiochus Epiphanes and then by his son Antiochus Eupater early in the second century B.C. These are discussed below. However, there are twelve Heb. references and one Gr. reference to ivory, mostly just under the name ivory, but two vv. describe it as elephant ivory (I Kings 10:22; II Chron. 9:21). This is a wonderful substance, almost indestructible, that has preserved numerous facts about the cultures of those far-off days.

Long-extinct species of elephant had roamed Palestine up to perhaps a million years ago; then the climate changed into one that did not suit them and they disappeared. The nearest elephants to Palestine in OT times were in N. Mesopotamia, around the upper reaches of the Euphrates, separated from Palestine by the Syrian desert. This was the western race of the Asiatic or Indian Elephant, *Elephas maximus*, that was wiped out by hunters late in the first millennium B.C. It had never been plentiful and the demand for tusks was insatiable. This is a much smaller animal than the African Elephant; it has smaller ears and its back is domed instead of sagging slightly in the middle. The Indian has much lighter tusks, which in the cows often do not project beyond the lips. Elephants' tusks are highly modified upper incisors, and so do not conform to the general rule that 'tusks' are canine or eye teeth; elephants' grinding teeth are also unique, for they gradually work forward throughout life at such a rate that only one pair is opposed on each side at any time.

Tusks of both species of elephant are made into a wide range of ornamental work, the main advantage of the African being its much greater size. Some of the finest work has been done in India, where these big tusks are shipped regularly. Other kinds of teeth, including hippos', are also carved into necklaces, knife-handles, etc., but they cannot easily be confused with the real article. Ivory was early recognized as a perfect material, and many useful and ornamental items, dating from early in the third millennium B.C., have been found in Palestine and Mesopotamia: these are mostly small figurines and cut-outs for inlay in wood. The first biblical mention is rather late – in the time of David. The craft flourished through many ancient civilizations all over the Fertile Crescent.

For a long time most or perhaps all of the ivory used in countries north of Egypt was obtained from the so-called Syrian elephant now extinct. As this became scarcer supplies were brought from farther afield – from India by sea to Babylon via the Persian Gulf, or to Eilat, up the Gulf of Aqaba. Some of the fourteenth-century B.C. ivory from Megiddo is shown by its coarser structure to be African and this had probably been brought from Ethiopia via Arabia. Syrian elephants had then become too rare to be worth hunting.

Ivory is one of the goods listed in I Kings 10:22 as brought in the ships of Tarshish; this verse also informs us that these ships made a convoy with the Phoenician merchant navy, and it was these ships that carried most of the ivory freight, some of which seems to have been used for making inlays on the boats (Ezek. 27:6). Carving small seated human figurines was a speciality of the XII Egyptian Dynasty, early in the second millennium B.C. We know that at about that time many wild animals were being imported from farther south and trained in Egypt, so it is likely that all this ivory would be African, from higher up the Nile and from Ethiopia. Centuries later Cambyses, son of the Persian king Cyrus, captured Egypt and was paid tribute in African ivory. Some of these big tusks found their way on to Palestine and to Tyre, being carried overland via Dedan in Arabia (Ezek. 27:15). Later still routes were developed right across the Sahara over which the traders took ivory, skins and other produce, even live animals, to the N. African coast ports. This traffic continued through the Roman period and until the Muslim advance into N. Africa, when the network was broken up and the people manning the staging posts were killed by camel-riding nomads.

The use of trained elephants in the Middle East followed Alexander the Great's campaign in India. By the third century B.C. they were being kept in Egypt and among other exotic items recorded in a special procession in Alexandria Ptolemy II had ninety-six elephants, four to a chariot; this strange outfit, known as a quadriga, is shown on coins of the time. Later that same century, Ptolemy IV won a great victory over the Seleucid king of Syria, Antiochus III, and captured his elephants. All these are thought to have been of the Asiatic kind, but now its western race had almost gone for good. The drying up of that supply and a desire to be independent of Syria perhaps prompted the effort to tame the African elephant for the first time; the small N. African or 'Saharan' race still survived, and coins show that this was the kind that Hannibal used for his crossing of the Alps.

The real value of war-elephants was as shock troops and the Seleucids went on using them. The next Antiochus, who called himself Epiphanes, struck back at Egypt and then went on to attack the Jews, the first time that these 'troops' had been used in Palestine. His son employed them again, and it is worth quoting some facts from the accounts in I and II Maccabees. In the first campaign there were thirty-two elephants exercised in battle, to form spearheads for 20,000 horsemen and 100,000 foot-soldiers (I Macc. 6:30). Each elephant was supposed to lead the way for 1,000 foot soldiers and 500 picked horsemen (v. 35), but it seems that these elephants went unwillingly into battle and had to be driven into a panic by showing them what might look like blood: 'the blood of grapes and mulberries' (v. 34). The elaborate *howdah* is described in v. 37: 'strong towers of wood . . . girt fast unto them with devices.' It goes on to say, 'there were also upon every one two-and-thirty strong men, that fought upon them, beside the Indian that ruled him'. It is not surprising to learn that the elephants still had their Indian mahouts, but one can hardly imagine thirty-two large soldiers on an elephant's back, however large the *howdah*! Later in the battle a brother of Maccabaeus rushed forward and killed the largest elephant from below, only to die when it fell and crushed him (vv. 43–46).

The figurative use of ivory is fairly consistent and II Chron. 9:17 is typical: 'Solomon made a great throne of ivory and overlaid it with pure gold.' This was probably one of the first big structures to be veneered with ivory. The use of this material in figurative passages suggests wealth and soft living, but Amos gave clear warning that this had no future: 'The houses of ivory shall perish' (3:15), and 'Woe to those who lie upon beds of ivory' (6:4).

VII

Cats

Big

and Small

Lion, Leopard, Cheetah, Lynx, Sand Cat and Fishing Cat. The Domestic Cat, its origin and spread.

PALESTINE WAS ONCE THE HOME OF MANY BEASTS OF PREY – THE wild beasts and the ravening beasts of the OT. The numbers of most species have decreased, sometimes alarmingly, but only the lion and cheetah have completely disappeared from the Middle East as a whole. This chapter is concerned with the cat family, including the domestic cat.

Lion

Throughout OT times the lion, *Panthera leo*, was widespread in Palestine and adjacent countries, and was sometimes common enough to be some danger to both humans and their stock. It is mentioned some 135 times in OT, only twenty-five being wholly literal, under several different names. Heb. *'ari*, with *'aryeh* (fem.) is used more often than all the other terms together. This is the general name for it, and normally does not indicate either age or sex; it is found in both literal and figurative passages. *Kephir* is usually tr. 'young lion'; this does not mean just young cubs but obviously applies up to the sub-adult stage, e.g., 'The young lions do lack and suffer hunger' (Ps. 34:10), yet Ps. 17:12 reads, 'a young lion lurking in ambush', which must be old enough to hunt for itself. *Kephir* is used only once in a literal passage – Judg. 14:5, describing the lion which Samson met, which is called *'ari* from then on. The other names *labi'*, *lebiyyah*, etc., and *layish* appear to be poetical names, perhaps also with specialist meanings, e.g. 'He lay down as a lion (*'ari*) and as a great lion (*labi'*)' (Num. 24:9).

The word whelp was Old English for the young of beasts of prey, especially the dog; now it is almost obsolete, having been replaced by cub

for most wild carnivores and pup for dogs. AV and RV use whelp throughout; RSV has adopted cub for young bear and, in one passage only, for a
young lion, which elsewhere is still a whelp. These are from two Heb.
words; the common word *ben* – son or young of – is found twice; in all
other cases a more technical term is used, Heb. *gur* which is very close to
cub or whelp. Lioness is the correct name for the female, found only in
Ezek. 19:2 and Nah. 2:12.

The two giants of the cat family are the lion and tiger; the former is
called the king of beasts in many languages, but the tiger is on average distinctly longer and heavier. These are usually regarded as African and Asiatic respectively, which is not wholly correct, for the tiger's range is now,
as it has always been, from the borders of Europe, in the Caucasus Mountains, through to NE. and SE. Asia, so that it is found in cold, temperate,
warm and tropical climates. The lion's main home is now in Africa south
of the Sahara, with a tiny outlier in the Kathiawar peninsula of NW.
India. Thus the lion and tiger overlapped for part of their range, probably
without meeting, for the lion kept to grassland and dry open forest, while
the tiger mostly lived in the dense jungle and closed forest, where its
striped coat served as camouflage in the broken light and shade. Man has
reduced the tiger's numbers more than its overall range, largely because it
often lives in difficult country where it is safe. Persia is the nearest the tiger
has been to Palestine.

The lion is now confined to warm regions, where alone it has room to
hunt, and it shows much less variation in colour, size and habitat than the
tiger. Lions once lived in most parts of Africa, though not in the true
deserts, and in pre-historic times they were still in Europe; even as late as
David's reign they were found more or less from Greece through Asia
Minor to India. The lion began to lose ground as soon as man began to live
in settlements, and bred flocks and herds of domestic stock that needed
protection, but for a long time this process was slow. Egypt was a special
case and all land available for cultivation was occupied quite early, with
the result that lions had gone from Lower Egypt many centuries B.C.
The Greek epics have much to say about lions, which were still plentiful
long after the Homeric period. Herodotus described how they attacked
camels in Xerxes's army invading Thrace, and Aristotle twice mentions
them in Macedonia. These Greek lions became extinct about first
century A.D., and they disappeared from Palestine during the time of the
Crusades, the last probably being killed near Megiddo in the thirteenth
century.

Burton reported seeing some in Syria as late as 1851 and Layard, ex-
cavating near Babylon and Nineveh about the same time, found their
tracks more or less daily, and heard of a man on horseback being attacked
by one, only escaping with the loss of his horse. Lions lived on in Persia
into the present century, but the last had gone before 1930. In recent

times in Africa those in the far south and north were the first to go, the former by about 1865 and the latter, known as the Barbary lion, in the early 1920s. Perhaps the tsetse fly has been the lions' greatest friend for it has allowed their prey to live in regions where domestic stock cannot thrive.

It is popularly believed that the African lion was long-maned and the Asiatic short-maned; in fact the mane, found only in males, is an individual rather than a racial characteristic, and this is also largely true of its colour, which ranges from black to tawny. The lion's body colour is tawny yellow, with little variation between different areas, and it is the only plain-coloured big cat. The cubs, born in litters of two to five, have more or less obvious darker markings which are sometimes not lost until they are two years old and fully grown. Unlike the rather solitary tiger the lion is sociable and lives in family groups called prides. Lions normally feed on fairly large game; zebra are a favourite prey on the African plains and they also take antelopes and gazelles; the latter were perhaps their main prey in Palestine, with onagers in nearby countries. A group of lions often combine in the hunt; the prey is sometimes pulled down first, sometimes killed outright with a tremendous blow. They feed to capacity and then rest perhaps for several days before killing again, which is suggested in Num. 23:24 (RSV) 'it does not lie down till it devours the prey'.

The lion's roar is frequently mentioned, using three Heb. and two Gr. words suggesting different moods. The most common one has a rather general meaning, e.g., 'a young lion roared against him' (Judg. 14:5), and 'the lion hath roared; who will not fear?' (Amos 3:8). The letter is written from personal experience as a herdsman. The usual roar, many times repeated and often at night, is of challenge and defiance and may have some territorial meaning

The numerous references, both literal and figurative, to lions in the OT clearly infer that they were found widely. The only actual localities listed are Timnah, near the edge of the hills west of Jerusalem; Bethel, on the road from Jerusalem to Samaria; and around Samaria, where they are mentioned twice. David's encounter, described to Saul, would have been in the hill country not far from Bethlehem and the lion which one of his mighty men, Benaiah, killed in a pit on a snowy day can only have been in these hills. In addition three of the figurative passages refer to lions around the Jordan. Jer. 49:19 and 50:44 both speak of a lion coming from the swelling of Jordan, i.e., flushed out of the thickets by the annual floods which follow the winter and spring rains. Other localities can be inferred from place-names. Laish, a Sidonian city in the extreme north, later became Dan. Beth Lebaoth – the place of lionesses – was a town in Simeon, in the dry country not far from Beersheba.

There is frequent mention of lions in wooded areas: thicket (Jer. 4:7); covert (Job 38:40; Jer. 25:38) the tr. of two Heb. words meaning thicket or copse; forest (Jer. 5:6 and 12:8). 'Den' has two distinct meanings. The word used of the lion enclosure where Daniel was put is found nowhere else; this was a type of stone pit in which lions were kept in captivity. Elsewhere lions are six times described as being in their dens. 'He lieth in wait secretly, as a lion in his den' (Ps. 10:9). The RSV renders this more accurately by the word 'covert'. In the other passages the word means a home, whether under cover or in a thicket; not necessarily a cave, though in the rocky country of Judaea they might use such a place, e.g., 'lay them down in their dens' (Ps. 104:22), 'will a young lion cry out of his den?' (Amos 3:4).

Few cases of attack on domestic stock are reported directly, but it can be assumed that lions were often a menace. When David was justifying to Saul his offer to go and fight Goliath (I Sam. 17), he speaks of rescuing his sheep from a lion. Amos, a herdsman himself, was probably speaking from personal experience when he wrote, 'As the shepherd taketh out of the mouth of the lion two legs, or a piece of an ear' (3:12). As regards attacks on humans the habitual man-eater, whether lion, tiger or leopard, has always been the exception. In Africa today there are very few human casualties, and many fatal incidents have been provoked by carelessness or foolhardiness, perhaps when hunting the lion. Such evidence as the biblical narrative provides suggests that this was probably true during a long period when lions were fairly familiar objects of the countryside.

Three cases are reported of men being killed by lions:

(1) The disobedient prophet of I Kings 13. It is interesting that although the man was torn and killed (v. 26), the body had not been eaten. This is typical of the chance encounter where, on the human level, it can be said that the lion panics and kills; it has no intention of eating the victim, for it is not a man-eater.

(2) A rather similar incident is reported in I Kings 20:35-6, when one of the sons of the prophets was killed on the road.

(3) A different situation is described in II Kings 17:25-6. After many Israelites had been carried away into captivity the King of Assyria tried to settle strangers in Samaria; as a result 'the Lord sent lions among them, which slew some of them'.

This is clearly recorded as a divine punishment, but it is one in which natural agents are used. As regards this 'first cause' a modern parallel is seen in the notorious man-eating lions of Tsavo in E. Kenya; these terrorized the labour force building the Kenya Railway for a year or two shortly before 1900.

Lions such as those to which Daniel was thrown were being kept in captivity in Babylon about 600 B.C. In Egypt at least 1,000 years before this lions were trained to help in the hunting field, and Rameses II even had a tame lion that accompanied him to battle. Ashurnasipal II (883-859 B.C.)

kept a group of lions at Nimrud in Assyria which bred regularly, and lion-hunting was a favourite pastime of these Assyrian kings. One of the most famous carvings found in the place of Ashurbanipal at Nineveh is the lion hunt (c. 650 B.C.). Lion-hunting is still practised almost ritually by some African tribes today, whose young men kill lions in single combat to acquire some of the lion's attributes. A similar motive could have been behind the hunting in ancient Mesopotamia.

It is possible that the lion killed on a snowy day had been caught in a pit made for the purpose, such as is still used in parts of Africa and India; a deep, steep-sided pit is dug and then so covered with branches, etc., that it is invisible, and the animal is gradually driven towards it or attracted by a bait. Palestine is so rocky that few places would be suitable for building such a trap, especially up in the Judaean hills, and it seems more likely that Benaiah killed his lion in some natural hole; this Heb. word (bor) is more often used of a rocky hole, such as is prepared for water storage. In Ezek. 19:4, 8 a different word (shackath) denotes that it was dug for the purpose of catching animals, usually alive, which were then tied up and taken away. These vv. are in a figurative passage which begins by comparing the subject of the prophecy to a growing lion cub. In v. 8 mention is made of a net, such as was used to take a variety of animals, and in v. 9 the captive lion is carried to Babylon. This is interesting in that this refers roughly to the time of Daniel. It is worth noting that Ezekiel contains many more references to catching animals by nets, hooks, etc., than any other book except the Psalms.

The tradition of animal-keeping was revived again in Egypt under the Ptolemies in the third century B.C.; in a fantastic procession in honour of Dionysus there were said to be twenty-four adult lions, as well as leopards and cheetahs. Soon after this a more brutal development took place, when the Romans began staging animal fights as public spectacles. Huge numbers of lions were trapped and exported to Rome for these 'games', most of them coming from the upper Nile. Seneca recorded that 100 lions were killed by javelin men, and Julius Caesar's extravagant shows included one with 400 lions. Even allowing for considerable exaggeration a lot of animals must have been killed in this way. Nero organized fights between cavalry, bears and lions and under him one of the standard sentences for Christians refusing to conform about Emperor-worship was being thrown to the lions.

Of the only two literal references in the NT – where one Gr. word, leōn is used nine times – one refers back to the Prophets (Heb. 11:33) and the single current one is in II Tim. 4:17, where Paul states that he was rescued from the lion's mouth, which a few commentators see as meaning the devil.[1] Others believe that this was a lion in the arena or that it may refer to his being sentenced to be thrown to lions, but then released. There is no

[1] cf. I Peter 5:8, 'the devil, as a roaring lion.'

other mention of such an experience, but the catalogue of Paul's troubles in II Cor. 11. 23–7 suggests that it was quite possible. Of the few NT occurrences the remaining six have a variety of symbolic meanings in Revelation.

Such a series is far too small to draw any firm conclusions from it, but the absence of the word 'lion' from the Gospels and Acts suggests that by NT times it had become rare in the main parts of Palestine, and no evidence to the contrary has been found. Conditions may have been different farther south. Diodorus Siculus, who wrote of events about the beginning of the Christian era, but was not always accurate, reported that the Nabateans were keeping flocks in their fertile farms in the S. Negev which they had to protect continually against lions and other beasts of prey. This could possibly be true; the Nabatean Arabs had worked out ways of farming parts of the desert, and any livestock that they kept would have been vulnerable.

The figurative mentions of lions in OT are so many and diverse that it is impossible to consider all. The five occurrences of the main word *'ari* in the Psalms can be listed to suggest this variety:

> 7:2 – 'lest he tear my soul like a lion'.
> 10:9 – 'he lieth in wait secretly as a lion'.
> 17:12 – 'a lion . . . greedy of his prey'.
> 22:13 – 'a ravening and roaring lion'.
> 22:21 – 'save me from the lion's mouth'.

Many attributes can be seen here – the lion is savage, stealthy, greedy, threatening and dangerous. Often the lion is a symbol of strength, as in Samson's proverb, 'What is stronger than a lion?' Another quality is emphasized in Prov. 28:1, 'the righteous are bold as a lion'. Yet the lion is several times named as an animal which may be in need of care and provision. In Job 38:38, 'Wilt thou . . . fill the appetite of the young lions?' is followed by 'who provideth for the raven his food?' (v. 41); see also Ps. 34:10, 'the young lions do lack and suffer hunger'. Among birds the raven is similarly mentioned.

Several assorted proverbs feature the lion. 'The slothful man saith, there is a lion in the way; a lion in the streets' (Prov. 26:13), giving this as an excuse for not getting on with his work. This is another passage where two different names for lion are used, *'ari* being preceded by the poetic form *shachal*. The words of Eccl. 9:4, 'a living dog is better than a dead lion' are still familiar as an English proverb. The fascinating comment in Amos 5:19, 'as if a man did flee from a lion and a bear met him', is equivalent to our 'jumping out of the frying-pan into the fire' and the basis of this is discussed under bear.

Many lessons can be learnt from the literal passages where the lion appears, as, for instance, David's encounter with lions and bears in defence of his sheep; here they clearly can be compared with the dangers and problems which the Christian is called on to face as he grows in strength and experience.

One of our Lord's Messianic titles obviously reflects the first mention of lion, in Gen. 49:9, 'Judah is a lion's whelp'. In a setting of judgement and power He is called 'the Lion of the tribe of Judah', reminding us of such prophetic writing as Hos. 13:7, 'I will be to them as a lion'.

In II Sam. 23:20 and I Chron. 11:22 one of David's mighty men is recorded as having killed 'two lion-like men of Moab'. Heb. *'ariel* is said by RSV to be of uncertain meaning and is merely transliterated. RV takes it as a proper name and tr. 'two sons of Ariel'. AV mg. has 'lion of God' and it is possible that these were champions of a heathen deity, perhaps comparable with Goliath of Gath.

Leopard

Panthera pardus, the leopard, is a large spotted carnivore and the biggest of its family still surviving in the Fertile Crescent. Heb. *namer* is similar to Arabic *nim'r*. The Gr. *'pardalis*, is seen in the scientific name. There is no doubt about the identification, the only complication being that the Cheetah, or Hunting Leopard, *Acinonyx jubatus*, may also be included in *namer*. The name leopard is compounded of *leo* (lion) and *pard* (panther, now a synonym of leopard), and was originally given to the cheetah, which was long thought to be a cross between lion and leopard. The cheetah's name is of Indian origin and means spotted.

Leopards can reach a head and body length of up to 5 ft. with a tail of 2 to 3 ft., but some are much smaller. The leopard's spots are in a characteristic pattern, best described as rosettes of almost black spots on a background which varies from deep chrome to pale grey or sandy. The underparts are very pale and hardly spotted. The proverb of Jer. 13:23, 'Can... the leopard (change) its spots?' is still current in English. The large, darker specimens usually live in the denser cover of forests; those from the steppes and desert are paler and smaller, the extreme of this being reached in Arabia. The black leopard is a melanistic variety mostly found in the wetter parts of its range.

The leopard is still the most widely distributed of the Old World cats, both geographically and as regards the type of country it lives in; it was once found over most of Africa and right across the warmer regions of Asia. Its secretive habits and ability to hide in the scantiest of cover have helped it to survive in some unexpected places but its numbers have been reduced critically and it has disappeared from many areas. The pressure has come from two directions – hunters have found its skin a valuable trophy, for ceremonial or ornamental purposes, and farmers saw it as a danger to their stock. In fact the removal of leopards has often resulted in a dangerous increase of such crop-robbers as baboons and other monkeys, and in many parts of Africa the killing of leopards is being rigidly limited or even banned.

The leopard takes a wide variety of prey, large and small, including many birds. It kills by stealth, the camouflage of its spotted coat allowing it to hide easily even in the open. This action is suggested by Hos. 13:7, 'as a leopard by the way will I observe them', and Jer. 5:6, ' A leopard shall watch over their cities'. The leopard seldom kills other than to eat and it is unusual for one to prey on sheep and cattle habitually, though it may be forced to do so if all wild game has gone. Wherever possible the leopard keeps out of man's way and there are very few records of one becoming a man-eater in either Africa or Asia.

There can be little doubt that leopards were well known over most of Palestine in biblical times and for long after, their numbers varying as the population rose and fell, with consequent changes of pressure on the land. This is suggested in an interesting way by changes in place-names. One of the cities allocated to Gad east of Jericho was called Nimrah, or Bethnimrah, the House of the Leopard. When John the Baptist was preaching beyond Jordan some 1,200 years later the human population had built up and this had now become Bethabara, the House of the Ford. Later the locality became more or less deserted and a century ago the Arabs called it Nahr-nimrim, the Stream of the Leopards.

'The waters of Nimrim shall be desolate' is forecast in Isa. 15:6 and Jer. 48:34 as the prophets pronounce judgement on Moab. This, too, derives its name from the leopard and is thought to have been near the southern point of the Dead Sea. Nimir is still a favourite Arab name given to boys in the hope that they will have the leopard's grace and boldness.

The leopard's status a century ago in Palestine is well recorded by Tristram. It was still common enough in the wooded ground north and south of the Jabbok river to be a nuisance to shepherds and herdsmen and in one village he saw four recently taken skins. There were a few leopards on Carmel, where they would find cover in the rocky scrub and forest patches, and the spoor of some of these was almost large enough to be taken for that of lion. He found their traces around the Dead Sea and Mount Tabor, but little evidence in Galilee. With the steady increase of population from the beginning of the twentieth century, and the much more rapid rise since World War II, the leopard has almost been driven out; even so, there are a few desolate bits of country where it still just holds on. In a letter to *The Field* (6. v. 1954), Brigadier Broadhurst reported having seen the body of a leopard killed near Safad, in Upper Galilee, in 1929. One leopard was shot by a hunter on 20th October, 1964, in the Wadi Darejah, on the west shore of the Dead Sea, in Jordan.[1] A few months later one was killed in Galilee, in the north of which there are still

[1] This is recorded, with a photograph, in the *I.U.C.N. Bulletin* (Jan/March 1966).

A SMALL FAMILY PARTY of Palestine Gazelles shelters under a thorn-tree in the almost waterless Negev, near Eilat (p. 92).

A YOUNG BULL AFRICAN ELEPHANT on a bank of the River Nile in Uganda. This species is now found only south of the Sahara (p. 102).

THE SYRIAN ROCK HYRAX (coney) is in less danger than most animals and is still found in scattered colonies in Israel and adjacent countries. It is shy and difficult to approach, so that pictures in the wild are rare. This was taken near the Dead Sea (p. 129).

areas of dense scrub. A year later another was seen at Darejah. The human population in these countries is bound to increase and it is hard to see how adequate reserves can be set aside to ensure the survival of animals which need large hunting territories.

Cant.4:8, 'from the lions' dens, from the mountains of the leopards', is in poetic form and may, or may not, be meant literally. Two purely symbolic references are found – in Dan. 7:6 and Rev. 13:2. The passage in Isa. 11:6 foretells the coming of the Messianic kingdom and is difficult to comment on biologically since it includes the statement that the lion shall eat straw like the ox.

Cheetah

The cheetah is thought to be referred to in Hab. 1:8. Speaking of the Chaldaean cavalry the prophet says 'Their horses also are swifter than the leopard'. The true leopard is certainly fast for a short rush but the cheetah keeps up its pace for perhaps three miles and this has been used in the hunting field since early times. In Egypt it replaced the Hunting Dog, *Lycaon pictus*, early in the second millennium B.C. for taking antelopes and gazelles. There are records of it being trained in Assyria, and a sculptured head of a cheetah has been found at Beth Shan, at the eastern end of the valley of Jezreel.

The cheetah is longer in the leg and lighter built than the leopard; the rather harsh fur has single spots on a tawny or buff ground. It is a true cat, even though its claws are blunt, almost straight and only partly retractile. Now dangerously reduced in numbers, it once lived in the open country of much of Africa and through to India. It was found in Palestine and nearby countries, and trained for the hunt, as is evidenced by a Byzantine carving of a cheetah wearing a collar. A century ago all knowledge of their use in the field had been lost; they have since disappeared, probably from the whole of the Middle East, the last record being in 1962, when a female was killed and her cub taken.

Lynx, Sand Cat and Fishing Cat

Three other small and very rare cats need only a brief mention. The Caracal, or Desert Lynx, is a uniformly coloured cat, when adult, with a body length of about 30 in. It is least rare in the S. Negev and in some of the inland deserts, but a few still survive on the coastal plains. The Sand Cat has recently been reported from the southern Negev. The spotted Fishing Cat has a contrasted habitat – the marshes and dense jungle along the Jordan Valley, where it is now fully protected.

Domestic Cat

Felis domestica or *F. ocreata catus,* the cat now has a world-wide distribution and is thought far to outnumber dogs in Britain and various other

H

countries, yet it has a very different history from that of any other major domesticated animal. Its claim for inclusion in this book is not a strong one, for it is certainly not found by name in either OT or NT, and the only mention of cat in the Apocrypha (Baruch 6:22) is now thought by some authorities to refer to a wild species. However, it had become popular in Egypt shortly after Joseph's time; possibly it had come on the scene long before that, and it can hardly have been unknown to the Israelites when they lived there. It must therefore be discussed.

Wild cats roughly the size of the domesticated form were once found through much of Europe and Asia, as well as in N. Africa; they still survive, mostly with their range and numbers reduced. They vary in colour and pattern of coat but are sometimes regarded as geographical races rather than species; the domestic cat breeds with some of these wild forms, including the Scottish wild cat of the forests.

There is general agreement that our cat began life in Egypt, and had as its wild ancestor the N. African Wild Cat, *Felis libyca*, rather than originating from several different forms in various countries. Some of these may have contributed later and the result is now a mixture, in addition to which there have been many mutations of colour, coat and shape. Various claims are put forward for earlier dates but the generally accepted period for its wide distribution throughout Egypt is the XVIII Dynasty, from 1570 B.C., which is just after Joseph's time. If this is so it is strange that it is so comparatively recent, for the Ancient Egyptians were masters of animal training and long before this they had tamed such unlikely kinds as hyenas, mongooses and monkeys.

An ivory statuette of a cat found at Lachish and dated about 1700 B.C. raises more questions than it solves. The form represented could be either wild or domestic and if the latter, it is equally possible for either the statuette or the cat from which it was modelled to have been imported. At that time there was regular commerce between Egypt and Lachish, at the southern end of the Judaean hills.

The cat is Ancient Egypt's only contribution to domesticated stock, in spite of the great expertise of its people, and the only important one to come from a wild animal not gregarious by habit. It is possible that it had started entering buildings and making itself useful for a long time before it was actually brought into a domesticated state. This sounds likely and also ties in with the theory that cats were deliberately encouraged to catch rodents in a country where large-scale grain storage was sometimes necessary, as it was under Joseph's administration; without proper control rats and mice could quickly destroy all the stocks. Delightful illustrations of about this period show cats doing battle with rats. It has been suggested that Egyptian priests may have recognized the causal connexion between rats and plague and therefore encouraged cats, at the same time protecting them by making them sacred to the goddess Bast who was patroness of the eastern half of the Nile delta, where the Israelites lived, The centre of this cult was at Bubastis, referred to as Pi-beseth in Ezek. 30:17 and the subject of grim warnings. These cats were venerated throughout Egypt and their mummies were preserved in tens of thousands.

Zeuner points out that some English names may confirm N.E. Africa as its starting-point. Cat itself probably comes from a very old Berber word and took over from *felis* when the cat arrived in Rome. Puss may come from *Pasht*, which is another name for the goddess Bast.

If the early history of the cat in Egypt is uncertain, this is even truer of its wider distribution. The Greek classics say little about it, though Herodotus tells of an unfortunate Greek who got into trouble by killing a cat while visiting Egypt, and a few specimens seem to have been kept in Greece itself from before 1100 B.C. The cat's real spread beyond the eastern Mediterranean dates from the Roman Imperial period, when it was taken far and wide by the colonizing legions. The remains of a cat of the domestic type have been found in Kent on the site of a house burnt down during the fourth century A.D.

There still remains the question of when the cat became known in Palestine and lands to the north-east. The earliest date for Babylonia is second century B.C., and from there it went to India. There is no evidence, other than the ivory statuette already discussed, of its presence in Palestine before Roman times. We must assume that the Hebrews at least knew it in Egypt before they left, but it was so intimately associated with pagan worship that it would surely have been unclean and *tabu*, even more so than the dog, which did at least serve as a town scavenger and cattle guard. This could explain the absence of any mention other than in Baruch, where they are associated with bats – always unclean to the Hebrews – and are actually sitting on the idols in heathen temples.

VIII
Other
Beasts
of Prey

Bear, Wolf, Domestic dog, Fox, Jackal and Hyena, Weasel, Badger and Mongoose

THE REMAINING BEASTS OF PREY BELONG TO SEVERAL DIFFERENT families. The wolf, jackal and fox, with the domestic dog, are true canines. The bear belongs to a family of its own and cannot be mistaken for any other animal. The hyena, of a small and highly specialized group, is the typical scavenger of the Old World. Brief mention is also made of a few smaller hunters of the weasel tribe, characterized by powerful scent glands around the tail; and the mongoose, of a related family which is common in many warm countries.

Bears

Brown bears were once found over a large part of the temperate N. Hemisphere. Some zoologists have divided them into a number of different species but the present trend is to regard them all as a single species, *Ursus arctos*, with many geographical races varying in colour and size. The Alaskan and Kodiak bears are the giants, weighing up to 1,500 lb.; in fact they are the largest living carnivores. The Old World races are much smaller, some of them scaling only 500 lb. or so. The biblical bear (Heb. *dob*) can be called the Syrian Bear, *Ursus arctos syriacus*, and except perhaps for the Isabelline Bear of the Himalayas, it had the palest coat of all.

The W. European race of brown bears lived in Britain until the tenth century, when the last few were killed in their strongholds in the Welsh mountains and in the Caledonian forest of Scotland. It had probably never been common – there was little country suitable for it. Throughout its range the bear has been pushed back farther and farther into the hills and dense forests, and reduced in number, though not exterminated, in most countries. Dense populations and wild bears are just not compatible.

116

In biblical times the Syrian Bear was found over most of the hilly wooded parts of Palestine, where the rock formation often gave it good cover. The only two localities plainly listed are in the Judaean hills, near Bethlehem, and east of Bethel. Bears obviously ventured down into the plains but kept away from the actual desert. It seems astonishing that bears have managed to find a living in Palestine until so recently. They had become scarce by a century ago and Tristram saw only one, near the lake of Galilee; farther north, on Hermon, they were still seen regularly, even above the snow line. The last bear in Palestine itself was killed in the hills of upper Galilee just before World War II, but a few managed to survive in the higher ground of Lebanon and Hermon, much of it above 6,000 ft., only to be shot by soldiers a few years later. This meant that this pale race was extinct in the wild and was now represented only by a few still living in Zoos. The nearest bears, belonging to a slightly different race, now live in the mountains of N. Syria, S. Turkey and Persia, where they should be safe for some time.

Bears form one of the most important groups of the carnivores, with not many species but all of them large. The Polar Bear, among the heaviest, is mostly a meat-eater; the others are truly omnivorous. Their food varies with the season and for much of the year they take vegetable matter, especially fruits of all kinds, but also roots and grass. They are fond of bees and their nests and combs, the thick fur protecting them from attack. Ants' nests are raided and rodents dug from their burrows; birds' eggs and nestlings are eaten, as well as carrion. Bears are seldom fast enough to catch such active animals as deer and antelopes. In suitable areas they take fish, especially in the rivers of northern Canada, where migrating salmon may be their basic food while the run lasts.

Even in cold and temperate climates bears do not hibernate in the strict sense of this word; they lie up in dens for varying periods, but are easily woken up. This is when the cubs are born and then suckled for some weeks. A litter may have up to four tiny cubs, relatively smaller than in any other ordinary mammal, and at under 1 lb. each they are less than one five-hundredth of the mother's weight. The growing cubs gradually begin to follow her around, and are dependent on her for some months more; sometimes they stay with her, or perhaps link up again, after the next year's litter arrives.

While accompanied by her cubs the she-bear, as the female is properly called, is more aggressive and potentially dangerous than usual. Three different OT passages, quoting what is obviously a proverbial saying, refer to a bear robbed of her cubs, and each of the settings is interesting. In II Sam 17:8 Hushai, sent back to court by David to counter the advice of the able turn-coat Ahithophel, describes the fleeing king as 'a bear robbed of her whelps in the field'. It made him sound formidable, but this was not perhaps just how David felt at the time. In Prov. 17:12 we find Eastern hyperbole at its best, when a man is advised to meet a bear robbed of its cubs rather than a fool in his folly – always a pet aversion of Solomon. In Hos. 13:8 God is protesting at Ephraim's unfaithfulness and says 'I will meet them as a bear bereaved of her whelps', perhaps the most suitable use of this simile. In all cases the same Heb. word is used, meaning bereaved, which could be accidentally or by human action, when cubs might have been taken alive; if so, one can only speculate whether bears were in use as performing animals, a practice that is very ancient but cannot be clearly traced back farther than the fourth century B.C.

Left to themselves bears usually avoid contact with man and his stock, though the occasional individual may become almost a man-eater, most often one of the tropical species. In countries such as Palestine there could be times in late winter and early spring when bears were tempted by hunger to come down to lower ground and try to take a lamb from the flocks feeding on the early grass, perhaps some distance from the nearest settlement. This could be the kind of incident that David described to Saul in I Sam. 17:34. The expression in v. 37 'out of the paw of the bear' is interesting, even though the Heb. *yad* could have a wider meaning than paw, for it is with the massive fore-paw, armed with heavy blunt claws, that the bear usually attacks, dealing a powerful blow that would crush the head of some animals. (The lion's paw is also mentioned in this verse; this sometimes, but not always, knocks down its prey with a smashing blow.) Even though a man might be killed in such an encounter as David re-counts, the bear would be unlikely to eat the body.

The passage in II Kings 2:24 in which forty-two 'children' were torn by two she-bears, has often been criticized. There is more to the story than is at first apparent, as any good commentary explains, and the Heb. *na'ar* would be better rendered 'young men'; it is the word used by Samuel of Jesse's sons, of which David was the youngest. There is a distinct element of divine justice here, with animals used of God to carry it out, and the locality was somewhere towards the top of the western side of the Judaean hills above Jericho, once well wooded but with narrow rocky valleys. Two bears meeting a provocative crowd of youths in a narrow defile could cause panic and heavy damage, as the passage suggests.

'A ranging bear' is mentioned in Prov. 28:15: this is a better tr. than 'charging bear' (RSV), for the root meaning is of quartering the ground searching for food. On the other hand RSV is preferred in Isa. 59:11, 'We all growl like bears', using a word that was not known when the AV spoke of roaring. Bears do not have much of a voice and their ears are poor; however, their noses are highly sensitive and used for locating food.

The only other OT passage needing comment is the proverb in Amos 5:19, 'as if a man did flee from a lion and a bear met him', which is like jumping out of the frying-pan into the fire. Almost any experienced zoo or circus man would agree that in general a lion is more predictable and therefore safer; a bear hides its intentions. This is also suggested in I Sam. 17:37, 'the lion . . . the bear . . . this Philistine', where the three are listed in order of increasing danger.

The only NT mention is in a purely symbolic passage in Rev. 13:2. Gr. *arctos* is seen in the bear's scientific name.

Wolf

The wolf is the largest wild canine and is generally thought to be the main, probably the only, ancestor of the domestic dog. It may be 4 ft. long with a tail of 15 in., often weighing over 100 lb. It is a powerful predator and it was as such that our Lord spoke of it four times and St. Paul once (John 10:12, etc). The OT picture is similar, though the wolf is less closely identified as a menace to sheep. There is no problem of identification. Heb. *ze'eb* and Gr. *lukos* are properly tr. 'wolf'.

In its breeding habits it naturally resembles the dog, having litters of up to a dozen, born in a den where they are suckled for some six weeks. The wild wolf's colour is variable, and also its size, as would be expected in an animal that ranges in many races over much of N. America, Europe and Asia, from sub-tropical areas to Arctic. The commonest European form is brownish or yellowish grey, usually with a mixture of black hairs; the underparts are pale. The thickness of the coat varies with the climate, northern forms having a thick woolly underfur, such as is seen in the Alsatian dog. On the edge of the Arctic wolves are white; southern forms tend to be darker than average, but the Syrian wolf is pale brown. The correct name for the whole species right across its range is Grey Wolf, *Canis lupus*, with a number of geographical races, some better defined than others. It was once found widely and commonly but it was a constant danger to livestock, and as man occupied more and more ground, so the wolf had to drop back; finally it was exterminated from most settled areas and it remained plentiful, and in its typical packs, only in large tracts of undisturbed forest and steppes. It is now realized that killing wolves in big National Parks is a mistake; they are essential to keep hoofed game on the move and take sickly and weak animals from the herds.

Wolves were common in Britain throughout the Middle Ages and the last English specimen was killed during Henry VII's reign. In parts of Ireland they were still a menace in Oliver Cromwell's time and were not exterminated until towards the end of the eighteenth century.

Because of its greater size the wolf can take much larger prey than its smaller cousins the fox and jackal. Hunting in packs, wolves can overcome deer and cattle; such kills are probably rare anywhere and it is noteworthy that some biblical writers refer to it as an enemy of the lamb. For the most part, wherever they live, wolves are content with smaller animals, including rabbits, mice, fish, crabs and insects, using their accurate noses to locate prey. They eat carrion and in hard times may also take vegetable food. As with the big cats, the odd individual may become a specialized cattle-thief, but genuine attacks on humans are very rare indeed.

Like some of the other large animals in OT times, the wolf's numbers tended to vary with the political situation. In periods of peace the land would be more effectively occupied and its numbers controlled, though the wolf has always been notorious for its ability to avoid traps of all kinds and to survive against heavy odds. There is no way of knowing just how common it was at any one time. The twelve mentions in the Scriptures show that it was a familiar beast of prey, yet it is never found in a literal passage.

Its status may well have changed little between the start of the Christian era and last century, when Tristram reported that he came across the wolf in almost every region of Palestine – in the forests of the north, among the Judaean hills and on the coastal and inland plains. They were in twos and threes, never in packs, but were regarded as a serious danger by the shepherds, who never relaxed their guard at night. Their numbers may have increased between the wars, and in the 1930s they were reported as widespread by naturalists in the British Forces in Palestine. In fact 'between the wolf and the dog' was then an expression for the early dawn when one could first distinguish between these two canines. The wolf still survives there, but since World War II it has been much reduced in numbers, especially by poisoning and hunting, and it is no longer a serious enemy of livestock. It is bound to be driven farther back still, into areas unsuitable for human occupation, where a few should be able to live in safety.

The picture in NT is consistent, beginning with Matt. 7:15, where false teachers are described as ravening wolves. The word 'ravening', used twice elsewhere, is now obsolete and is rendered 'ravenous' by RSV. Both are from the same root; the older one suggested savage plundering, which is nearer the original, whereas ravenous has now come to mean little more than very hungry.

The first mention is in Gen. 49:27, where it is prophesied that 'Benjamin shall ravin as the wolf'. This well described the tribe's character, as several episodes in their history were to prove, especially in the bitter fighting with other tribes (Judges 20). Wolves are three times associated with the evening. (In fact the AV of Jer. 5:6, 'a wolf of the evenings,' is not correct and it should read as RSV, 'A wolf from the desert shall destroy them'. The word is Arabah, the name still given to the broad valley running south from the Dead Sea). The half-light of the evening is one period when wolves are active and when their typical howling is often heard. Barking is peculiar to the dog but wolves kept in captivity have been known to copy it.

It is interesting that in more than half the passages, including all in NT, the wolf stands for someone in authority who is misusing his position e.g., 'Her princes . . . like wolves ravening the prey' (Ezek. 22:27);

'her judges are evening wolves' (Zeph. 3:3); and 'False prophets . . . inwardly they are ravening wolves' (Matt. 7:15). The change of nature that will characterize the Messianic kingdom is twice illustrated e.g., 'the wolf and the lamb shall feed together' (Isa. 65:25).

Domestic Dog

Without doubt the dog is man's oldest animal companion, the earliest of all the assortment of animals to be enlisted, and for a far wider range of jobs than any other. There is ample evidence that late Stone Age man used dogs as general helpers in many parts of the world; modern methods of dating, including the identification of pollen grains in peat bogs, suggest that by 7500 B.C. dogs could be considered as domesticated. Some of the oldest remains, including whole skeletons, came from Denmark and other parts of N. Europe where conditions were ideal for their preservation; two distinct types were found in some places, so at least one must have been introduced from outside. Remains are also present in some of the earliest levels at Jericho, dated soon after 7000 B.C.

There will always be argument as to how it all started, just as there is about the dog's wild ancestors. On the latter point many authorities agree that the wolf is the father of all domestic dogs, which are known collectively as *Canis familiaris*. This finding is based on anatomy and behaviour, and to some extent it is confirmed experimentally by work done on taming wolves in Canada. Another school of thought, headed by the famous naturalist Konrad Lorenz, believes that the dog has two ancestors – the wolf and the jackal – and that some breeds have more of the one, some more of the other. There is a further theory that their forebears were wild dogs very like the Australian dingo but now long extinct.

The dog had been around for several thousand years before written records began, so its early history can only be conjecture, based on our knowledge of the gregarious wolf and of the behaviour of dogs that have escaped and become more-or-less feral. The association began long before men thought of making agricultural settlements; they still lived mainly by hunting and so had a common interest with the wild wolves, which were always prepared to clean up the remains of a kill. As fear of man was lost they would take refuse from around the crude encampments, gradually regarding them as territory to be defended against other packs. From this stage it is a small step – though perhaps taking a long time – to the assumption of guard duties and assisting in the hunt, perhaps in that order, perhaps reversed, although the process could have been hastened by bringing in young cubs and hand-rearing them. Later would come the herding work for which dogs have been so valuable in all ages and in all continents. But this is guess-work, and we shall never know what actually happened.

The dog reached Egypt very early and at least three breeds can be distinguished in the pre-dynastic period, i.e., before about 3000 B.C. Over 1,000 years before that they were making white-painted pottery dogs of a definite greyhound type, a breed which is illustrated time and again in Egypt and other parts of the Fertile Crescent.[1] Dogs were highly regarded in Ancient Egypt, where they were probably among the animals worshipped, perhaps associated with the deity Anubis, whose name is given to the dog-faced baboon, but this name is now thought to refer to the jackal rather than the dog. Dogs also came to be considered a desirable goal for the human soul after death. These facts are likely to have made the dog even more abhorrent to the Hebrews, who seem to have used it for none of the jobs for which it had been bred and trained in Egypt.

Dogs were just as highly esteemed in Mesopotamia where, among other forms, a big hunting mastiff was in use in the earliest Babylonian period (third millennium B.C.), so Abram must have known about dogs before he moved to Canaan. From those days the development of breeds has been almost continuous, with nearly 200 now recognized, of all shapes, sizes and colours, and serving a multitude of purposes, of which the most recent and valuable is to act as seeing eyes for the blind.

In Palestine and Egypt in Biblical times, as in some parts of the east today, the dog was mainly a scavenger and did in larger towns what hyenas helped to do in the villages and outside the walls. In most other countries other dogs were used for herding, hunting and so on, but the Hebrews' low view of the dog as utterly unclean meant that most dogs in Palestine were semi-wild, like the pariah dogs that still haunt some countries.

The incident in II Kings 9, where the dogs ate Jezebel after she had been thrown down from the city wall and killed, was nothing unusual, for dead bodies were sometimes left out for the scavengers to dispose of; this was not generally practised by the Hebrews and was probably done deliberately as a mark of disrespect. Dogs are classed as carnivores but now take a wide range of food; these town dogs lived on refuse, vermin such as rats and mice, the corpses of animals, etc., and were thus potential carriers of various diseases.

The dog is not specifically proscribed in the Mosaic law though, except for a few comments that are neutral, the many Scriptural references leave no doubt that it was regarded as such. Only one Heb. word is used for it – keleb. Contact with corpses alone would have made it ritually unclean (Lev. 22:4). Our Lord's command, 'Give not that which is holy unto the dogs' (Matt. 7:6), shows that dogs were still regarded similarly. There was everything to be said for avoiding contact with dogs, and this is yet another case of Hebrew hygiene being ahead of its time. Conditions have now changed radically, and refuse disposal is no longer left to animal scavengers. We now know much more about human and canine diseases and the

[1] The word 'greyhound' is found once in Prov. 30:31, AV and RV, unsupported by any modern VS. It is agreed that the Heb. is obscure and speculation about it is pointless.

dog has assumed the role of honoured assistant and intimate companion of people all over the world. It can still carry rabies, one of the most horrible diseases to affect man, but this can now be prevented. Probably due to local influence the dog occupies a different position in Tobit, one of the books of the Apocrypha written during the Exile in Babylonia or Persia. The young Tobias is accompanied by his dog when he sets out as a bachelor (5:16), and it later follows him home when he returns with his wife (11:4).

The first reference in Exod. 11:7, 'not a dog move his tongue', is thought to be a proverb, and the meaning is not clear. The next, in Exod. 22:31, orders that any cattle killed by wild animals shall be thrown out for the dogs; this clearly shows how they were regarded, and it possibly suggests that dogs followed them into the desert as scavengers. All six mentions in I Kings concern dogs eating human flesh and licking blood; nothing could have been more horrifying to the Hebrews. 'The dog that returns to its vomit' (Prov. 26:11, RSV), quoted in II Pet. 2:22, is a proverb that features a well-known habit of dogs. Another, in Eccl. 9:4, 'a living dog is better than a dead lion', is one of the few comments not positively black-listing it.

Goliath, laughing at David's simple weapons, asked him contemptuously 'Am I a dog?' David, speaking to Saul, compared himself humbly to a dead dog, even more despicable than a live one. The mention of dog in Deut. 23:18 seems to be as a technical term, perhaps a euphemism, for a male temple-prostitute; this could be echoed by Rev. 22:15, which lists dogs and whoremongers among those excluded from the Holy City.

Two passages can be interpreted as referring to guard dogs. In speaking of the dogs of his flock (Job 30:1) Job must mean sheep dogs, though not in the specialized sense that we know. However, it is not certain that Job was a Hebrew. Isa. 56:10, 'his watchmen . . . are all dumb dogs, they cannot bark', is preceded by 'beasts of the field come to devour', which suggests that it was then the custom to use dogs to guard the flocks and herds from beasts of prey. This context is figurative, and again there is no proof that this was Hebrew practice.

The point made in Judg. 7:5, 'Everyone that laps the water with his tongue, as a dog laps', seems to conflict with v.6, 'that lapped, putting their hands to their mouths'. The Heb. text is not clear.

The incident of the Syro-Phoenician woman is the only passage where the Gr. *kunarion* is found. This can be tr. 'little dogs', in contrast to *kuōn*, the normal word for dog. The woman replied, 'the dogs under the table eat of the children's crumbs' (Mark 7:28), showing that they were dogs allowed in the house, and she could well have meant small pet dogs. However, she was not Jewish and this is no exception to the rule that the Hebrews regarded dogs as animals to be avoided at all costs. In modern Israel there is no official ban, except presumably among the Orthodox Jews, but house dogs in a city like Tel Aviv are rare enough to be remarked on. In general the Mohammedans view the dog in the same way as the Ancient Hebrews. There are exceptions, such as the greyhounds and salukis that are kept for coursing hares and gazelles.

Foxes and Jackals

These are members of the dog tribe, similar in size and appearance, and in some habits. Both are referred to in the Scriptures but except in RV and RSV the position is rather confused, which seems due to two separate factors. First the local people seldom distinguish between these two animals even today, and this is likely to have been true in all times. Both are therefore included in Heb. *shu'al*, which is the root from which Arabic *jakal* and English *jackal* are derived. Second, the biblical writers use two Heb. words, of which the above is found only in literal or simple metaphorical passages, the context sometimes indicating fox and sometimes jackal. The other word, *tannim*, is tr. 'dragon', AV, and it is always pl.; it appears to be almost a convention to indicate desolation and is used only in this symbolic way. One could infer that *tannim* is a nickname or solely used in poetry. RV and RSV now tr. 'jackals' in all these passages, which is generally accepted as correct. The word jackal did not come into use until early seventeenth century, just too late for the AV translators to know it. Fox, on the other hand, is an old name belonging to a well-known animal.[1] Only one Gr. word is used – *'alōpex*.

RSV has also substituted jackals for foxes in two figurative passages where this is clearly better (Ps. 63:10; Lam. 5:18). In the following section the more accurate rendering of the RSV will be followed.

Three species of fox are found in Palestine and Egypt. One of them is a race of *Vulpes vulpes*, the Red Fox of the cold and temperate parts of the Old World; this form is about 24 in. long, with a tail of half that length, and it is greyer than its red British cousin. This lives in the hilly and more wooded areas; in 1962 we were lucky to see one in full daylight near the Sanhedrin tombs on the outskirts of Jerusalem. The rather similar Desert Fox, *V. rüppelli*, is from the drier parts and the Fennec Fox from the desert itself. This is not closely related and is known as *Fennecus zerda*; only 15 in. long and with a 10-inch tail it is easily recognized by its huge ears and pale colour. This is the most strictly nocturnal of all, for it lives in country where the ground temperature by day may be far too high for life, but all foxes are basically nocturnal, spending the day in their holes, or earths, as our Lord pointed out in Matt. 8:20, comparing them with the birds that have their nests. In this case fox best fits the context. The fox tends to be a

---

[1] The position has been further complicated by the existence of two Hebrew words *tannim* and *tannin*. AV treats them as more or less identical and tr. all as dragon or similar, but in spite of their being almost identical they are not now considered cognate. Their more detailed treatment is given in App. B.

solitary hunter, taking a wide range of prey, from worms and insects to birds and furred animals; its diet includes fruit and other vegetable matter, but this varies a lot with the locality, and it normally eats less refuse and carrion than the jackal. The fox's fondness for fruit is stressed in Cant. 2:15, 'the little foxes that spoil the vines'. Most vines in Palestine trail on the ground and these too could be damaged by foxes running along the rows.

The pair are known as fox and vixen, or dog-fox and she-fox; the cubs are born in an 'earth', which may be large and deep underground.

Brer Fox has appeared in stories and fables since Greek and Roman times, and features in some attributed to Aesop, who was more or less contemporary with Daniel. In these stories, which were certainly known in NT times, the fox is crafty and cunning, and our Lord used this metaphor in one of his rare critical comments when He called Herod 'that fox' (Luke 13:32). The Greeks and Romans had the actual fox in mind, but it was the jackal that featured in the tales told in Palestine and Iraq, so we cannot tell which is meant here; it would have been equally apt to compare Herod to the jackal, dancing attendance around the 'kill' and eating what the lions leave. One of the few passages where the word is singular is in Neh. 4:3, where the opponents suggested sarcastically that 'if a fox go up, he shall even break down their stone wall'. Either foxes or jackals might wander around the ruined city at night.

Jackals are related to foxes and even more closely to dogs, for like them they belong to the genus *Canis*. Several species of jackal live in the warmer parts of Asia and Africa, and this one is *C. aureus*, the Oriental or Golden Jackal, which also extends into parts of S. Europe. About the same size as the fox, its coat is dirty yellow mixed with reds and blacks. Jackals differ from foxes in going about in packs of up to a dozen, and it is interesting that in all cases where the tr. 'jackal' is preferable the Heb. word is plural. The jackal is basically a nocturnal scavenger and in game country it lives rather as a hyena, though lower in rank, and is allowed to have the remains only when the others have eaten their fill.

The narrative in Judg. 15:4 ff. has caused considerable comment about both its ethics and its accuracy. Samson's action in tying fire-brands to the tails of foxes was far from humane – as were many other things which he and his enemies did. As regards the practical problem it seems likely that he could catch larger numbers of jackals than foxes, and it is not stated that it was done overnight. Such fire-raising would be far more effective spread over a wide area, as the context seems to imply, and this would take time. The effect of sending 150 fire-brands rushing through the dry crops in the late spring would be devastating. A similar cruel custom is recorded a thousand years later, when Romans used to tie torches to foxes' tails and hunt them in the circus at the feast of Ceres, goddess of corn.

Jackals are more typical of dry and desolate places than the common fox, which likes some woody cover. Most of the contexts confirm this, e.g., Isa. 13:22, in the oracle about Babylon 'hyenas will cry in its tower, and jackals in the pleasant palaces'. Other lands are promised the same fate; 'Hazor shall become a haunt of jackals' (Jer. 49:33). Because of their own disobedience the land of Judah would suffer similarly; 'I will make Jerusalem a heap of ruins, a lair of jackals' (Jer. 9:11).

Striped Hyena

This is another species whose existence in Bible lands right down to the present day is undisputed, and whose voice and habits make it difficult to overlook, yet its biblical mentions are few and rather uncertain. However, it is generally agreed that Zeboim, a place-name, is derived from a Heb. root meaning hyenas, and this was given to three towns in different periods:

(1) A city of the plain destroyed with Sodom (Deut. 29:23);

(2) A valley in Benjamite country north of Jerusalem, in the high ground near the eastern edge of the Judaean hills;

(3) A town built in post-exilic times on the coastal plain near Lydda (Neh. 11:34).

A much debated word, *tsabua'*, meaning 'spotted' or 'striped', is found only in Jer. 12:9; it is mostly rendered 'speckled bird' (of prey), while LXX has 'hyena', which is supported by both Tristram and Bodenheimer. The former points out that *doubba*, Arabic for hyena, is similar and it seems related to *zebo'im*. Isaiah twice used the word *'iyyim*, which has also puzzled translators, who suggest 'wild beasts of the islands' (AV) 'wolves' (RV) and 'hyenas' (RSV). On the other hand Tristram regards this as another name for the jackal, since its root meaning is 'howler'. This could apply equally to the hyena, with its fantastic call from which it is often named Laughing Hyena. These are figurative passages from which one gets no clues other than that the creatures in them suggest uncleanness and desolation. Hyenas are indeed animals of the desolate places, one of their favourite haunts in Palestine being ancient tombs; *'iyyim*, is always found parallel with *tsiyyim*, tr. 'wild beasts of the desert', and these could be more or less mythical creatures, or nicknames for some others, perhaps hyenas and jackals.

However, there is no doubt whatever that the Striped Hyena, *Hyaena hyaena*, has long been a member of the Palestine fauna. It is still there today, rarer than it once was and living only in the less populated and less developed areas. It is likely that in biblical times it was less common generally in the areas occupied by the Hebrews than in comparable places nearby, for the hygienic sections of the Mosaic code would have meant that less pickings were left for it. Elsewhere it was sometimes the custom for even human bodies to be left exposed for hyenas to eat during the night, which they quickly do, leaving little trace. Such habits would make hyenas unspeakably defiling to the Israelites, and this may help explain why there is so little, if any, direct mention in the Scriptures. By occasionally throwing bodies to the dogs and hyenas, as happened to Jezebel (II Kings 9:35), they were perhaps deliberately fouling the name of a wicked person, though here they seem to have had second thoughts and sent later to have the corpse buried, only to find that it had already been eaten.

Hyenas belong to a small Old World family of specialized scavenging carnivores, looking vaguely like dogs but belonging to a completely different section of this order. The species in our area, the Striped Hyena, ranges from India through SW. Asia to E. Africa, where it is replaced by the Spotted Hyena. It is about 40 in. long with tail of 16 in. The hair is rather long, and an even longer mane runs right along the back; the very irregular dark brown or blackish stripes are on a yellowish or grey background, the markings becoming much less distinct with age. The head is massive, to give room for muscles and jaws which can crush the biggest cattle bones, which are then swallowed. Carrion is perhaps their main food. It was once thought that hyenas seldom attacked healthy animals and this is probably true for most areas, though careful observation has now shown that where there is plenty of game they do quite a lot of actual hunting.

The hyena's numbers had probably been fairly level for many centuries up to the beginning of the present one and all this time it served as a useful scavenger, disposing of corpses, human and animal, that might otherwise have allowed diseases to spread. It was still found everywhere a century ago and the jackal was the only sizeable beast of prey reckoned more numerous. The twentieth century has brought a big change; the introduction of modern hygienic methods of refuse disposal and sewage treatment, and the great extension of animal health services have reduced the hyena's opportunities. The use of unsuitable poisons against rodent and insect pests, with shooting by thoughtless hunters, did further severe damage. Even so, there are still areas where they are likely to survive for a long time, and in country parts it is still wise to bury corpses really deep to make them secure from the hyena's digging. As recently as 1963 no less than twenty were shot in a period of three months around the Azraq oasis in NE. Jordan.

Weasel
Although there is no positive confirmation, Heb. *choled* is widely thought to be the weasel. It is found only in Lev. 11:29, as one of the creeping things that creep on the earth, which fairly well describes this short-legged, stream-lined little hunter. In this list of unclean animals it is followed by the mouse, which is of the same order of size. The powerful anal glands found in all members of this family, including the skunk, make it too evil-smelling to be considered as food. In Greece and Rome weasels were used to

control mice before cats became available. In Ancient Egypt they were considered sacred to the moon, which would be an additional reason for the Hebrews to avoid them. The Palestine weasel is the same as the well-known British kind. The same name could have been given to other members of the same family, including the much larger polecat.[1]

Badger

This is about the largest of the weasel family and its range extends from W. Europe through into Asia. There is no support for the tr. 'badger skin' in Exodus 26, etc. (see p. 138) and the badger does not seem to be mentioned. Another relation, known as the Honey Badger, is found in warm countries from central Africa to India, and this is reported very rarely from Arabia and Iraq.

Mongoose

The Egyptian Mongoose could perhaps have been included in the group-name 'weasel' for it is of a similar build, even though it is much larger, with a total length of over 3 ft. It takes a wide variety of prey, including lizards, birds and small mammals; still common in Palestine it may do damage to poultry.

[1] Although the word 'ferret' is found in AV, this is corrected to 'gecko' in RV and RSV (*q.v.*). The ferret is not a wild animal but a domesticated form, usually albino, of the polecat.

CAMELS ARE ALLOWED to roam in suitable parts of the desert to browse on thorny shrubs and seasonal greenstuff. Jericho is in the distance, and a rare spring storm covers the eastern outliers of the Judaean Hills (p. 68).

CAMEL TRAINS STILL carry some groups of Bedouins and their loads to new camp sites. A leading rope has become detached and the camel kneels while a lad reties it to the tail (p. 69).

THIS ALBINO FOAL, born to a donkey of normal colour, has no trace of the dark stripe over the shoulder. The setting is barley stubble on the edge of the Negev, near Beersheba (p. 70).

THE BLACK KITE is usually a winter visitor, flying north in spring to nest in many parts of Europe. Like the slightly larger Red Kite, it lives on both carrion and small live animals, including many locusts (p. 146).

IX

All

Manner

of Beasts

Coney, Hare, Mouse, Hedgehog, Porcupine, Mole-rat, Bats, Ape, Whale and Dugong.

THE ANIMALS INCLUDED HERE ARE A STRANGE MIXTURE RANGING from the mouse to the whale. They are, in fact, all those that do not fit into the natural groups of the preceding chapters, and they are not listed in any particular order. Some can be identified quite positively; others will always be the subject of argument.

Coney, or Rock Hyrax

The true identity of the coney has been known for over a century, perhaps for much longer, and it is unfortunate that no commonly read EV seems to have taken note of it. The use by RSV of badger and rock badger for Heb. *shaphan* is surprising, for neither is supported by any authority. A badger fairly closely related to the European and American species is found in Palestine, and is discussed briefly elsewhere; the term rock badger has no meaning, no animal being popularly known by this name. Badgers' habits do not fit the biblical passages quoted below.

The word coney first meant rabbit and was derived from the Latin *cuniculus*. In the Middle Ages rabbit was used only for the young animals; it then became the basic name, making coney obsolete in general use though retained in biblical and a few technical senses, as for instance in the fur trade and in heraldry. Its use in the Scriptures is acceptable since it has long ceased to mean rabbit when applied to the live animal. The name coney was already being given to the Cape Hyrax, or Dassie, before the end of the sixteenth century, by merchants who called at the Cape on their way to India. It is just conceivable that the translators intended this meaning of coney, but much more likely that they meant rabbit.

It is not known yet when the biblical coney was first identified as the hyrax. It is described unmistakably by William Carpenter in his *Scripture Natural History*, published early nineteenth century, but given only the native name of *Ashkoko*. He quotes from a Mr. Bruce, whose comments could apply to no other species, '. . . . gregarious; several dozens sit upon the great stones at the mouths of caves and warm themselves in the sun'. He had obviously handled them for he goes on to say, 'All over his body he has scattered hairs, strong and polished like his mustachioes.' This is typical of all species. The impression is that it had not yet been firmly named, and Canon Tristram may have been the first to do this in the 1860s.

The hyraxes form a very small order with no more than ten species found in suitable parts of Africa and SW. Asia. All have the same general shape and are roughly rabbit-sized, weighing up to 6 or 8 lb. They are completely unlike any other small mammals in their anatomy and habits, which is reflected in their long gestation period of about seven months, and they are classified near the elephants. Round-backed and with no visible tail, they have short sturdy legs, and feet whose flexible soles are ideal for gripping rocks. Each digit ends in a tiny hoof-like nail. One species has taken to living in the tall trees of the tropical forests; all the others are at home among the rocks. As the Psalmist noted in Ps. 104:18, 'The rocks [are a refuge for] the conies.' Solomon also included them in his wise creatures and added, 'The conies are but a feeble folk, yet they make their houses in the rocks' (Prov. 30:26). The Syrian Rock Hyrax is the one that he knew; it is also the species most commonly kept in captivity. Its general colour is grey-brown, with a yellowish patch on the back surrounding a surface gland. There is no visible tail. To zoologists it is *Heterohyrax syriacus*.

In both the above passages the word is pl. and it is indeed a gregarious animal, living in colonies of a few dozen. They seldom venture far from their rocky retreats and they usually post a sentinel whose high warning note is quickly heard and acted on. In a sense they are a feeble folk, with little means of defence against their enemies, of which the most dangerous in Palestine are perhaps the large eagles. We saw a pair of Verreaux's Eagles prospecting a site high in the cliffs above a *wadi* in Upper Galilee while we watched and filmed a colony of hyrax. Conies are basically vegetarian, taking a selection of leaves, roots, bulbs, etc., but some are also said to be fond of locusts. They are day feeders, with periods of activity and feeding, interspersed with times when they return to their holes.

The Mosaic law specifies the coney as unfit for food in a statement that has often been misunderstood, 'Because he cheweth the cud but divideth not the hoof'. The precise meaning of the Heb. word here tr. 'chew the cud' is not quite clear; it is suggested that it may mean 'chew again', without necessarily implying the possession of a ruminant stomach. The hyrax never seems to stop chewing as it sits outside its hole, and it could easily be said to 'ruminate'. It is not clear why it was prohibited as food, except that circumstances demanded a simple and easily applied code, which might exclude some good with the harmful. The Arabs today consider the meat tough and dry, so the hyrax is a prey hardly worth shooting; it is too wary to be caught in most traps. However, hyraxes are eagerly hunted in some parts of Africa.

Much of Palestine is rocky and provides numerous suitable habitats for the Syrian rock hyrax. Precise details of present distribution are hard to obtain, especially from the more isolated and frontier districts. Its range is probably less reduced than that of many other animals, thanks to its choice of terrain, and it is still found widely, from the desert edge right up into Galilee, where it is perhaps most easily seen today, even from the road.

The Hare

Several hares are known in the area with which we are dealing. The long-eared Egyptian Hare, *Lepus capensis aegyptius*, was often depicted in wall paintings in Ancient Egypt. The Iraqi Hare, *L.europeus connori*, is the hare of the Mesopotamian lowlands; this is often shown on Assyrian reliefs and seals, also in larger pictures, being hunted by falcons or dogs, and being prepared for the table. The hare of Palestine and Syria is another sub-species of the European Hare and is known as *L.europeus syriacus*, similar to the British form in general appearance and habits, but smaller and with shorter ears, and rather paler; there are slightly different forms of it in the various regions. It is found most commonly in the rather greener country and it must have been helped to some extent by irrigation.

Hares look like rabbits, to which they are related, but rabbits are not found in Palestine. The hare grows larger than the wild rabbit (but not quite as big as one or two of the domestic breeds); it stays above ground all the time and jumps much farther. However the most important differences are in their breeding habits, even though the gestation period of both is about thirty days. Rabbits have large litters which are born underground, hairless and with the eyes not opening for about eleven days. Baby hares, called leverets, are dropped above ground, usually up to four at a birth; these are fully furred and are born with their eyes open. They can move about almost at once.

The hare (Heb. *'arnebeth*) appears in the Bible only as an unclean animal (Lev. 11:6; Deut. 14:7), and new light has recently been thrown on the reason given for this ban. 'Because he cheweth the cud but divideth not the hoof' was either considered false or taken to be based on the observation of mouth movements characteristic of this group. We now know that rabbits and hares practise a strange habit called 'refection'; at certain times of the day, when the hare is resting in its 'form', it passes droppings of different texture and appearance which it at once eats again, swallowing them after little or no chewing. It thus seems to be eating without taking any greenstuff into its mouth. This is not, of course, the same thing as chewing the cud, but it has a similar effect. Like the ruminants, hares feed on bulky vegetable matter of which only a part can be digested, and the yield is largely the result of bacterial action inside the gut; the process of breaking down into assimilable substances is started on the first passage through and taken a stage further on the second.

As with the hyrax, which is banned on identical grounds, it is not clear why the hare was regarded as unclean, other than to allow the application of a simple rule. Rabbits are alternate hosts of the dog tape-worm, which can also invade humans if infected rabbit-meat is eaten incompletely cooked; the hare may also be a host. In Europe and SW. Asia the hare is now in big demand as a game animal and for food.

In contrast, over large areas of Africa the hare is never killed deliberately but regarded as the magic hero of folk tales. These stories are told in the open savannah country from Senegal in the west through to Rhodesia, and even around the Kalahari Desert, and this magic hare crossed the Atlantic in the memory of the first slaves several centuries ago to become the Brer Rabbit of the same stories translated into English.

The hare was well known in Ancient Greece, where it was said to do considerable damage to vegetable gardens and in vineyards; one would expect this latter to be to the foliage and stems, but there are several Palestine mosaic pavements showing the hare feeding on grapes. Catching hares in traps is illustrated in the mosaics at Beth Shan, and they were also hunted by dogs and taken in nets.

Mouse

Even to a naturalist the word mouse covers a number of different animals; in Britain the ordinary person would probably lump field and house mice, voles and shrews, dormice and harvest mice just as mice, but he would not include rats, which are sufficiently bigger to demand a name of their own. This is not the rule everywhere; in parts of Africa for instance, it is usual to refer to all uniformly coloured rodents up to the size of a brown rat just as mice, the word rat being reserved for much larger rodents that are hunted.

It seems likely that this was also true of Heb. 'akbar, and of Arabic farah, and that these words have been given to a whole range of small rodents, including true mice and rats, dormice, jerboas, hamsters, etc. The ordinary people would use this word on its own; those in closer touch with nature might qualify it for certain species. The word has the root meaning of corn-eater, which is how farmers normally regard any mouse.

The prohibition of Lev. 11:29 therefore covers a whole group, but the main object of the ban could have been to exclude Black Rats, which are specific carriers of dangerous diseases; as destroyers of food and goods they are second only to the larger and stronger Brown Rat that was later in starting to spread across the world from the East, but has now replaced it in towns and away from seaports.

In many countries a wide range of small rodents is eaten, though never the black rat, except perhaps in times of famine. In the Middle East generally many small rodents are considered well worth hunting, especially the jerboas and the larger sand rats, which belong to entirely different families from the black rat. In Roman times, a large dormouse was a great delicacy and was fattened on walnuts while being kept in special cages called *gliricidia*; so much so that this is now known as the Edible Dormouse, with the Latin name of *Glis glis*. It is not native to Britain but was introduced and became established here early in the twentieth century. To the Hebrews this and all the others were forbidden in the Mosaic law. Many centuries later Isaiah spoke of punishment due to those who ate swine's flesh, and the abomination and the mouse (Isa. 66:17), and the inference is that the defilement had been deliberate.

Apart from these two passages the word mouse is found only in I Sam. 6:4 ff. This chapter describes the events preceding the return of the Ark by the Philistines, and for a long time no connexion seemed likely between the plague of mice that ruined the crops and the deadly disease which killed large numbers of the Philistines. Some commentators are still cautious on this point, but many consider that the disease that struck the Philistines, and perhaps later the Israelites, was bubonic plague and that the 'mice' were black rats. The bacillus responsible for plague was first identified in 1894 and a few years later its strange mode of transmission was discovered. It is primarily a disease of black rats, passed on by fleas peculiar to them, and it is only when the host dies that the fleas seek another, which may well be man, seeing that these rats are now seldom found far from human dwellings. Very recently it has been found that some gerbils are also carriers of plague, which makes the identification less certain.

In this passage the rats are not precisely blamed for the outbreak, but it does seem that the causal relationship between the rats and the tumours or buboes, which form in the groin and elsewhere and are so characteristic of the plague, was recognized by the priests of Dagon, for the presents sent back with the Ark were golden models of rats and tumours. The miraculous defeat of the Assyrian army of Sennacherib after the siege of Jerusalem has sometimes been attributed to plague, but this is less likely. Another account of it, by Herodotus, speaks of a multitude of mice which ate the army's equipment and left it without bows and quivers. If this is true, the rodents concerned are likely to have been house mice and rats, which are mixed feeders, rather than field mice and voles, which are largely vegetarian.

Black rats originally came from the east, gradually making their way across Asia and Europe, reaching Britain early in the Middle Ages and bringing plague with them; it is possible that they arrived much earlier, even with the Romans. There is also argument as to when rats reached Palestine but they were present in Mesopotamia many centuries before the Philistine incident, and they had probably travelled on ships trading out of India, for the black rat is the true ship rat and, as such, has colonized seaports the world over.

If the diagnosis of bubonic plague is not correct the rodents that spoilt the Philistines' land were almost certainly voles, *Microtus guentheri*; these have long been notorious for sudden multiplication into massive outbreaks, which were attacked by all possible means, especially smoking out and allowing domestic pigs to root up the land and so catch and eat them. These voles still cause trouble in the intensively cultivated areas, and in recent years they have sometimes been controlled by the use of poisons which have long-lasting and deadly effects on other animals. (See Chap. II.) Very many small rodents are still found in Palestine, including Jerboas, Jirds, Gerbils, Sand Rats, Spiny Mice and Dormice.

Hedgehog

This popular little animal is mentioned only in RSV, as the tr. of *qippod*. This is discussed under *Bittern* in Chap. XIII, where it is concluded that this word's meaning remains unknown. Hedgehogs are easily recognized; they are up to 10 in. long and are densely covered above and on the sides with short spines. Their colour varies from brown to sandy and one kind is white beneath. With the much smaller shrews they belong to the order Insectivores – the insect-eaters – but this is a far from accurate name, for as well as taking a wide range of insects they eat many worms, small reptiles, baby mice and birds' eggs, mostly found on their night prowls. When alarmed hedgehogs roll into a characteristic defensive ball, spines pointing outwards; they even do this on the road, apparently expecting that they will then be safe from cars. As a result many are killed, in Palestine as well as in Britain. Three species of hedgehog are found, two being desert or semi-desert forms, and the one in the north almost the same as the British species.

Porcupine

This is RV tr. for *qippod*. The Crested Porcupine has strong sharp spines, mostly on the back, and it is possible that both this and hedgehog would have the same native name, though in fact the spines are their only common feature. The porcupine is by far the largest rodent of the area and may weigh over 40 lb. It is basically vegetarian, feeding on roots, fruits, nuts, etc., and also chewing bones for the calcium content. In most countries where they are found porcupines are considered good eating, and in spite of the discomfort involved they are a favourite prey for lions and leopards. Because of its size even a single porcupine can do serious damage to root crops and they are now found only where there is ample rocky shelter.

Mole-Rat

Two Heb. words are rendered 'mole' in one or other EV. *tinshemeth*, whose meaning is obscure, is discussed under 'Lizard' (see p. 199). *chaphar-parah* occurs only in Isa. 2:20, 'their idols to the moles and to the bats.' This is a most unlikely pair and it seems best to accept the AV mg. suggestion that this tr. is conjectural. Moles belong to the Insectivores and are widely distributed, but they are missing from this area. However, some other burrowers go by the name of mole-rats and the result of their activities are a common sight in all areas with a rainfall of more than 4 in. and enough soil for them to work in. They have become fully modified for a strange underground life and are completely blind. They tunnel extensively just beneath the surface, pushing up heaps of soil, very like molehills, at irregular intervals. Their feet have become flat scrapers but the huge protruding gnawing teeth do most of the work as the mole-rats search for roots, bulbs, etc., which they store in special chambers. In farmed areas mole-rats may do serious damage to grain and root crops. In winter they build breeding mounds which may be 5 ft. long and 3 ft. high. The largest of the species is 8 in. long; others reach only about 3 in.

Bats

In some warm countries bats can be very numerous and this is certainly true of Palestine, where they are found in all regions from the desert through to the moister country of the north. It would be truer to say that they hunt over all regions, for they would scarcely find breeding or roosting places in such specialized habitats as the swamps and the coastal dunes. Well over twenty species are recorded from Palestine, some of them found more or less across Europe and as far west as Britain, others being African species on the northern edge of their range. Many other kinds live in Egypt and Mesopotamia. Only experts distinguish most of these species, especially in the field, and though bats would be known to the Hebrews one would certainly not expect them to have more than one or two names. It is generally agreed that Heb. *'atalleph*, meaning 'night flier', is properly tr. 'bat'. Two of its only three occurrences are in the food laws, where it is bracketed with unclean birds, e.g., 'the stork . . . and the lapwing and the bat' (Deut. 14:18). Bats are included among the birds with some logic, for they are the world's most expert fliers. Some commentators also see bats in 'all fowls that creep' (Lev. 11:20), from their manner of crawling on a surface, but RSV renders this insects. Bats form a distinct order of mammals called *Chiroptera* (hand-winged); their efficient wings are the fore-arms, with elongated fingers and thumbs entirely covered with fine membrane.

It would hardly seem necessary to class the bats as unclean, for nearly all kinds have a powerful and persistent musky smell, and few groups of mammals are more odorous. This is not quite so true of the larger bats, some of which weigh up to 2 lb., that feed on fruit, and these are killed and eaten in vast numbers in parts of Africa where more orthodox meat is scarce. These bats were also eaten in Ancient Assyria, after being preserved in salt.

Most bats on the Palestine list are insectivorous and they catch their prey by using their highly specialized echo-location sense; this is illustrated well in several of the *Fact and Faith* films made by the Moody Institute of Science. Many bats roost communally in caves, old buildings, hollow trees, etc., and their numbers are such that they quickly build up large deposits of highly-smelling guano which is often used as manure. These bats do good by killing insects of many kinds, but the Egyptian Fruit-bat, *Rousettus aegyptiacus*, is liable to become a pest in the increasing areas of fruit orchards now being established in Israel. Its numbers were probably negligible in biblical times.

In the warmer parts of Palestine, especially in the lower Jordan valley, bats can be active during the winter; in the colder north they must hibernate for several months. It is also possible that in the extremely hot, dry weather food may become scarce enough locally to enforce a resting period. Bats normally become active at dusk, having spent the day asleep hanging upside-down in their roosts. Their unusual appearance and habits have long made them the subject of strange beliefs, often with evil associations. In Ancient Egypt charms in the form of a bat's head were recommended for use in dovecotes to stop the pigeons from leaving it. The only biblical reference, other than in the food laws, is in Isa. 2:20, 'In that day a man shall cast his idols . . . to the bats.' They are mentioned in rather similar circumstances in Baruch 6:22, 'Upon their bodies and heads sit bats', referring to the Babylonian idols worshipped by the Israelites. Bats, like several other animals which are hard to identify precisely, were used almost to set the scene of desecration or desolation.[1]

Ape

The sole mention of apes in the Scriptures is in the list of imports made by Solomon in I Kings 10:22, the other animal products being ivory and peacocks(q.v.) Traditionally Heb. *qoph*, which is from a foreign root, has always been rendered 'ape' and today is generally accepted as such, but two different interpretations are put on it, depending on the origin of this cargo. As discussed under the other two items, this may have come from India, with which trade was being done long before Solomon's time, or from Africa via Egypt. The one school, including Tristram, claims that *qoph* is derived from a Tamil word for monkey; the other, including Albright,

---

[1] One of the few books giving any field notes on bats in Palestine is *Footsteps in the Sand* (1959) by David Harrison who was a doctor with the R.A.F. and had a special interest in small mammals.

that it is Egyptian in origin. If it is the former it could have been one, or several, of the macaques or langurs found in S. India. It is worth noting that several Indian monkeys, including the Hanuman Langur, are depicted on ancient Assyrian monuments of Solomon's time and just afterwards, showing that such traffic existed. These illustrations are also thought to include baboons from Africa. If the name is of Egyptian origin the apes would have been either baboons or vervet monkeys, from the open country of NE. Africa.

The word ape is used here in its more popular meaning, i.e., as monkeys in general. Technically it is confined to the man-like apes – chimpanzee, gorilla, etc., and it cannot possibly be taken in this sense.

No monkeys seem to have been native to Palestine within recent geological ages. The nearest occurring naturally today is the Sacred, or Hamadryad, Baboon of the Arabian coast; this was once found in Egypt, where it was sacred, and other species also may well have been there until biblical times. The existence of monkeys in Ancient Mesopotamia seems uncertain.

Whale

Jonah's 'whale' is a favourite of the critics and much has been written about it from many angles. In this book it will suffice to emphasize two points – that the miraculous element is stressed as the narrative opens, 'The Lord had prepared a great fish to swallow up Jonah' (Jonah 1:17), and that our Lord stated explicitly that this actually happened (Matt. 12:40). Regarding such passages it is useful to remember Mark Twain's often quoted comment, that it was not those parts of the Bible that he could not understand that worried him, but those bits whose meaning was quite clear.

The tr. 'whale' is found three times in OT, from the Heb. *tannin* or *tannim*, which are rendered 'sea monster' once in AV and three times in RSV. These are discussed in App. B. In NT Gr., *kētos* is found once only, in our Lord's reference to Jonah, where the Heb. *dag* is used four times; this latter word, while usually tr. 'fish', has a much wider meaning. It is generally agreed that the rendering 'fish' is not possible anatomically, at any rate as regards any species of the E. Mediterranean – where the incident took place, not far out of Joppa. However, some of the toothed whales are physically capable of such a feat, for several species are known to swallow whole seals and dolphins weighing several cwts. each. Although the documentation may not be fully acceptable in some quarters, there do seem to be cases of reasonable authenticity, of men being swallowed alive by such whales and liberated shortly afterwards. The Sperm Whale, a member of this group, comes into the Mediterranean and is recorded from time to time off the Palestine coast. The male may reach a length of nearly 60 ft. and the female about half as much. It could have been such an animal that was 'appointed' for this particular task, but there is no point in speculating in detail about the possible physical explanation of an incident that is primarily metaphysical, i.e., miraculous.

This is perhaps the place to discuss briefly the word sea-monster, found only once in AV, 'Even the sea-monsters draw out the breast' (Lam. 4:3). The RSV rendering is 'even the jackals give the breast and suckle the young'. The whole setting is desert rather than sea, so that RSV, reading *tannim* instead of *tannin*, must be preferred. If it were tr. whale, as it is in other AV passages, this statement would contain a literal truth, for whales do indeed suckle their huge young.

Dugong

Heb. *tachash* is found in three passages only. The skin appears as the material used for covering the Tabernacle when erected (Exod. 25:5 ff.). The following year it was specified as the covering for the Ark of the Covenant when on the march. It occurs only once more, in Ezek. 16:10, where it is used for making women's sandals. This word has given great difficulty. It is thought to be derived from an Egyptian word for leather, and to be related to Arabic *tuhasun* or *tuchash*, a general word for all sea-mammals found in the area. AV has 'badgers' skins' in every case. RV tr. 'sealskin', with margin 'porpoiseskin'. Unfortunately RSV failed to make use of any recent work on the subject and has 'goatskin' in the Tabernacle passages and 'leather' in Ezekiel. LXX has *hyakinthos*, merely suggesting skins of the colour of hyacinth, a shade which is not now known for certain.

In trying to establish the identity of this animal three facts seem relevant:

1. The instructions for the Tabernacle and its fittings were issued early in the march, while the Israelites were in the vicinity of the mouth of the Gulf of Aqaba. This is desert and while it is not entirely lifeless it can support only very low populations of land mammals. The badger cannot be considered.

2. The skins were of large size. The net size of the top of the Tabernacle was about 13 by 44 ft. i.e., 572 sq. ft. RSV has 'goatskins' throughout, reflecting the pl. in the Heb. The Ark was much smaller, about 4 by 2½ ft., and it was covered over for the journey by a single skin. The consistent use of pl. and sing. in these two passages must be significant. Nothing smaller than a large antelope could provide a skin of this size; no desert animal was plentiful enough, or obtained with sufficient ease, to make the larger cover. Thus all land mammals seem to be excluded.

3. The passage in Ezekiel infers that the material is valuable, for it is placed alongside embroidered cloth and fine linen, yet it was strong enough for sandals and was not just ornamental. This makes the RSV rendering of 'goatskin' unlikely, for this was common, everyday material.

The only likely source of such animal skins is therefore the sea, and various authorities have made the following suggestions:

1. *Seal.* The nearest species is the Monk Seal of the Mediterranean, where it is rare.

2. *A small whale.* Several species of dolphin are recorded from the Red Sea and may be expected to venture into the Gulf of Aqaba. Their skins would be quite unsuitable for these purposes; also, their wandering habits and high water-speed would make it impossible for the Israelites to catch them.

3. *Dugong.* This is the only truly marine species of Sirenia alive today. Until about the beginning of the nineteenth century it was fairly plentiful in the Gulf of Aqaba, and for centuries its skin had been the standard material for making sandals in the eastern Sinai peninsula. As regards size an adult dugong is upwards of 10 ft. long and one skin would very easily cover the Ark. For the larger cover a maximum of twenty would be needed, a number which should have been obtainable without too great difficulty.

On this evidence the dugong seems a probable source of these skins, if not the only practical one. All the above argument had been developed before I obtained a copy of Tristram's valuable work, in which he had reached almost the same conclusion. He considered that since the name probably included seals, these skins were perhaps used for making women's sandals, but he was not aware that the Monk Seal was absent from the Red Sea. His findings were obviously noted when the RV was tr.

Dugongs are not truly gregarious but go about in groups of up to six when they are not heavily preyed on by man, who is their only important enemy. Once found in coastal waters from the Red Sea all the way round to Australia, dugongs are now much reduced in numbers through hunting for food, and in some areas they are in serious danger of extinction, for they are quite unable to survive against modern weapons. The dugong was not included in the species forbidden as food to the Israelites and the flesh was perhaps eaten after the skin had been removed for preparation into leather. More probably it was banned by Deut. 14:9, 10, being aquatic but without fins and scales.

The dugong is fully adapted to aquatic life; its fore-limbs have become paddles and its hind-limbs have completely disappeared, so that it cannot leave the water. Its only living relative is the manatee, of W. Africa and the American coast from Florida to Brazil, and this lives in brackish water and in many sluggish rivers; the dugong is much more marine. Both are entirely vegetarian, the dugong's food including many seaweeds.

The dugong was once divided into a number of species, to one of which, living along the coral banks of the Red Sea, the German zoologist Rüppell gave the name *Halicore tabernaculi*, from the belief that its skin had been used to cover the Tabernacle. All dugong are now regarded as belonging to the one species *H. dugong*.

X

Birds

of

Prey

The difficulty of identification. Eagles and Vultures, Osprey,
Buzzard, Kites, Falcons, Hawks, Owls.

PALESTINE, LIKE MANY OTHER COUNTRIES OF THE E. MEDITERRANEAN, has always been rich in the birds of prey, especially those that fly by day. As has already been explained in Chap. II, some of the finest birds of prey have suffered very serious, and in some cases disastrous losses that will take years to replace. Even so, the ordinary naturalist is still likely to see more of these birds in Palestine than in any part of W. Europe. Identification is not easy, but their very numbers in earlier times would lead us to expect several to be mentioned in the Scriptures. In one or other EV the following names are found, most of which probably refer to day birds of prey: buzzard, eagle, falcon, gier eagle, glede, hawk, kite, osprey, ossifrage and vulture. These are discussed individually below, but a few introductory remarks are first necessary.

1. Although some of these birds are resident and may be seen at all seasons in the wilder places, most are birds of passage and are obvious only in spring, when the larger species travel northwards by using thermals for a lift into the sky before gliding as far as possible. Their movements are dependent on weather but at times they go through in great numbers, often at hundreds an hour, and mostly over places where there are few resident birds of prey. The smaller kinds travel nearer the ground, and the commonest – or, at least, the one most often seen – is the Lesser Kestrel; this travels in large flocks and roosts in hundreds, in such conspicuous places as the trees around Capernaum.

2. These birds are usually seen only once or twice a year as they migrate, often at heights too great for details of plumage or even colour to be seen,

for they appear as little more than silhouettes. There are further difficulties in identification. Some kinds have light and dark phases and are also variable in pattern. Smaller species may reach full adult plumage by the second winter but eagles and vultures take four to five years, with the colours and pattern changing a little at each moult. In many of the smaller kinds the cocks have a different plumage from the young and hens (in the harriers the former are grey and the two latter brown), while the cock is typically smaller than the hen. Because this is a main migration route these birds are headed in all directions, so there are many more kinds than most countries could have on their regular list. Even to experienced observers this is one of the most frustrating groups, and one cannot expect more than the vaguest reports from non-naturalists, among which most Biblical writers must be included.

3. The above collection of names is far from being an accurate list. Most, such as eagle, falcon, hawk and vulture are not individual kinds but names of groups with a number of different species. Glede is now obsolete and ossifrage is clearly taken over from the Latin. Night-hawk is a vague term for various night birds. So it is not surprising to find great variation both among and within the VSS, and the position is so complicated that listing all these variations would be a rather academic task. These Heb. group names are probably best tr. by equally vague English names, but this is such an interesting group of birds that the whole Palestine list is given in App. A, and some attempt will be made to suggest tr. for each Heb. name and give some background.[1]

4. Many of these feature only in the two lists of unclean birds, so that context is of little help, except that G. R. Driver sees the lists drawn up logically and in descending order of size. Birds of prey are, by definition, carnivorous and this alone disqualifies them as food for the Hebrews. The smaller hawks, falcons and harriers rarely take other than living prey and for these the ritual defilement would arise from eating food unclean to man or killed in the wrong way, but the practical reason for the ban becomes plain when the larger birds, especially the vultures, are considered. They feed on carrion and dying animals, while the eagles are more likely to take sick and injured animals than those that are fit. These birds are always liable to carry infection, especially the carrion-feeders, and the prohibition was sound on grounds of hygiene.

5. The scavenging and predatory habits of the ravens and crows might tempt the layman to class them with the birds of prey, but they are members of a completely different family and are discussed elsewhere.

---

[1] The fullest recent work on these birds, and some others, is by G. R. Driver (PEQ 1955 pp. 5–20). The Heb. names are analysed in the light of philology and natural history; unless further important material is found his work must be considered definitive, but it must be accepted with caution, not because his findings differ largely from the traditional, but they imply more detailed knowledge of birds by the ancient writer than seems likely.

Eagles and Vultures

There is general agreement that Heb. *nesher* and Gr. *aetos* cover the large eagles, especially the Imperial Eagle, and the Griffon-Vulture. Seen mostly as they glide high overhead on almost motionless wings they are not at all easy to identify. Shortly before writing this page I was visiting Delphi with a big party of students, and earlier arrivals reported that they had already seen the eagles we had been told to watch for. Shortly afterwards two huge birds glided over the top of the tall cliffs and the cry went up 'there are the eagles'. In fact they were Black Vultures, but it needed the binoculars to make quite sure. Before we left a Golden Eagle came along, a good deal lower but almost in line, giving a wonderful chance to compare them. To the ordinary person they were all eagles, and my experience there that day convinced me that this would be even truer of the Hebrews travelling over the desert. It seems best to make this the starting-point and then examine any clues suggesting that one or other is intended in the various passages.

Nesher is found a total of twenty-eight times, which is more than all other birds of prey together. In the main VSS it is uniformly rendered 'eagle', except that RSV has 'vulture' on three occasions. Driver considers that its root meaning is of a gleaming flash or rushing sound, a bird that streaks through the air; in contrast, Canon Tristram believes it to mean 'to tear with the beak'. It heads the tables of unclean birds, which can reasonably be taken to show it is the biggest. Great size and strength is implied in several passages, e.g., 'I bare you on eagle's wings' (Exod. 19:4). Other attributes are swiftness and the ability to fly high, 'Fly swiftly like an eagle' (Jer. 49:22, RSV). 'Though you soar aloft like the eagle' (Obad. 1:4, RSV). These apply equally to both eagles and vultures.

In a few passages it is clear that vultures are meant, e.g., 'There will the eagles be gathered together' (Matt. 24:28). The big vultures hang high in the sky, soaring or cruising slowly great distances apart, and can see at once when a neighbouring bird drops down. In a short time vultures have gathered from a wide area. This is a habit of vultures generally, but in Palestine it is the Griffon-Vulture of which this is truest. The Black and Egyptian Vultures have rather different feeding patterns, which are discussed below. An ancient proverb, quoted in the Talmud, says that a vulture in Babylon can see a carcass in Palestine, which typically emphasizes a truth by exaggeration, but perhaps also has a political slant. Mic. 1:16 twice speaks of baldness 'as the eagle', presumably a reference to the Griffon-Vulture whose head is covered with short creamy down that gives the impression, at a distance, of being bare.[1]

The word eagle twice has a fully literal sense, where it is forbidden as

---

[1] The American national bird – the 'Bald Eagle' – is quite different; the distant appearance of baldness comes from the white feathered head.

food. In the remaining 26 vv. it is used in a wide variety of figurative ways, which seems to confirm that it has a general rather than a narrow meaning. Several passages reflect interesting old beliefs, which, because of their context, need not be taken as statements of fact, e.g., 'as an eagle stirreth up her nest' (Deut. 32:11), implies that the hen bird deliberately disturbs the eaglets, persuades them to take off and then, if need be, catches them on her wings, but naturalists agree that this is not confirmed by observation. Young birds spend long periods alone at the nest, especially as they grow older and need more food; this is hunted over great stretches of country and the parents may visit the nest only two or three times a day. After eight to twelve weeks they become fully feathered, exercising their wings increasingly and finally becoming air-borne. All this applies equally to most eagles and vultures, all of which nest high on cliffs or in tall trees. Add to this long period the six weeks or so of incubating the one or two eggs, and then the fact that they do not breed until four or five years old, and it becomes all too clear that once their numbers are badly down they take a very long time to build up again. So it is well that they are long-lived. Firm evidence is hard to obtain but there are reasonably reliable records of over a century, including one kept in captivity in Vienna for 104 years.

This long vigorous life is probably the thought behind one of the best-known passages, 'Thy youth is renewed like the eagle's' (Ps. 103:5). Some commentators see here a suggestion of the ancient Phoenix legend in which, according to one version, the eagle disappeared into the sun every ten years, to dive down into the sea, like the sun, and emerge refreshed. Pliny wrote of the eagle forcing its young to look straight into the sun.

The list in App. A shows that most of the large eagles pass through Palestine or stay just for the winter; they can fast for two or three weeks without difficulty and most that go straight through need not feed on this part of the trip. The status of these birds is changing so rapidly at the moment, due to the contradictory factors listed in Chap. II, that comment can soon be out of date, but the Short-toed Eagle probably outnumbers all the other breeding species. It can live in all sorts of country other than the desert, it nests in trees and feeds mostly on reptiles and frogs, so it may have kept out of the chain of events started by the rodent poisons. Bonelli's Eagle is about the same size – between the Osprey and the Golden Eagle – and is a hunter of small game in the rocky, mountainous areas. It nests high above the carved temples of Petra. The much larger White-tailed Eagle (once a rare resident in Scotland) makes its home on remote high crags within reach of the sea, where it lives by snatching fish near the surface. Very few are now left but it is still on the Israel list.

One spectacular bird has just been added to the Israel fauna and we were fortunate to film what was perhaps the original pair when they returned to their prospective nesting-site in a remote gorge in upper Galilee. This is Verreaux's Eagle, one of the world's biggest; apparently it just decided to extend its range beyond Africa and chose a nature reserve for its new home.

The vultures are fewer in species and all four nest in Palestine. Although the big ones habitually go for many days without food, these scavengers find life more difficult in countries where sanitary methods of refuse disposal are used and where large wild animals have become very rare. This is true for increasing areas of Palestine, and almost the only carcasses likely to be thrown out today are those of sheep, goats and camels which have died of disease and are useless as human food. Improved animal health services are cutting down even this source.

The griffon-vulture is between 3 and 4 ft. long, with a wing span of almost 8 ft. Canon Tristram, describing his experiences in Palestine in 1863-4, noted that no landscape was ever without its circling vultures. There were breeding colonies wherever it could find suitable nesting-sites – especially in the rocky gorges in and leading off the Jordan valley, some of which held hundreds of birds. Those days are gone for ever. In upper Galilee, around the lake itself and in parts of the Judaean hills one sees the odd pair most days, but that is all. Breeding-places are few and well protected, one of the last – and safest – being high above the Valley of the Doves, just west of the lake.

The vivid description in Job 39 must surely refer to the griffon-vulture. Vv. 27, 8, 'Doth the eagle mount up at thy command, and make her nest on high? She dwelleth and abideth on the rock, upon the crag of the rock, and the strong place.' This passage well describes a typical nesting-site. Vv. 29, 30, 'From thence she seeketh the prey, and her eyes behold afar off . . . Where the slain are, there is she.' The ability to spot distant food and the habit of feeding on carcasses have already been noted.

The Lappet-faced and Bearded Vultures are birds of the desert edge, where they still nest, in tiny numbers, on cliffs and escarpments. The former is rather like the griffon, but the Bearded Vulture, or Lammergeier, more resembles a giant falcon, with long narrow wings and diamond-shaped tail, and it is yellow beneath. They are usually solitary birds, and they share a habit that almost certainly lets us identify them with *peres* (the breaker) of Lev. 11:13, a name variously tr. 'ossifrage', 'geier', 'eagle' and 'vulture'. These birds do not compete with the larger groups of griffons but come in when these have finished; they take over the picked bones, carrying them aloft and dropping them time and again on to hard rock until the bones are broken and their favourite marrow exposed. Ossifrage was a splendid invention of the AV translators to describe this method. A few animals are also caught and given the same treatment, especially tortoises and snakes. In Spain, where they live on high cliffs, they are known as *Quebrantahuesos* – bone-breakers. Unfortunately it is no longer true, as

THE KIBBUTZ at Ma'agan Mikhael (background) depends on agriculture and fish-farming. A drained fish-pond provides a resting place for herons of several species on their northward journey in spring (pp. 176, 221).

THE RAVEN is found in most parts of Palestine and breeds on crags or in trees. This nest was in a thorn tree alongside the main road 12 miles north of Eilat (p. 182).

HARVESTER ANTS' nest, Huleh valley, mid-April. This colony is storing grass seeds, and the husks, removed at the nest, surround the entrance (p. 247).

THE SAND VIPER perfectly matches its surroundings but because of the high surface-temperatures it must remain buried in the sand for most of the day (p. 206).

Canon Tristam could report, that most ravines have a pair and that one or two could usually be seen on a day's journey.

Following *peres* in the list is the word *'ozniyyah*, found nowhere else, but said to be derived from the root 'goat' and hence meaning 'bearded'. It has been suggested that this is the Bearded Vulture, which, by reason of size, would stand next to the big vultures. This is not impossible, but it seems rather doubtful whether this bird of the high crags would ever be approached closely enough to note its beard. The tr. 'osprey' in all EV is most unlikely.[1]

The Egyptian Vulture is perhaps half the size of the others and the adult has black and white plumage which at once distinguishes it, even when high above. It is a true scavenger, picking its living from town rubbish heaps and being seen everywhere from its arrival in spring to its departure, after rearing a family, in the autumn. Canon Tristram regards this as the *racham* of Lev. 11:18, noting that this is identical with Arabic *rachmah*, by which this vulture is known. This sounds probable, and it is strange that Driver rejects it, preferring osprey.

Unlike many biblical words which are used consistently in metaphor, the eagle/vulture has several contrasting figurative applications of which some have been mentioned and some others merit comment. The vulture was a symbol of Egyptian power, which gives special point to Jehovah's message to encourage the Israelites early in their journey, 'I bore you on eagles' (vultures') wings and brought you unto myself' (Exod. 19:4). It was ironical that many centuries later, after repeated disobedience and national sin, they were again taken into captivity, this time by the Assyrians, whose deity Nisroch (possibly from the same root as *nesher*) was vulture-headed.

In several passages the eagle is a symbol of a punitive power allowed by God. The warning is found in Deut. 28:49, 'The Lord shall bring a nation against thee ... swift as the eagle flieth'; this was fulfilled when the Chaldeans came 'As the eagle that hasteth to eat' (Hab. 1:8).[2] There seems to be no particular figurative meaning in Jer. 49:16, 'Though thou shouldest make thy nest as high as the eagle I will bring thee down from thence, saith the Lord,' but it is an interesting comment on the nesting habit of this group. The eagle also appears in two important prophetic settings – as one of the four living creatures of Ezekiel and in the Revelation.

As regards the remaining birds of prey the evidence on which the names are based is largely philological and often rather slender; the suggestions made can be only tentative for we cannot even be certain that all the names refer to birds of prey. The Osprey is one of the obvious birds of

[1] The word gier, also spelled geir and geier, is first recorded in 1567 and noted as vulture 1615. It came from a word now found in modern German *Geier* – vulture. In English it is known only in combination, as Gyr Falcon and Lammergeier. The name otherwise is meaningless and should be dropped

[2] See also Hos. 8:1 and Lam. 4:19

K

spring passage, for instead of riding the thermals some, at least, work their way north in easy stages. As we travelled north from Eilat we saw ospreys in the most improbable places – sitting on telegraph poles in the middle of the Negev. Farther north they looked more at home, on trees around the Huleh nature reserve where they could snatch a few fish from the lake before moving on towards their breeding-grounds. Although most VSS include osprey in the unclean birds list, this tr. of 'ozniyyah is unlikely, as is also Driver's suggestion that it is racham. It seems doubtful if this passage migrant would be well enough known to the Hebrews to rate a name, far less a place in the list.

Buzzards and Kites

Buzzards are broad-winged soaring hawks and probably the best-known day birds of prey in Britain, for in the past thirty years or so they have become much more common. Several species of buzzard in dark and light colour phases, that would hardly be distinguished by most observers, pass through or live in Palestine. Only RSV includes buzzard – for 'ayyah, where AV has 'kite' and RV has 'falcon' – and it agrees with Driver, who regards the Heb. name as derived from the mewing call. The Honey Buzzard is one of the travellers, a bird that specializes in raiding wasp and bee nests; the others catch mostly small mammals and reptiles, as well as feeding on carrion. Some authorities prefer to follow AV with its tr. 'kite'. dayyah (da'ah), is rendered 'kite' in RV and RSV, with which Driver agrees. The root is disputed, but it is generally considered to be either hawk or kite. In any case, one or other of these Heb. words is likely to be the kite, of which two species are known in Palestine. The Red Kite is rather larger and paler than the Black Kite, and it is seen only on passage or in winter. Kites are distinguished from all other birds of prey by their long forked tails and, like all large Raptores, they are masters of flight, catching flying ants and locusts with skill and grace. In size and also in feeding habits they fall between vultures and hawks, taking a wide range of prey, as well as carrion.

When the AV was being tr. the Red Kite was very familiar in English towns and cities, where it was useful as a scavenger.[1]

Hawks and Falcons

Heb. nets, coming well down the list, is tr. 'hawk' in all EV. The ornithologist defines hawks as having rather short rounded wings like the Sparrow-hawk. The falconer uses the word for any species that he trains, while the ordinary person gives the name to any small bird of prey. This could be the Heb. use for it, and it is interesting that in Lev. 11:16 the words 'after its kind' are added, suggesting that a number of species are included

[1] The word 'glede' (Deut. 14:13) is obsolete or dialect for kite; it is omitted from RSV because Heb. ra'ah is now regarded as a textual error.

in the group; so it seems reasonable to include the falcons, true hawks and harriers under this heading. (RSV suggests that *'ayyah* be tr. 'falcon', but this is unlikely.)

The falcons, with their long pointed wings and long tails, catch most of their prey by sheer speed. Palestine has a wonderful range of them, from the Peregrine and Lanner of 18 in. down to the Merlin and Lesser Kestrel, of about 12 in. As the list shows, they include both residents and migrants. Falcons take only living prey, which varies from Rock Doves, the main quarry of the Peregrine, to small birds, rodents and insects on which many of them feed. Kestrels and Lesser Kestrels are very common, breeding right in the towns, often forming small colonies in old ruins and towers. The latter is one of the commonest migratory hawks and is doubtless included in the comment in Job 39:26 RSV, 'The hawk spreads his wings towards the south', setting off on the autumn journey to Africa.

The true hawks, by comparison, are poorly represented and only the Sparrow-hawk is likely to be seen. My only meeting with it was at the Italian *Hospice* on the Mount of Beatitudes, where it arrived at rather before 5 a.m. and kindly dispersed a crowd of house sparrows that had woken me by chattering in the eucalyptus trees outside my window.

Lastly there are the harriers, whose name comes from their unmistakable method of hunting – by quartering the marshes and fields in search of almost anything small that moves. These are some of Britain's rarest breeding birds, with only a handful of nests each year for each of three species, and we were delighted to have the chance of filming a Marsh Harrier hunting grasshoppers in the alfalfa fields at Yotvata in the S. Negev.

Heb. *'ayit* has not so far been mentioned. This is tr. 'bird', 'fowl' and 'ravenous bird' (AV); RSV is more accurate here with 'bird of prey' throughout, e.g., 'birds of prey came down upon the carcases' (Gen. 15:11) The root meaning is 'screamer', a good name for members of this group, and *'ayit* is now thought to be a general name for all day and night birds of prey. As such, it is therefore omitted from the detailed food lists.

Owls

The owls are night birds of prey varying from sparrow-size to a length of 30 in.; all are unmistakable and unlikely to be confused with other birds, even by the layman. Palestine has a typical range of these legend-surrounded birds, four more-or-less resident species and four migrants. They are as secretive there as in most countries and only three are likely to come to the attention of the ordinary folk – the Little Owl, which is partly a day bird and enjoys sunning itself on roadside posts and wires; the Barn or Screech Owl, whose strange calls are heard around buildings; and the Scops Owl, whose single whistling note is familiar, though perhaps seldom recognized as such. The others would usually be known only by the field naturalist.

The owls have always been a translator's problem. The AV uses the name sixteen times, from five different Heb. words; two of these appear only once each (Isa. 34:14, 15) and their meaning is very uncertain. Owl features only seven times in RSV and several traditional renderings are changed. These, with RV tr. of the Heb. words and Driver's suggestions are set out in this table:

Heb. translit.	AV	RV	RSV	Driver
1. *bath ya'anah*	owl	ostrich	ostrich	eagle owl
2. *tachmas*	nighthawk	nighthawk	nighthawk	short-eared owl
3. *shachaph*	cuckoo	sea mew	sea gull	long-eared owl
4. *kos*	little owl	little owl	little owl	tawny owl
5. *shalak*	cormorant	cormorant	cormorant	fisher owl
6. *yanshuph*	great owl	great owl	ibis	barn owl
7. *tinshemeth*	swan	horned owl	water hen	little owl
8. *qa'ath*	pelican	pelican	pelican	Scops owl

Several efforts have been made to identify these owls, including H. B. Tristram (1867), and J. G. Wood (1869). For the most detailed analysis we are again indebted to G. R. Driver, whose work has already been mentioned. Though based on the same facts, opinions vary widely and further lengthy discussion is not justified here; anyone wishing to examine all the arguments should compare these treatments. The following points seem relevant:

1. There is a general agreement that numbers 1, 4 and 6 refer to owls and that the first is not the ostrich as suggested by some authors and followed in RSV: *bath ya'anah* is found eight times and accounts for the big difference between AV and RSV in the occurrence of 'owl'.

2. Three owls are each mentioned twice in the food lists; otherwise they appear solely as a symbol of desolate places, e.g., 'the owls shall dwell therein; and it shall be no more inhabited forever' (Jer.50:39). In such figurative settings we cannot reasonably look for data to identify species of a bird that has been held to be of ill omen since ancient times, as Pliny recorded.

3. Their nocturnal habits make owls hard to observe and except to a few experts all are just owls. There is no reason to suppose that such secretive birds would have been well enough known to have individual Heb. names, especially the Fishing Owl and Long-eared Owl, so that Driver's tentative findings, while most valuable for their analysis of Heb. roots and bibliography, seem improbable, and the AV recognition of only three types more likely. It is, indeed, reasonable to recognize three groups – the huge Eagle Owl, rarely seen; the big series of medium-sized owls; and the Little Owl, diurnal and common. But it is not really possible to suggest which is which.

The following are brief notes about these owls now on the Palestine list and mentioned by the various authors. The Eagle Owl, in many species and races, is the world's largest. Its range includes Palestine where a beautiful pale form lives in the deserts. This owl nests in trees or among rocks. The Short-eared Owl is a bird of the open ground, where it hunts at dusk and in daylight; in Palestine it is only a passage migrant. The Long-eared Owl is one of the hardest to see, for it lives only in forests and hunts at night, staying silent outside the breeding season. This is a winter visitor. The Tawny or Wood Owl is found in woods all over Europe and SW. Asia. It is some 15 in. long and feeds mostly on small rodents. The very pale Barn Owl is a little smaller; it is easily recognized by its long-drawn flight-calls from which it gets its other name of Screech Owl. This has perhaps the widest range of all owls and is everywhere associated with farms and buildings, though it is the Tawny Owl that has moved into the bigger towns and cities, including London, to hunt for rats and mice.

The Fishing Owl, which hunts in the manner of the Osprey and White-tailed Eagle, is probably absent from Palestine itself, where the tapping of rivers for irrigation has reduced its fishing areas, but it is well known from the Nile and Iraq. The Little Owl, about 8½ in. long, breeds in most regions other than the desert. This is the owl sacred to Athens, the goddess of wisdom in Greek mythology. Like the next species, which is slightly smaller still, it feeds mostly on insects. The Scops Owl is a summer visitor and one of the most elusive birds I have yet tried to see. All through the late evenings in April we heard it calling from the trees around our hostels in Tiberias and upper Galilee, but we never managed to catch a glimpse of it.

Nighthawk (Lev. 11:16) is an indefinite name, only as old as the AV, which SOED defines as a name for various birds, especially the nightjar. It may well refer to an owl, but it is impossible to suggest which it could be.

Tsabua' (spotted) is found only in Jer. 12:9 and translated 'speckled bird' (AV), 'speckled bird of prey' (RV and RSV). This is discussed under 'hyena' (see p. 126).

XI

Birds

of

Passage

*Palestine as a major flyway. Migration Patterns. Some important
birds of passage – Pelican, Storks and Cranes*

LTHOUGH IT IS NOT MENTIONED BY NAME, AND SEVERAL THOUSANDS
of years were to pass before its significance was fully appreciated,
the fact of bird migration is plainly implied in a number of OT
passages. This is hardly surprising, for when the spring migration is in full
flood one can hardly fail to be aware of it all over Palestine. The earliest
of these references is in Exod. 16:13 ff., where the escaping Israelites
received a regular provision of meat in the form of quails. These tiny
game birds at one time travelled between Africa and Eurasia in vast flocks
totalling several millions, crossing the Exodus route as they did so and
coming within range of the hungry nomads. The passage in Jer. 8:7 is just
as clear, even though it is in a figurative setting: 'The stork in the heaven
knoweth her appointed times; and the turtle, the crane and the swallow
observe the time of their coming, but my people know not the judgment
of the Lord.' Both turtle and stork are correctly rendered here, and though
there is some argument about the identity of the other two there is no
doubt that they were conspicuous migrants, and that this is a picture of the
position in early April, when the birds are streaming through.

Palestine's position and geography combine to make it a great natural
flyway. It is a comparatively narrow strip of land, for most of its length
not more than fifty miles across, and running more or less north and south
at the eastern end of the Mediterranean. The mountains, by and large,
also run north and south, offering no difficult barriers for the birds to cross.
This is the most easterly route available to birds which have spent the
winter south of the Sahara and are now known to travel across more or
less the whole of the Mediterranean. At the western end large numbers

150

cross the narrow Straits of Gibraltar, and there are probably other concentrated take-off points. Some attempt has been made to calculate the
total numbers involved and a conservative figure for the migratory birds
that travel over or round the Sahara from Europe west of a line drawn
north and south through Berlin is 600 million. No estimate has yet been
made of those passing through Palestine.

This number was once very much higher but it has gradually been
reduced by centuries of merciless trapping at both take-off and arrival
points, with tremendous bags year after year. This is done in most countries
around the Mediterranean; in parts of Italy the pressure is still such that
birdsong is rarely heard today[1]. Crossing the desert – nearly 1,000 miles in
some places – and then the Mediterranean – as much as 500 miles – makes
the journey hazardous enough. Add to this the terrible toll taken by the
hunters and the surprising thing is that any get through to breed. It is
fortunate for the birds that much of the N. African coast is sparsely
inhabited.

The cultivated strip along the Nile may be only a few miles broad but
it is enough to carry what is probably the greatest single concentration of
birds, and from there the most natural route to go north is over Palestine;
a more direct line across to Asia Minor, even via Cyprus, involves at least
300 miles of sea. A more easterly course would involve another desert
stretch of at least 500 miles – over Jordan and Syria – in which they might
see a few oases but would find little available water for most of the year.
The coastal strip offers several advantages that will be discussed below,
but there is much variation in the patterns followed by the various species,
developed over long periods of time and impossible to explain today. For
instance, the Lesser Whitethroats now use the eastern route almost
exclusively and in spring are seen daily throughout Palestine. In contrast
the Common Whitethroat, which is heading for a similar breeding range
in Europe, travels up the west side and is rare in Palestine.

Too few recoveries of ringed birds have yet been made in Israel to know
the full range from which birds come but the following are typical and
suggest that the range is large:

Starling – Moscow.
Pintail – Astrachan, U.S.S.R.
Lesser Black-backed Gull – Helsinki.
White Stork – Heligoland.
White Wagtail – Stockholm.

Winds affect the routes taken and in the autumn they modify the return
journey; the birds are then more spread out and some travel south over the
Syrian deserts with the help of strong tail-winds that increase the ground
speed to well over the 25 m.p.h. average for many of them. The return

[1] Legal action has now been taken to stop this slaughter.

migration in autumn is less concentrated for another reason also, even though total numbers have been augmented by the summer's broods; departure for the south is spread over a longer period. In the case of cuckoos, for instance, the first adults leave early in July and the last of the year's youngsters towards the end of September. In contrast the majority had arrived at their breeding grounds in the first half of April.

The importance of Palestine as a migration route becomes even more apparent when its bird list is analysed. For such a small country it is a rich list, with nearly 350 species, and for our purpose we may recognize five different classes: Resident, Summer Breeder, Winter Visitor, Passing Migrant and Straggler. It is impossible to classify every one exactly, for many of them belong to two of the three middle groups. Less than seventy are described as Resident, which means that they stay within Palestine all the year round; these include some that occupy specialized niches, for instance Tristram's Grackle of the oases around the Dead Sea, and the Blackstart of the rocky desert. This means that no less than 80 per cent of all species are to some degree migratory and since these latter include some very common birds, the proportion of resident individuals may well be considerably less than this.

The Winter Visitors are those that come south after breeding in Europe and W. Asia – Rook, Black-headed Gull, Woodcock, White-fronted Goose, Mute Swan and other well-known kinds. These number about fifty, and some have come a very long way; for instance the White-fronted Goose breeds in the far north of Russia and in Greenland. Many individuals do not stop in Palestine but go on farther, so they are also Passing Migrants. Many waders are in this category; the Curlew, for instance, is as much at home probing the rich mud of the Israeli fish-ponds as it is on the warm beaches of Kenya. The Red-throated Pipit is another of them, for some stay in Palestine while others fly on to E. Africa. My first meeting with this neat little bird was early in April 1960; after a few weeks in Jordan and N. Israel my wife and I had flown down to Eilat especially to see some of the migrants as they arrived. At dawn the next morning the tiny patches of grass, kept green only by conserving every scrap of dirty water, were alive with wagtails and Red-throated Pipits, fearlessly racing round and snapping up green-fly and other insects. Exactly two years later I was back there again, and there were the pipits, refreshing themselves for their long journey north – and it is a long one, for they breed only among the tundras and swamps of Lapland.

The true Passing Migrants are the most numerous class, with 130 species. For most of them Palestine is merely a station along the route, a country to be flown over as quickly as possible by some; to be used as a refreshment stop by others. The thirty or so Stragglers are, to some extent, also Passing Migrants, for most of them have been displaced from other flightlines by freak weather or some mischance. Nearly always they have been carried east or south-east of their normal wintering grounds, and they include many well-known British species, such as the Goosander, Bean Goose and the Whooper Swan. If bird-watchers were as thick on the ground there as they are in Britain this bit of the list would probably be much longer, for many rarities must slip through without being spotted.

The remaining fifty are called Summer Breeders, but few are classed only as this. Having wintered south of the Sahara they make their way north and many breeding grounds begin at Palestine, so they gradually drop out, a few at a time, with the bulk of the flock pushing steadily on. One conspicuous member of this group is the black-headed form of the Yellow Wagtail, one of several forms that use this route, heading in all directions. This one, the neatest of all, builds its nest in Palestine, Asia Minor and the Balkans. Another Summer Breeder is the Purple Heron; only a few spots in Palestine are still suitable for it, and it uses them; most fly on many hundreds of miles to its main breeding grounds in the swamps of S. Europe.

One summer visitor makes an exceptional journey; as far as is known the Black-headed Bunting is the only member of this group which winters in NW. India.

As far as we can see, this tract has been a major flyway for birds since long before the first civilization began, and there is no reason to think that the pattern I observed on my spring journeys in the Holy Land is substantially different from what it was in our Lord's days and for several millennia before that, except that the total numbers are now less. There have been great changes in the flora and fauna, as discussed in Chap. I and II, but these have most affected the large mammals. The more intensive occupation of the country since the early 1950s has changed the status of some resident birds, some for the better and some for the worse, and certain factors have hit the large birds of prey severely – let us hope only temporarily. By and large the small migrants have been less hurt, and change in public opinion about conservation should bring them help.

Jeremiah's list, quoted above, is an interesting one; of the four birds two are large, one is of medium size, and one is small, and they belong to four widely different families. In putting these together he emphasized a real truth – that all sorts and sizes of birds are among the long-distance travellers. Some fifty bird families are on the Palestine list of which only four have no migrants; these are all rather special families with only one bird representing each – Palestine Sunbird, African Bulbul, Palestine Babbler and Wren.

The smaller birds travelling this route may already have had several hundreds of miles of desert crossing, averaging about 25 m.p.h. and often having no help from the wind, though there is sometimes a favourable wind a few thousands of feet up if only they can find it. The lucky ones were those that came down the Nile Valley and avoided being trapped. For most of spring and autumn, when the birds are on the move, the Sahara offers neither water nor food; the scattered oases there have been compared with a few dozen tea cups sunk at irregular intervals in the surface of a football field! There is hardly any shade if they are forced down by day into the lethal temperatures at ground level. To these birds Palestine is luxury, for both food and water can be found at intervals made much shorter by the spread of cultivation, with irrigation, into the Negev. There is argument as to how much the birds need such help, for migration has gone on successfully without it, over the vast Sahara desert and over the desert areas to the north-east, but access to water and shade, at intervals during a critical desert stage, must surely help rather than hinder.

All over Palestine in the weeks of spring, one is conscious of the passage of these birds and my memory of places is often tied to the birds that we met there. It was in the valley of Elah – scene of David's victory over Goliath – that we began meeting the main stream of European Rollers, perhaps the most colourful of them all. At that point they preferred the branches of the roadside eucalyptus; farther south, for mile after mile, they watched for their prey from the telegraph or power lines alongside the road, one pair to every two or three lengths. At Hazor we looked up to see a flock of White Storks almost filling the sky; after being held up by a few days of broken weather they had at last found a thermal to give them a lift up. And among the ruins of this ancient city which Joshua burnt (Josh. 11:13) – now excavated and tidied up – we watched and filmed a pair of Bee-eaters hunting grasshoppers and dragonflies.

Perhaps the migrant that gave me the biggest thrill was a Wryneck snaking its way through the weeds in a pocket-handkerchief-sized garden at Mitspeh Ramon in the central Negev, a garden made possible by the effluent from the tiny community's sewage plant. I had known this bird well as a schoolboy but had not seen it since before the war, for it has almost gone from the British list.

These small birds seemed to make their landfall around Eilat and then work their way north across the desert. How many times they stopped it was impossible to guess. Some of them certainly did some fairly long hops; for instance, after finding the pipits just about the commonest birds in Eilat we did not see them again. On the other hand, we met the wagtails, all the kinds, time and time again, especially in alfalfa fields around the big desert *kibbutzim*, where they rushed around hunting all manner of insects. These small migrants must find the long sea passages both tiring and dangerous, yet they do it habitually and seem to manage just as well as those who travel more comfortably by the eastern or western routes.

The larger birds seem less willing, perhaps less able, to do the long stretches unaided by thermals. Even on a short sea crossing like the Bosphorus the eagles sometimes lose so much height on their glide over that they are down almost to sea level. The general pattern is to ride a thermal to a height of perhaps 6,000 ft., and then glide north, making every possible use of rising currents, until so much height has been lost that another thermal must be found. This makes them much more dependent on local weather conditions and they therefore travel in longer hops and tend to come through in rushes. In the northern part of the Rift valley a cloudy spell, possibly with heavy rain, may occur even in April and in these conditions thermals do not form. We had a striking example of this on our 1962 visit. For some three weeks the weather had been wonderful, with just enough cloud to make the skies interesting for photography, and then it broke – to the joy of all the farmers, to whom every drop of rain then was a bonus. The White Stork migration was at its peak and they just had to pile up in the upper Jordan valley and wait. Wave after wave came in until we reckoned there were perhaps 5,000 in the area. It reminded us of a busy airport where something had happened to stop the planes landing and so they were stacked up at various heights. Sometimes we would see some six or seven flocks circling as they searched for thermals.

Their mode of travelling is perhaps best seen in the desert. Just inland from Eilat we had seen the odd eagle and kite looking for a lift, but even when a patch of rising air was located a single bird was not much to see, and just then there were few large birds about. Later in April we were more fortunate, when we were making for En Gedi. We had dropped many hundreds of feet after passing the Sea Level sign on the roadside and stopped above the Dead Sea to get some shots of the desert hills, when we noticed a long line of birds flapping slowly towards us at a few hundred feet. They had found a thermal above a dome of rock; when they reached it they set their wings to circle within the rising column of air and just went up. They were almost out of sight when they straightened out and made for the north, keeping along the line of the Dead Sea hills where they would also get some help from the rising air. We needed an expert to identify them all – several species of buzzard and large eagles, as well as the clearly recognizable Short-toed Eagles and Egyptian Vultures. Several hundreds came by in perhaps half an hour and then a flock of White Storks entered the column, their differing upper and under wing patterns making their banking movement easy to follow. They, too, sailed off to the north, losing just enough height to maintain cruising speed. It is not clear where the birds of prey stay overnight. There are no thermals then, so presumably they must sit it out on rocks or on the ground – or fly the hard way. Spring nights in the desert can be cold and it may be well into the morning before the rocks really warm up again.

The more detailed pattern of travel is decided by the food habits of the various groups of birds; in general this gliding involves little effort and thus the minimum use of food reserves. The birds of prey are discussed in more detail in Chap. X. As flesh-eaters they can go for days at a time without food and over some of the stages probably take nothing at all. However, it is clear that they sometimes drop out of the procession to feed, for some of the big eagles suffered serious casualties after eating poisoned corpses in the Jordan Valley. A few other important migrants will now be discussed.

Pelicans

The most spectacular – and quite the most unexpected – migrants that fly over Palestine are the huge White Pelicans, *Pelecanus onocrotalus*. They were, in fact, the first that we saw in real numbers on our 1962 visit; two long skeins, perhaps 500 in all, flying and gliding north high over the Huleh valley. It seemed hardly possible that these massive birds with a 9-ft. wing-span and weighing perhaps 30 lb., could have come all the way from Central Africa, where I had watched them only a few months before.

All members of this small family are specialized water birds, and though most are more or less resident in areas where fish supplies are unlimited, some of the White Pelicans travel between their breeding grounds in the Danube delta in the Black Sea and their winter quarters in Africa, probably on the great lakes of Uganda. They use the Nile valley route, with the chance of coming down to rest but probably not to do much fishing. For the Palestine stretch of the journey their main stopping-place in earlier times, perhaps their only one, was the old Huleh lake with its surrounding swamps. Reclamation has now turned this into productive arable land flanked with fish-ponds, and a lake of some 400 acres, part of the carefully protected Nature Reserve, is the only open water in the area. The pelicans do not seem to favour the Lake of Galilee, some 1,000 ft. lower. If they are in this part of the country when the weather breaks, as it did while we were there, they must sit it out in safety either on the small lake or in the centre of one of the vast ploughed fields. They are not made welcome at the fish-ponds, for a flock of 500 pelicans could eat an average of a ton of fish per day – worth perhaps £200 in the wholesale market.

There is no doubt at all that the pelican passes through Palestine but it is unlikely that it can be identified in the Scriptures. Heb. *qa'ath* is three times tr. 'pelican', twice in the list of forbidden meat. The third is in a familiar text 'I am like a pelican of the wilderness' (Ps. 102:6), which sounds somewhat self-contradictory; it would not be typical of such a desert and pelicans are never solitary, but wilderness in this verse could also mean open fields or pasture. Elsewhere this word is twice rendered cormorant, one of several birds of ill-omen in Isa. 34:11 and Zeph. 2:14, and this problem is discussed further in Chap. X. This tr. can probably be rejected on other grounds also. These birds are seldom seen by the ordinary person, certainly not at close quarters, for they fly over once or twice a year as quickly as possible, using the thermals to mount high in the sky and glide north on almost fixed wings, usually so high that they can be identified only through field glasses.

Before naturalists began making accurate observations early writers had stated that pelicans fed mainly on shellfish and later brought back their shells as an owl produces pellets. Both statements are false, though the odd crayfish may be taken along with the fish which are the main food. They mostly work in teams, using their beak pouches, which hold four times the contents of their stomachs, as nets and scoops when the fish have been concentrated. In contrast the American Brown Pelican dives into the water after fish, in the manner of a gannet. All pelicans feed their young by partly digested food, taken by the chick as it puts its head down the parent's throat. This regurgitation was the basis of the LXX and Vulg. tr. pelican, for Heb. *qa'ath* is said to mean 'vomiter'.

Many strange legends have arisen about pelicans, most of them from this method of feeding the young. As the food is taken the lower beak is pressed against the breast, from which it was believed that the young were fed by blood. Thus in heraldry this bird was always shown pecking at its breast, and in this form it was sometimes used as a pattern for church lecterns, though less commonly than the eagle.

Storks

Two kinds of stork pass through Palestine every year, the White Stork, *Ciconia ciconia*, in great numbers, and the Black Stork, *C. nigra*, in small groups or singly. The scavenging Marabou Stork is a very rare straggler from Africa. To most folk there is only one stork – the White Stork, the popular bird that still builds its huge nest in many European towns. It is unmistakable on the ground, standing well over 3 ft. high on its long red legs; and equally so in the air, with neck outstretched (in contrast to the pelican) and legs trailing. The red beak and black-and-white plumage are obvious in all positions. This is another bird that migrates the lazy way, by riding the thermals, so it is largely committed to an overland route as it flies north from its winter haunts; these extend from SW. Arabia through Central Africa to the far south.

The Black Stork is slightly smaller, and glossy black except for most of the underparts, which are white. It passes in smaller numbers and is more solitary in habit. Its route lies up the Rift valley, which it leaves before it reaches the Dead Sea, crossing over to the coast, which it then follows.

Unlike pelicans, storks are mixed feeders, taking some vegetable matter but mostly a wide variety of small animal life – mice, snakes, fish, worms and insects; also frogs, which are their main prey in the breeding season. Some winters they may live largely on locusts. With such catholic tastes they can find food *en route* much more easily than pelicans. In Palestine the big concentrations mostly look for food and water in the safety of the broad acres of Upper Galilee, but from February to early May they may be seen, in greater or lesser numbers, following the plough, whether ox or tractor-drawn, or striding over the fields and marshes in many parts of the country. The pattern varies from year to year. On our first visit, in 1960, we saw storks several times, but never more than a dozen or so at a time and usually single birds. Two years later, also in April, we saw them literally in thousands. Their return migration is less obvious; the different wind pattern lets them take a course farther inland and they move on a broader front.

Heb. *chasidah*, from a root meaning constant, loyal, loving, has had a wide range of renderings. In his concordance Young lists it as white goshawk, kite, stork or heron; the LXX has heron, pelican, hoopoe and 'asida', but from AV onwards the accepted tr. is stork, though it may also include herons. Three points seem to confirm this rendering:

1. It is in the list of unclean birds (Lev. 11:19). Its basically carnivorous diet, taken in dirty places, would make it unsuitable; in any case, the meat is not edible.

2. It is obviously migratory. It is likely that Jeremiah drew his hearers' attention to a flock passing high overhead as he told them that 'the stork in the heaven knoweth her appointed time'.

3. It is a very large bird. This is implied in Zech. 5:9, 'they had wings like the wings of a stork; and they lifted up the ephah between the earth and the heaven'.

The only other mention tells us that the stork once nested in Palestine. 'The stork has her home in the fir trees' (Ps. 104:17, RSV). A century ago a few storks still stayed in Palestine to nest but they have not done so for many years now; with protection perhaps they may return. The few birds that stay for the summer are thought to be youngsters from the previous year. The useful nature of the stork, especially as a destroyer of snakes, is now widely recognized and it is carefully protected in most countries; even so, its numbers are diminishing everywhere, partly due to draining swamps which had provided much of their food. In recent years a big factor has been secondary poisoning, when storks have eaten pests killed by too powerful chemicals.

Secular literature has many references to the character implied by its Heb. name. All observers agree that the parents are devoted to their young, but some writers have gone much farther and have suggested that the young ones recognize their parents throughout life and come back to look after them in old age!

Crane

This well-known bird certainly visits Palestine regularly but it cannot be identified with complete certainty. Some confusion has resulted from what is thought to be the transposition of two words by an early translator. In Isa. 38:14 and Jer. 8:7 Heb. '*agur* is tr. 'swallow' (AV) and 'crane' (RV and RSV); *sus* is tr. 'crane' (AV) and 'swallow' (RV and RSV). No authority now supports the AV even though there is some disagreement about the identity of '*agur*. The tr. of *sus* is discussed under swallow; it is enough to note here that it may well stand for both swift and swallow, which belong to separate families but live similar lives and have calls which could be the basis of the name.

There is fairly general agreement that '*agur* is the crane; in the Jeremiah passage it is mentioned as a migrant, while Isaiah speaks of its voice 'Like a crane . . . did I chatter' (AV). 'Like . . . a crane did I clamour' (RSV). The call can certainly be described as a clamour; it is said in textbooks to be a 'loud, clanging, trumpeting note'. (See p. 186 [Chap. XVIII] for comment on this call.) The Common Crane, *Grus grus*, is such a conspicuous bird that one would expect it to be named, especially since it is a passing migrant and also a winter visitor to the southern part of the country. Migrating cranes are mentioned by Homer in the *Iliad*, *c*. 1000 B.C. In the air it compares in size with pelicans and large vultures in having a wingspan of 8 ft., but flies with neck stretched out and long legs trailing. It stands 4 ft., the tallest bird of the area today, very erect, mostly grey with a touch of red on the crown. Perhaps it is not surprising that the name is included in the AV, for this was a familiar bird in Britain during the Middle Ages; it bred regularly until the early seventeenth century, and was then a winter visitor for many years. It seldom comes to Britain today and its main breeding grounds are in secluded marshy areas across N. Europe, with a few colonies in Spain, Rumania and elsewhere.

In winter most cranes move south, going by the Palestine route to Africa, but varying numbers stay in S. Palestine and Arabia, where they roost communally on hillocks. They arrive over Sinai from the south in March; just over a century ago the Rev. F. W. Holland reported flocks of as many as 2,000 passing over the desert south of Beersheba.

A rather smaller species, the Demoiselle Crane, is a less common passing migrant which breeds mostly in Asia but goes down into Africa for the winter by the same route.

The crane was considered good eating when it was common in Britain; it is not among the prohibited birds and so was presumably eaten by the Hebrews. Although it may seem to live rather like the stork it is, in fact, largely vegetarian, taking a wide range of seeds and leaves, as well as some animal food. Prof. Driver suggests that '*agur* is the wryneck. This sparrow-sized bird is an uncommon passing migrant, of skulking habits and hard to recognize when on the move. We saw just one bird in our two spring visits of a month each. It certainly has a penetrating call, but this is heard only in the breeding season. It does not seem likely that the wryneck would have a Heb. name; still less that Isaiah and Jeremiah would quote it in what are almost proverbial sayings.

Many migrants are included in other chapters, in particular among the *Birds of Prey* and the *Birds of the Waterside*, and still more could be discussed here of the great variety that pass through Palestine every year. Enough has been said to show that this historic tract is a wonderful avian crossroads and worth a visit by naturalists for that reason alone.

A DETAIL FROM the famous Lion Hunt relief of Ashurbanipal at Nineveh (7th Cent. B.C.). Much earlier than this dogs had been bred for special purposes, including a huge mastiff-type used in the chase (p. 122 middle).

FOR SEVERAL WEEKS in spring the White Storks fly north in their hundreds, using the thermals to help cover the long distance between East Africa and Europe, but they take time off to search the fields for food (p. 157).

XII

Fowls after their Kind

The layman's difficulty in distinguishing between clean and unclean birds. Domestic fowls, Partridge, Quail, Peafowl, Sandgrouse, Doves and Pigeons.

ONLY A FEW OF THE BIBLE BIRDS ARE EASY TO NAME EVEN THOUGH, as a group, they must have been familiar to the Israelites. They are more numerous and in more kinds than any of the other animals with backbones; they range in size from the Palestine Sunbird at about five to the ounce right up to the Ostrich with its 300 lb., while in shape and colour Palestine's 350 or so species are about as varied as they can be. Today just a handful of experts could name them all, and competent naturalists would know at least half of them by sight, but the average Hebrew was no bird-watcher. Between thirty-five and forty Heb. words are thought to be names of birds, some standing for single species, e.g., *selav*, quail; others for larger or smaller groups, e.g., *tsippor*, small perching birds usually clean, and *nesher*, the large eagles and vultures. Nearly 3,000 years were to pass before a system of classification was worked out; how was the ordinary person to know which of these feathered creatures should be eaten and which left alone when the majority were probably unknown to him?

The clean mammals had been fairly easy to define, for meat came from the ruminants. As animal was edible only if it both had cloven hoofs and chewed the cud, not just one or the other, like a few specially named – pig, camel, hare and coney. Birds cannot be classified so simply and so the Mosaic law lists over twenty birds to avoid; as already discussed, many of these seem to be birds of prey, and others are hard to place. This proscribed list in Deut. 14 is enclosed between v. 11 'of all clean birds (*tsippor*) ye shall eat', and v. 20 'of all clean fowls ('*oph*) ye may eat', and the only fair assumption is that if a bird is not classed as unclean then it may be eaten.

An ancient Jewish definition was that any bird seizing food in its claws was unclean; any that had an extra talon and craw (i.e., crop) and the skin of whose stomach can be stripped off (i.e., like the gizzard of a chicken) is clean. This rough and ready rule is comparable to that concerning the cloven-hoofed ruminants.

The law probably did little more than codify what has been generally accepted as sound practice by civilized man down the ages. Three easily-recognized groups of mainly vegetarian birds have always been utilized:

(a) The Game or Gallinaceous Birds (i.e., related to the cock) from which have been derived the domestic fowl, turkey and guinea fowl.

(b) The Pigeon/Dove family which produced the Carrier Pigeon and tame Barbary Dove.

(c) The Waterfowl, of which ducks, geese and swans have been domesticated.

All over the world these are the birds which man eats in great numbers, mostly bred for the purpose, and there are a few others. The Shore Birds or Waders, which are the greatest travellers of all; the mysterious Sandgrouse; Bustards, which are now about the world's biggest flying birds; these are also eaten but, except for some Waders which live in great flocks outside the breeding season, they are all scarce or only of local interest. There is also the biggest bird family of all – the perching birds; the Crows are the giants among them, and they are specifically banned, but the others could legally be eaten, then as now. Unfortunately, this is still the case in many Mediterranean lands, and so their songs are seldom heard. It is interesting that even in countries where almost every kind is eaten because meat is scarce, as it is in the West African jungles, those carefully avoided are the vultures and crows, which are the mostly clearly identified in the Mosaic list.

The Birds of Prey of Chapter X form a neat natural unit. This chapter will go on to treat the obviously clean birds of the game bird and pigeon families. The rest are sorted into chapters as well as their wide variety allows, and we shall have to bring in many that find no biblical mention.

It might be helpful at this point to define some of the names used for birds generally. When the basic tr. into English were being made, culminating in the AV, 'fowl' was commonly used for adult birds, while 'bird', which also had its origin in Old English, meant a young or small fowl, or a maiden. (This is closely comparable to the progress of the words swine and pig; see p. 97.) In the sixteenth century 'bird' began taking over generally and 'fowl' started to become obsolete except in a few specialist uses, e.g., we talk of a boiling fowl and of a wildfowler who shoots ducks on the marshes. This latter is a biblical use, as in Ps. 91:3, 'deliver thee from the snare of the fowler'. This early meaning of bird determined its usage in AV, where it mostly tr. Heb. *tsippor*. As is discussed under sparrow, this sometimes has a more specific use but mostly means any small bird, and most contexts show that it is a clean bird. RSV is not completely consistent in its treatment of the Heb. words, but it has dropped fowl entirely except for birds that can be eaten (Lev. 7:26 and Neh. 5:18) which is nearer current English usage.

Domestic Fowl or Chicken

It is ridiculous that the world's most important bird commercially has never received a proper English name. We often refer to it as a fowl in the sense the dictionary defines as a barnyard fowl, a domestic cock or hen, which does not get us far, for these are the correct terms for the sexes of any bird. Across the Atlantic turkeys and ducks may also be regarded as fowls! Or we may speak of it as a chicken, which, as its use in Matt. 23:37 confirms (Gr. *nossion*), first meant a young fowl – 'as a hen gathereth her chickens'. This was soon shortened to chick, which is now used for a very young bird of any kind, but some southern dialects have chicken for its plural!

There is no doubt about the presence of domestic fowls in Palestine in NT times, but there will always be speculation whether they can be recognized in the OT, for they were probably not spread generally around the eastern end of the Mediterranean until towards the end of the monarchy. The two passages which may refer to them are discussed below.

At least the wild ancestors of this important egg- and meat-producer are easy to recognize in the Red Jungle Fowl, *Gallus gallus*, which is one of the very few forebears of domestic stock whose status as a wild bird is still secure. Its jungle haunts have obviously been reduced as land has been brought under cultivation, but it is still common enough in much of India and many countries to the east and south-east. In general size and shape the wild cock is very like the Game Bantams still kept by specialists. It lives a similar life to domestic fowls, scratching the soil with its powerful feet to find seeds, ants and grubs, and running at good speed through the bushes, but, unlike them, flying powerfully when needed and roosting high in the jungle trees at night. Only a few small domestic breeds can fly any distance; in the others the bodies have grown too heavy for their wings.

Domestication took place in its homeland very early, during the Indus Valley civilization, known through the digs done at Mohenjo-Doro, where a great city was founded about 3300 B.C. That the fowl was fully domesticated before 2000 B.C. is proved by the finding of leg-bones half as long again as in the wild form; this big increase in size is one of the characteristic changes in the chicken, the numerous colours and shapes coming much later. Bringing birds into human service is a less forbidding task than taming wild oxen, for instance, especially species whose chicks can feed themselves by pecking scraps soon after emerging from the eggs. Perhaps these eggs were collected and hatched – but how would this be done before the age of broodies and incubators, and with no way of measuring the hen's body temperature?

From India the chicken spread west by two main routes. It was brought to Egypt by sea before the fourteenth century B.C., so it is conceivable that the Hebrews knew it before the Exodus. The other route was overland via Persia to Mesopotamia, where it was well distributed by about 800 B.C. Fifty years later it had reached Greece, as is reasonably proved by its representation on proto-Corinthian pottery, and by the sixth century it was common throughout the Greek world. There is another way by which the chicken could have come to Palestine – imported directly by ship from India. Critics differ widely about the cargoes brought to Solomon, as to both contents and origin, and this is discussed further under 'peacock' (p. 168). If, as is quite possible, the shipments were from India they could well have included these poultry. This may perhaps be related to the first text having possible reference to poultry – I Kings 4:23, which lists *barburim*, fatted fowls, among the daily provisions for Solomon's table in the mid-tenth century B.C. This Heb. word is of unknown root and found nowhere else, so that experts' opinions have ranged from swan to fish!

The other passage in question is Neh. 5:18, RSV, 'Fowls were likewise prepared for me'. This is dated after the return from exile in the middle of the fifth century B.C. A different Heb. word is used – *tsippor* – which is applied to small 'clean' birds. The inference is that they were fattened in confinement, whether or not actually domesticated.

All we can say is that Solomon might have enjoyed roast chicken, but it is more likely that the *barburim* were other poultry, perhaps geese, which are discussed on page 179. As regards Nehemiah there is a much greater chance that his birds were chickens, which by that time could have come in from several directions; they might even have been brought by the exiles themselves among the gifts organized by the King of Persia.

The earliest evidence unearthed in Palestine itself is a seal showing a fighting cock; it was found at Tell en-Nasbeh, dated *c*. 600 B.C. and bears the name Jaazaniah, officer of the king who is listed in II Kings 25:23, but this is not proof that it was made there, or, if it was, that it was based on a local bird.

The fact that a fighting cock is illustrated raises a further query. The earliest records in the Indus valley also show this breed, and the motif is found so widely that experts are now suggesting that this could have been its main, even its only, use for many centuries, possibly for 2,000 years. It also acquired many religious associations among the Greeks and others, while later the Jews took to carrying a cock and hen in front of bridal couples because its large clutches of eggs suggested fertility. It was apparently a long time before the chicken was valued primarily for its eggs and then its meat.

By NT times it had become economically important and was regularly eaten by the Romans who took it everywhere, even as far as Britain. The cock had long been used to indicate time and was widely carried on camel caravans as an 'alarm clock'. It gave its name to one of the four night watches recognized by the Jews in Roman times, as in Mark 13:35, 'at even, or at mid-night, or at the cock-crowing, or in the morning'. The cock (Gr. *alektōr*) itself features in only one incident – Peter's denial of our Lord (Matt. 26:34 ff.). In such countries chickens still roam freely among the buildings and in the courtyards, finding most of their own food, and the cock is a useful sentinel, with an alarm note to warn his flock if a bird of prey comes overhead. The cocks would roost in some out-building, probably locked up for safety; the first crowing is well before dawn, but there is no suggestion that any precise hour is meant.[1]

Finally there is the only direct mention of a hen in one of our Lord's most poignant sayings, 'O Jerusalem . . . how often would I have gathered thy children together, even as a hen gathereth her chickens under her wings, but ye would not' (Matt. 23:37). This could well have been spoken as He indicated a mother hen urgently calling her tiny brood together, using a special call for this purpose, quite unlike the alarm note of the cock. The Gr. *ornis* is a rather general word for bird; the context fully confirms the rendering 'hen'.

Partridge

It seems likely that three fairly closely related game birds shared the Heb. name *qore'*, the caller, a name derived from the call made by the commonest of the three. The Rock or Greek Partridge, *Alectoris graeca*, lives in a variety of country, from the mountains of Lebanon in the north across the coastal plains to the dry hills of Judaea, but its range also extends westwards through Greece and all over Italy. It is of typical partridge build and at a distance looks exactly like the Red-legged Partridge. This is a native of SW. Europe that has been widely introduced into other parts of Europe and into America as a sporting bird. The Rock Partridge is about 14 in. long and easily recognized by its white cheeks, clearly bordered with a broad black line; the upper parts are greyish and the flanks strikingly barred. Cock and hen are alike. This is still the commonest game bird in Palestine and its voice is widely heard, a ringing 'cok-cok-cokrr'. Rock partridges are masters of concealment and are best spotted when perched on a boulder sending out a challenge; however, when we were there in the spring of 1960 and 1962 we probably heard ten for every one of which

[1] Prov. 30:31 has a disputed phrase which RSV renders 'the strutting cock'; that is almost certainly incorrect.

we had a glimpse. It is no longer true, as Canon Tristram could report a century ago, that it abounds everywhere and can be seen in great coveys in autumn. The great increase in the farmed acreage, the demand for tasty meat and wide possession of guns have combined to reduce its numbers, and, as in Britain and America, pesticides have done their damage. Fortunately this active bird makes good use of broken terrain and it is not in danger; like most kinds of game birds, it lays a dozen or more eggs to the clutch.

The Desert Partridge, *Ammoperdrix heyi*, about half the size of the first, is also resident, but only in the desert hills, especially around the Dead Sea, and in the Sinai area. We found it plentiful around En Gedi, where wild life is now protected. Had an early *Khamsin* not cut the light to far below photographic level we could have filmed some fine sequences from our Jeep. That was the only day in a month that we ran out of light! The Desert Partridge is pale sandy-coloured and when it squats in its almost bare surroundings it just about disappears; sexes are nearly alike, the cock having more colour on the flanks.

The Black Partridge, *Francolinus francolinus*, is also resident, but in yet another habitat. It likes the denser vegetation and marshy patches of the plains, and was once common, but these are the areas that have been reclaimed and heavily occupied, so its numbers are badly down. It is the size and build of a Red Grouse, about 15 in. long, and the name comes from the cock's black breast and flanks.

Although nowadays these seem to have separate local names, all are likely to have passed under the one Heb. name *qore'*, for they were obviously related in shape, habit and voice, and all would be equally edible; the snare of the fowler would often have been set for them (Ps. 91:3). All are typical game birds with powerful legs which are used rather than their wings; they seldom fly until forced out of cover, and then usually drop into the next suitable shelter. This habit is reflected in one of only two biblical references – I Sam. 26:20. David was being pursued from one refuge to another: when Saul finally caught up with him David confronted him not far from En Gedi, and described himself as being hunted like a partridge in the mountains, usually driven by beaters armed with sticks which they hurl when it breaks cover.

The partridge finds mention again only in Jer. 17:11, a verse that has been variously tr., 'As the partridge sitteth on eggs and hatcheth them not' (AV); 'Like the partridge gathers a brood she did not hatch' (RSV); 'As the partridge gathereth young that she hath not brought forth' (AV mg. and RV). There is agreement that the verse ends 'so he that getteth riches and not by right, in the midst of his days they shall leave him'. Many explanations have been suggested and it may reflect an old natural history belief that the hen removes eggs from another nest and incubates them, only to find that the birds leave when reared. This sounds unlikely, yet some old legends contain a strange grain of truth. Some Arabs think that a hen partridge lays in two nests one of which is looked after by the cock, and there is some evidence that this may be true of the closely related Red-legged Partridge. But the real meaning may be much simpler. Partridge's eggs have always been collected greedily for eating and Canon Tristram reported that 800 eggs were brought to his camp one spring. So the AV could be nearest, and it might have something to do with not counting chickens before they are hatched.

There is also one mention in Ecclus. 11:30, 'like as a partridge taken and kept in a cage'. This almost certainly refers to a bird that is tamed and then used to decoy others into snares.

Both a place and a person in the Scriptures are named after the partridge; 'En-haqqore' (Judg. 15:19), 'the well of him that cried'; Qore', the Crier (I Chron. 9:19).

Quail

Scholars now accept this as the correct tr. of Heb. *selav*. Professor Driver regards the root as unknown and suggests that the bird's liquid note, often the only sign of its presence, is reflected in the 'l' of the name. He differs, on etymological grounds, from Canon Tristram, who equates it with Arabic *salwa*, from the root 'to be fat', which would certainly suit its chubby shape. The quail fills the requirements of the narrative – that it was a clean bird encountered in vast numbers on its seasonal migrations.

Quails are the smallest of the game birds and they include the only truly migratory members of that family. The Common Quail, *Coturnix coturnix*, is the best known and most widespread, for it breeds in many parts of Europe and W. Asia and goes south in winter, many reaching Africa. It is only 7 in. long, mottled brown and looking like a miniature partridge. This is the species whose migration routes cross the line of the Exodus twice a year, and which was thus used to bring the Israelites the supplies of meat that God had promised. Two specific occasions are described. The first was about six weeks after leaving Egypt, when they had reached the wilderness of Sin, in the SW. Sinai peninsula. The second was a year later at Kibroth Hattaavah, and they had not progressed very far.

Such concentrated flocks as are described may have been exceptional, but these little birds can be numerous almost beyond belief. The mention of two cubits (3 ft.) in Num. 11:31 has caused confusion and prompted odd suggestions, as for instance, that the birds were storks. Again the VSS vary. 'Two cubits high upon the face of the earth' (AV) is indefinite. 'About two cubits above the face of the earth' (RV, RSV) suggests that they were flying at about this height, which makes sense. 'They flew in the air two cubits high above the ground' (Douai) is similar.

Though quail are powerful fliers over short distances their build makes migration journeys almost impossible without help from the wind, and the narrative says that they came in with the wind. Then a change of wind can bring them down to the ground and make them an easy prey. We learn that they came in during the evening, which is still usual with the much smaller flocks of today. Collecting went on for two days; it is true that birds are sometimes so exhausted that they must rest for a day or two to regain strength. Num. 11:32 tells us that the people 'spread them all abroad'. Centuries later Herodotus reported that the Egyptians were still preparing quail like this, cleaning them and drying them in the sun.

The quantities involved are admittedly difficult to understand, for it is impossible to imagine the situation if the smallest volume collected for a family was ten homers, a unit about the size of a tea chest. One man working on this problem calculated nine million as the total kill, and figures of exports in the past century show that this need not be entirely fanciful. Heavy exploitation in Egypt took place through the nineteenth century and well into the twentieth, yet for many years the annual export was over two million. The peak was reached in 1920 when they took three million, which left too few breeding pairs and put a stop to the mass migrations that had been going on since long before Moses.

On the other side of the world equally large numbers were being taken in China as they massed before crossing the Yellow Sea. Now the Japanese have domesticated them as meat and egg producers in a sort of battery system.

Peafowl

The splendid Peacock, *Pavo cristata,* is mentioned three times, of which one is generally accepted to be an error. This is Job 39:13, where the RV and RSV tr. of ostrich is preferred. The other two are in one context only – I Kings 10:22, repeated in II Chron. 9:21 – which is the list of freight brought back every three years by Solomon's merchant navy. Two items are simple enough – silver and gold – but the other three are found no-where else and are thought to have foreign roots, possibly derived from Tamil, spoken in parts of India and Ceylon, from which the consignment is thought to have come. They are *tukkiyyim* – 'peacocks'; *habbim* – 'elephant', to which was added the standard word for ivory, and *qophim* – 'apes'. *Tokai* (Tamil) means 'tail' but is not now known to refer to the peacock itself, while *qophim* could be related to a Sanskrit word for ape. Clearly the question must be left open, but an eastern origin of these words seems likely, for India had been trading with Egypt by sea well before this period.

Peafowl are the largest Old World game birds and are found wild in the jungles of India and Ceylon, living rather like the Red Jungle Fowl with which they share them. The wild form lives on and the one that we know best is technically a domesticated bird, virtually unchanged in every way except that it is sometimes found with white or nearly black plumage. Even assuming that Solomon did have these splendid birds, his were not quite the first in the Fertile Crescent, for the Phoenicians had already shipped some to Egypt, and Tiglath-pileser of Assyria (745–727 B.C.) had received peafowl as tribute from Arabia. Greece received the peacock from Persia, probably towards the end of the fourth century B.C., though perhaps earlier, and from there it gradually worked west. From the start it has been mostly an ornamental bird and it was eaten only until the Middle Ages, when the turkey came from America and was recognized as a much better table bird. It is hardly the bird for small gardens, where it can do much damage; its raucous voice is less offensive in large parks, where it is used to protest at intruders. However the cock's brilliant train, held up like a fan by the stiff tail feathers, makes it a most colourful bird in springtime. In fact it was just the sort of novelty that Solomon's sailors knew their master would appreciate.

Sandgrouse

Sandgrouse have been suggested as a possible alternative for quail, though no expert now accepts this. No other Biblical name can be fitted to them, but the Arabs recognize them, so these birds deserve a brief description. There are several species, all rather alike in general shape, and though they are birds of the driest country they occasionally stray into W. Europe. They are generally sandy in colour and can best be described – in appearance only – as half grouse, half dove; they are gregarious and sometimes travel in flocks of many thousands. They live deep in the desert but need water daily, for which they may have to fly great distances. It is strange that the young are reared in the hot weather; the cock brings food and water to its sitting mate and later both carry water for the chicks and feed them by regurgitation, rather as pigeons do, but in contrast to pigeon squabs the sandgrouse nestlings start moving round when a few days old.

These sandgrouse must have been a familiar sight to the Israelites during their forty years in the desert; ways of catching them may have been devised, but they are extremely wary, especially when approaching water. Once the Israelites had reached their main areas of settlement they would be unlikely to see sandgrouse again.

Pigeons and Doves

These are by far the most important birds in the Scriptures for they were the poor man's sacrifice and widely kept as domestic birds; as will be discussed in detail below, two species, or perhaps groups of species, can be clearly recognized and the tr. is fairly consistent, any confusion arising from the over-lapping of the two English words pigeon and dove. The latter is the slightly older word; pigeon at first meant a young bird of this group but this use soon became obsolete, and in many ordinary contexts now the two words are almost synonymous. The compact and easily-recognized group to which they belong is known as the Pigeon Family (*Columbidae*) or the Pigeons and Doves. In Britain the two sections are easily separated: the genus *Columba*, with the Wood Pigeon or Ring Dove, the Stock Dove, and the Rock Dove, which is the wild ancestor of the carrier and all fancy pigeons: and the genus *Streptopelia*, with the migratory Turtle Dove, and the Collared Dove, which is a recent arrival from SE. Europe. All these five are found in Palestine, and also the Palm Dove, *S. senegalensis*, which has colonized much of Palestine since the 1950s.

The whole family is strictly vegetarian at all ages, taking seeds, fruits and greenstuff. This habit meant that all were clean to the Hebrews, and suitable for eating and for sacrifice. It also brings a danger of their becoming farm pests, as the Wood Pigeon is now in Britain.

Of the various words involved one can be dealt with quickly. Heb. *gozal* is tr. young pigeon in Gen. 15:9 only. Its real meaning is 'young bird', as it is rendered elsewhere. The main word is Heb. *yonah*, which is tr. about twenty times 'dove' and ten times 'pigeon'. Without exception pigeon is used for sacrificial birds, always prefixed by 'young'; dove is used in all other literal passages and for all figurative uses, so the use of the two words is not so confusing as it might be. In the NT Gr. *peristera* is tr. 'dove' except in Luke 2:24, which has 'young pigeon' (AV). In RSV it is rendered 'pigeon' throughout. It is a rather general name for pigeon. The other pair of words are Heb. *tor* and Gr. *trugōn*, which are tr. 'turtle' or 'turtle-dove'.

Heb. *yonah* is from a root meaning a moaning sound, cf. Isa. 38:14, 'I did mourn as a dove'. This would describe the call of many species of dove. Jonah is the same word and can be taken to mean dove – or moaner! Perhaps this is a play on words, also referring to his mission; by this time the carrier pigeon may well have come into use for sending messages. Like many Heb. names of animals this seems to have had a general and also a more specific meaning, being applied first to the pigeon section of the family, i.e., the three species of *Columba*, which are generally grey-blue and distinctly heavier in build than the doves; second, and more exactly, to the Rock Dove itself, *C. livia*.

This Rock Dove has a wide range in Europe, Asia and N. Africa, the local races varying a little in colour but looking generally like the blue-grey type of racing pigeon. Jer. 48:28 (RSV), describes it as the 'dove that nests in the sides of the mouth of the gorge'. This is precisely where we watched them – in the great Avdat gorge that cuts deep into the N. Negev; the level-bedded rock strata leave little ledges ideal as nesting sites. Many other such rock faces are available in the Jordan valley and among the hills where the birds are fairly safe from man. The parents must often fly many miles to find food and water but desert irrigation has now brought water supplies within easy reach of some colonies. Just alongside the main

Beersheba road on the edge of the Negev we found a leaking surface-main that had formed a pool of open water several feet across; we made a rough hide and filmed the birds making good use of the pool – mostly migrating finches and buntings, but also some Rock Doves whose nearest nesting site must have been forty miles away.

It seems likely that the pigeon was domesticated independently in several different areas. It was already established in the earliest Dynasties of Ancient Egypt, and the first clear record of its use as a table bird is in the IV Dynasty, about 2500 B.C. In Mesopotamia it goes back even further and is known by a terra cotta dove of around 4500 B.C., from the lowest levels excavated. Some authorities consider that it was first domesticated for eating and it was not long before it became important as a sacrificial offering. It was among the clean birds taken on board by Noah and thus included in the first offering made immediately after the flood. It is specifically mentioned as a sacrifice for the first time in Gen. 15:9, together with a turtle dove, heifer, she-goat and ram.

Pigeons were widely used by the Romans for taking messages and the emperor Nero used them for sending results of the games to his friends. There is no record of the first message ever to be sent; it was long before this, but not as early as 1204 B.C., when four pigeons were sent in different directions to mark the coronation of Rameses III, for it is not seriously suggested that these were carrying messages.

These pigeons were the only domesticated birds kept in any numbers by the Hebrews. Rather later it became fashionable to build huge towers where breeding colonies were established on the ledges formed on the inside of the walls. In Roman times one of these dovecotes sometimes housed 5,000 birds. Even large caves were adapted for the purpose and called *columbaria*; one such can still be seen at Beit Guvrin, in the south-west part of the Judaean hills.

White varieties were well known and highly regarded during the Roman period, and are illustrated in mosaics, but the great range of colours and shapes that we know now are of fairly recent origin. The so-called town pigeon, living in thousands in cities like London and Venice, is only a semi-wild form of the domestic pigeon. Odd specimens are always escaping from lofts to augment these flocks and they find the ledges of tall buildings a good substitute for the cliffs used by their ancestors. The more fancy patterns of the fantails, tumblers and others are soon lost and the birds become a more or less standard shape, though varying in colour.

The Wood Pigeon or Ring Dove, *C. palambus*, is a winter visitor to the more wooded areas of Palestine, though never in the vast flocks that have become such a feature of the British countryside in recent years. The much rarer Stock Dove, *C. oenas,* easily distinguished from it by having no white on wings or neck, is also a winter visitor.

All pigeons and doves make scrappy nests of twigs and scraps, sometimes on rocks or in holes, mostly in trees or bushes; without exception they lay two oval white eggs and feed their squabs by an unusual type of re-gurgitation, giving them a sort of curd, sometimes called pigeon's milk, formed in their crops. The sexes are alike.

In many references to the use of pigeons for sacrifice the usual phrase is 'two turtle doves or two young pigeons'. It is often assumed that these were young domestic birds, largely because the wild breeding colonies of Rock Doves are now inaccessible; this may be so today but they were once much more numerous and widespread, for few countries offer more suitable nesting grounds, and squabs could well have been collected from the nest by poor folk who had no livestock of their own. They breed for much of the year and the young stay in the nest for about four weeks, by which time they are nearly as heavy as their parents.

Heb. *tor* and Gr. *trugōn* are comparable to the other pair of names in that they would be used mainly for the Turtle Dove itself; also, more generally, for the dove section of the family which includes the Collared and Palm Doves. This latter was probably its normal use. The Heb. *tor*, the English turtle, and scientific name *turtur*, are all based on the well-known call.

The Turtle Dove, *Streptopelia turtur,* is by far the commonest of this group and during the northern passage it is seen and heard everywhere. This begins early in April and soon it is impossible to see a stretch of telegraph lines without a flock of doves clinging precariously in the wind. This is indeed the time when 'the voice of the turtle is heard in our land' (Cant. 2:12). Like most migrants that go through at low level they seek food and water, mostly on the farms. In the north we found them drop-ping down in swarms to raid the sacks of damaged grain used for feeding to the pond carp, and left wide open. Most turtle doves move on towards Europe and W. Asia, but some stay in Palestine to breed.

The Collared Dove, *S. decaocto,* is a resident, especially in the warmer parts of the country, and until recently it seemed that Palestine was about its western limit. Less than twenty years ago it was not on the British list even as a straggler but within the last few years it has spread right across Europe and is now firmly established as a breeding bird over much of Britain, mostly in the towns. The Barbary Dove is very similar and this was also domesticated far back, though little is recorded about it. It is just possible that this was the turtle dove used for sacrifice, for it does not seem to have been the general practice to use wild animals for this purpose; however, we know that birds were trapped and snared in great numbers and when Hos. 7:11, 12 speaks of spreading the net for doves it could be that these were for use in the temple. Canon Tristram sees a significance in the invariable description of birds for sacrifice as *young* pigeons, pointing out that the turtle doves are easily trapped as adults whereas the larger pigeons are almost impossible to catch except as fledgelings in the nest. This suggests that both species were used as wild birds.

In most cases the turtle doves or young pigeons were the alternatives allowed to those too poor to bring a larger animal; Mary's offering in Luke 2:22–24 is such. One exception is recorded; if a Nazarite was accidentally defiled the obligatory offering was two turtle doves or two young pigeons (Num. 6:10). The stalls set up in the temple precincts sold all classes of sacrificial animals, including doves (John 2:11–16).

The first five mentions of *yonah* are purely literal, referring to the dove sent out from the Ark (Gen. 8:8 f.); the dove is dependent on greenstuff and could survive on its own as soon as the receding flood left trees exposed. After that it is translated dove only in figurative passages. In Ps. 55:6, 'Oh that I had wings like a dove', the writer envies the dove's ability to escape, perhaps to another country by migration. Ps. 68:13, 'The wings of a dove covered with silver', is thought to refer to a work of art and not a live bird.

The frequent use of dove in Song of Solomon is largely as a term of endearment, from the behaviour of pigeons which pair for a long time and show obvious signs of affection in and around the nest. Cant. 2:14, 'in the clefts of the rock, in the secret places of the stairs' (lit., rocky ascents) is another confirmation of their nesting habits. The moaning of doves is mentioned in several passages, e.g., Isa. 38:14.

In NT the dove is best known as the figurative description of the Holy Spirit descending on our Lord at His Baptism (Matt. 3:16), a figure widely used in Christian art ever since. Its use in the simile later in Matthew (10:16), 'Be ye wise as serpents and harmless as doves' seems to imply a meaning of gentleness.

Finally the dove has given its name to several gorges known as Wadi Hamam, from the same root as Arabic *hamamatu*, and also Jemima, the daughter of Job (Job 42:14).

XIII

Birds

of the

Waterside

The Leviticus food list. Brief review of some important groups living in or near the water. Herons, Gulls and Terns, Kingfishers, Waders, Ducks and Geese.

IN THIS CHAPTER THE APPROACH MUST BE RATHER DIFFERENT FROM THAT used with some of the other groups, for few of the names to be examined can be recognized with any confidence, though it seems certain that several must refer to birds typical of the waterside. Among them are the most obvious of the passing migrants and winter visitors, if only because the choice of resting and feeding places restricts them to certain areas where they are easily seen. The storks and pelicans, which have been dealt with already as migrants, could qualify equally for inclusion here, and the same applies to others also.

The fact that these are largely, if not entirely, birds of the marshes and open water has perhaps been under-emphasized in discussions of this problem. While a number of them, perhaps many of them, might have been familiar to the Hebrews during the captivity in the Nile delta, they would have seen nothing of them during the wilderness journey, except possibly passing high overhead far out of range as regards either catching or recognition. While actually on the Red Sea coast they would have seen such species as gulls, terns and cormorants. When they reached the Promised Land they lived mostly in the hills, whereas these birds would have been confined to the Jordan valley and to the coastal belt, with its marshes, estuaries and beaches. The Israelites would therefore be no more familiar with these birds of the waterside than the ordinary inland town-dweller in Britain today and their naming of these water birds would be equally vague.

Outside the food lists these disputed names are found only in the prophets Isaiah and Zephaniah, and in one Psalm of the Exile, and none of these writers would be expected to know the birds of the marshes and open water. These Heb. names will now be discussed briefly although some are mentioned elsewhere; the rest of the chapter will deal with the more important water birds that live in or pass through Palestine today.

shalak (Lev. 11:17 and Deut. 14:17) is rendered 'cormorant' in all VSS. Driver points out that a suggested root meaning is 'to dart on its prey' and that some early Hebrew writers describe it as drawing up fish from the sea. However, he sees this section of the food list as a catalogue of birds of prey and prefers 'fishing owl'. On logical grounds the cormorant may be more likely, for it is numerous, of fair size and found along some of the coastal stretches that the Hebrews would have covered in their march. One or other species of cormorant is found more or less all over the world, from the freshwater lakes of the tropics to the cold seas of the far north and south. They feed on fish and nest colonially in most unsanitary conditions.

qa'at, in AV, is three times tr. 'pelican'; in Lev.11:18 and Deut. 14:17 it is forbidden meat, while Ps. 102:6 includes the statement 'I am like a pelican in the wilderness': and twice it is tr. 'cormorant', in Isa. 34:11 and Zeph. 2:14, which are nearly identical and both of which bracket it with bittern *(qippod)* as a sign of desolation. In all five vv. the RV has pelican; RSV also has pelican in Lev. and Deut. but vulture (mg. uncertain) in Ps. 102:6 and Zeph 2:14, and hawk in Isa. 34:11.

This word is discussed further under 'owl' (see p. 148), which is Driver's suggestion, and 'Pelican' (see p. 156). The meaning of *qa'ath* remains uncertain.[1]

dukiphath occurs only in Lev. 11:19 and Deut. 14:18, where it is banned as food under the name 'lapwing' (AV) and 'hoopoe' (RV and RSV). The latter is much more likely and is treated in Chap. XV. There is no evidence to support lapwing, which is one of the plovers. This family is discussed below as wading birds.

qippod is tr. 'bittern' (AV), a bird of the heron family living in marshes and famous for its perfect camouflage and the strange positions that it assumes. Found three times, the word in RV is 'porcupine' throughout and in RSV it is 'hedgehog' twice and 'porcupine' once. These vv. (Isa. 14:23, 34:11; Zeph. 2:14) all speak of a place being occupied by *qippod*; e.g., 'The bittern shall lodge in the upper lintels (of Nineveh)'. Driver, who has made a new tr. of these passages (PEQ, 1955, pp. 129–140), very tentatively suggests the ruffed bustard. None of these is supported generally and its meaning remains unknown (see also p. 134).

'anaphah occurs only in Lev. 11:19 and Deut. 14:18 and is tr. 'heron' (AV, RV and RSV), one of the few such cases where all three agree. Unfortunately the word has been disputed since early times. Driver notes

---

[1] This is a good example of the uniformity usual in the RV contrasted with two different renderings in AV and three in RSV.

that Ancient Heb. manuscripts suggested a black hawk for the first verse
and a white one for the second. The Vulgate has *charadrius*, from the LXX,
a name now given to a genus of plovers. Driver himself suggests cormorant, largely because the most likely root from which this word is derived
is nose, i.e., it has a nose-like beak. In spite of the above agreement
'anaphah cannot be identified.

tinshemeth, listed only in Lev. 11:18 and Deut. 14:16, must also remain
undetermined. Names suggested have been 'swan' (AV), 'horned owl'
(RV), 'water hen' (RSV). Some of the older VSS such as LXX had ibis
and *porphyriōn*, from which RSV has derived waterhen. Swan cannot
possibly be correct; it would be entirely unknown in the desert, and such
a plant-eating bird would not be classed as unclean. Tristram considered
one of these old tr. the most likely. Both the Purple Gallinule *(Porphyrio)*
and the Sacred Ibis could have been well known to the Hebrews in
Egypt, where the latter was once common, though it is now found only
on the Sudan and farther south; its close association with one of the
Egyptian deities would have made it unclean, as well as its habit of feeding
in the mud.

yanshuph, which AV and RV tr. 'great owl' in Lev. 11:17 and Deut.
14:16, and 'owl' in Isa. 34:11, is rendered 'ibis', 'great owl' and 'owl'
respectively in RSV. The context of Isa. 34:10, 11, 'It shall lie waste . . .
the owl and the raven shall dwell in it' makes ibis impossible, even the
Glossy Ibis, which is an uncommon passage migrant to the coastal fish-
ponds. The root of *yanshuph* meant either 'evening' or 'one that hisses',
and the AV and RV are probably correct. Driver suggests screech owl.

shachaph has a wider range of tr. than most disputed names. Found only
in the food lists, AV renders it 'cuckoo', which is highly improbable.
RV has 'seamew', an older word for 'seagull' of RSV, and here they
follow early VSS such as LXX and Vulgate. Driver regards it as an owl.
Other old commentators have suggested shearwater and various sea-birds,
including gulls. Perhaps it can best be regarded as meaning sea-birds
generally and gulls in particular.

The Herons

These form an easily recognized family of birds. Long in leg and upright
in stance, the heron has a dagger-like beak well fitted to take the slippery
fish which form its basic food, though many other items are also eaten,
including frogs, mice and insects. Herons fly with legs trailing and
neck pulled back and tucked well into the shoulders. Palestine has about a
dozen kinds on its list; one of them is the biggest of all, the Goliath Heron,
a rare straggler from tropical Africa that stands about 5 ft.; also the Little
Bittern, which is just over a foot long. The three commonest are the Grey
Heron, which is the one that breeds in Britain, the Night Heron and the

A MIGRATING FLOCK of Pelicans rests on the lake in the Huleh Nature Reserve while Spoonbills fly over them.

Behind are the dense papyrus beds and, beyond, on the far side of the Jordan valley, the Syrian hills (p. 156).

ROCK PARTRIDGES are more often heard than seen. The cock bird, on the left, is
in a typical position for sending out its challenging call (p. 165).

Purple Heron; all are migrants, but some stay over to breed, mostly in the bird sanctuaries in Israel. The elegant Great White Heron stands as tall as the Grey Heron – nearly 3 ft. – and always has snow-white plumage, with the long aigrette plumes growing only in the breeding season. Some winter in Palestine; others pass right through, reaching as far south as the equator.

Only one member of this specialized family is habitually seen away from the marshes and water – the Cattle Egret or Buff-backed Heron; the latter name is true only in the breeding season. It is closely associated with cattle and game animals, keeping close to them and snapping up any small animals, from snakes to insects, which they disturb. Since the 1930s this egret has colonized large areas of America and has reached Australia. Until 1948 it was only a winter visitor to Palestine; now it stays to breed and may be seen almost anywhere in the farmed country.

Gulls and Terns

Gulls are well known in Britain, for we see them at the seaside and more and more come inland every winter to scavenge and follow the plough. We probably do not associate these birds with the Holy Land, yet eighteen members of the family are known there. Five are rare stragglers and the rest are migrants of which four usually nest there as well; these are the Herring Gull, and the Black, Common and Little Tern.

All are day birds and the adult plumage is always a combination of black, white and grey, often with red and yellow on beak and feet, so they are easy to observe but often hard to identify exactly. The well-known Lesser Black-backed Gull comes through in the greatest numbers, some staying the winter on the Mediterranean coast and around the ponds, where the fishermen do not encourage it, and others flying right through to the Red Sea, which involves crossing at least part of the Negev desert. While we were staying at Eilat we saw many small parties fly in from over the Gulf and make their landfall; then they rested on buoys and hawsers just off the beach before continuing their flight north. The Black-headed Gull is also common in winter, but without its dark hood.

Many of the gulls are immature and these are as hard to name as young eagles, for they take several years to go through varying brown stages and assume adult plumage. Gulls are mixed feeders, taking fish when they can but scavenging for much of the time. Whether or not they can be identified with Heb. *shachaph* in the list of prohibited meats, they would certainly rank as unclean.

The terns belong to this family but are distinct in many ways; their elegant build and graceful flight have earned them the name of Sea Swallows. Common and Little Terns live on fish, caught by diving into the water, and they are seen mostly on the coast, though the former is also nesting in the wild life sanctuary in the Huleh valley. Members of another

M

group of terns, including the Black Tern and White-winged Black Tern, go through in spring on their way to inland breeding grounds in Europe; these all feed on insects picked off the surface of the water.

Kingfishers

Visitors to the lake of Galilee can hardly fail to see some kingfishers; in fact they may see three different kinds in one morning, as we did on our first visit. The European Kingfisher is the smallest; it returns north in spring after spending the winter away from frost and snow. The Pied Kingfisher is the commonest and biggest, black and white all over and about 10 in. long. Like the first it lives entirely on fish, which it spots when hovering or watching from a perch, but the third takes a wide variety of animal food. This is the brown, blue and white Smyrna King-fisher which spends a lot of time away from the water, catching mole-crickets and other harmful insects, but well able to take fish for a change.

Waders

The Waders, or Shore Birds, form a big group which include some of the world's greatest travellers. This is suggested by the fact that the Palestine list of about forty species includes just one resident, the Spurwing Plover, and only about one other that may stop to breed, the Black-winged Stilt. Many of the hundreds that we watched in spring were heading for the marshes and tundras of N. Europe and Siberia; typical of these were the Curlew-Sandpiper and Spotted Redshank, resplendent in their full breeding plumage that we seldom see in Britain. In contrast not one of the numerous Ruffs showed any colour yet. There were Curlews and Grey Plovers on their way back from the sunny beaches of Kenya; the latter were making for the Arctic Circle. The most numerous of the true sand-pipers were the Wood Sandpipers; they, too, had come from East Africa, where we watched them the following winter, feeding in tiny pools alongside many kinds of tropical animals.

Great Snipe, Grey Phalaropes, Turnstones, Greenshanks and Godwits were there, with just about all that regularly pass through western Europe, and many others too. Like the other migrants, they have been travelling over this narrow strip of land for a very long time; the marshes have gone now but the fish-ponds and the sanctuaries are nearly as good and more permanent, so that on this stretch of their journey, at any rate, they are as safe as they have ever been.

Ducks and Geese

The last family that must be mentioned are the ducks and geese which, as producers of food, rank next in importance only to the game birds, which have provided the chicken. Some twenty-five kinds visit Palestine, including eight classed as stragglers. This high proportion of rarities is easily explained, for these birds have an open season and are regularly hunted, whereas many other rarities probably go through unharmed and unnoticed. The pattern is like that in the Waders, for only two breed here – the handsome Marbled Duck, which nests only around Huleh, and the Mallard, the common Wild Duck of Europe, whose numbers are greatly increased by winter visitors.

Many other ducks, both surface and diving, fly down for the winter or pass right through, including such familiar kinds as the Pintail, Wigeon, Shelduck and Smew. Several geese are regular winter visitors or passing migrants, specially the White-fronted and Grey Lag Geese. The Mute Swan is seen only in winter and the Whooper Swan very occasionally.

Most of these, and others too, would have been familiar to the Hebrews when they lived in the Nile Delta and they doubtless trapped many for food, copying methods worked out by the Egyptians centuries before. Ducks were taken in snares and nets, using corn as bait, and carefully carved wooden decoys enticed geese into position for a clap net to be sprung over them. Ancient Egyptian paintings illustrate many species so accurately that they can be identified at a glance – White-fronted, Bean and Red-breasted Geese, Shelduck, Teal, Mallard, Pintail, Wigeon, Pochard and Tufted Duck. Even greater numbers of these waterfowl visited the extensive marshes of Mesopotamia.

Finally, we must discuss the possibility that domestic geese were the fatted fowl – Heb. *barburim* – supplied daily to Solomon's table. There is little firm evidence about their development and distribution, but there is no doubt that geese were kept by man as long ago as the Stone Age. Except that their increase in body-weight makes flying difficult, tame geese today have undergone little change, and some breeds retain the grey plumage of their wild ancestor – the Grey Lag Goose. This is in part due to the ease with which they breed with the wild geese that may look in as they pass on migration.

This wild goose breeds naturally in N. and central Europe and may well have first been domesticated there. It was kept, perhaps already fully domesticated, very early in Ancient Egypt and Mesopotamia, probably as a result of trapping some of the many winter migrants. An illustration of mid-third millennium B.C. shows geese being artificially stuffed with food – the beginning of the cruel process of producing extra large livers: 1,000 years later, about Joseph's time, it was fully domesticated; perhaps much earlier still, but the similarity of wild and tame forms makes the pictures of little help on this point.

There is thus little doubt that the Israelites knew about goose-keeping before the Exodus but it is unlikely that any would be taken with them, for geese are basically grazers and would have been very difficult to feed on the journey. We have no data as to when they first reached Palestine; ivories of the eleventh century B.C. from Megiddo illustrate tame geese being tended, and this is the century before Solomon, so there is no doubt that they were available. It seems likely that geese formed part of the royal menu, whether or not they were, or were included in, the fatted fowl regularly supplied.

The keeping of geese flourished most of all under the Greeks and Romans, who regarded them very highly after their cackling helped save Rome from the Gauls in 390 B.C. Since then they have often served as efficient watch-dogs, and the idea of geese being stupid is never found in ancient literature, and seldom in the great array of proverbs which feature them.

XIV

Black

as a

Raven

Palestine members of the Crow family – Rook, Jackdaw, Jay, Fan-tailed Raven, Hooded Crow and Raven.

IN THE MIDDLE OF THE MOSAIC CATALOGUE OF UNCLEAN BIRDS IS ONE whose identification has never been questioned. This is '*oreb*, the Raven. Like some other animal names it probably has both this specific meaning and a more general one, as when it applies to the crow family as a whole, with the possible exception of the colourful Jay. This is closely parallel to English practice; we refer to the Crow Family – the *Corvidae* – and speak of them as crows, while this word is reserved more narrowly for the (Carrion) Crow.

It is quite logical to include the raven at this place in the Mosaic list, for it shares the predatory and scavenging habits of many birds of prey, even though it belongs to an entirely unrelated order of birds. Crows are the giants of the Perching Birds – the Passeriformes, as the zoologist calls them. This forms by far the largest order of living birds, one that includes 40 per cent of all species on the Palestine list.

It is interesting that this ban on eating crows is fairly general. The larger members seem to be entirely avoided, though it is not always said to be because of their scavenging habits. The very vocal Pied Crow of W. Africa is left untouched on superstitious grounds – its voice is regarded as human. One of the few exceptions seems to be in Britain, where there is a time-honoured custom of shooting young rooks (to control the numbers) and making them into pies, but in contrast to the largely carnivorous and scavenging raven and carrion crow the rook takes about 60 per cent of vegetable matter.

As will be shown below, some contexts clearly involve the raven itself. Lev. 11:15 forbids the Hebrews to eat 'every raven after his kind', a construction obviously suggesting that the ban was on the whole group, of which Palestine has six species. Several of these can be dealt with fairly briefly:

1. The Rook, *Corvus frugilegus,* is only a winter visitor, returning north to breed in Europe. It is about the size of the Hooded Crow, black all over except for a bare face-patch, and, being more vegetarian than the others, it has a slighter beak. It is everywhere associated with farmland and villages, but avoids the larger built-up areas.

2. The Jackdaw, *C. monedula,* often mixes with flocks of rooks but is easily distinguished by its smaller size, quicker wing-beats and different call, a sharp 'chak' from which it may get its name. At closer range its shorter beak and grey nape are obvious. This is a common winter visitor to Palestine but stays to breed only in the columbarium caves of Beit Guvrin, S W. of Jerusalem.

3. The Jay, *Garrulus glandarius,* is the only Palestine member of the family not dressed in black or grey. With its pinkish brown body and white wing patches, and neat black and blue wing coverts, it is a handsome bird, different from the European form only in its black cap. It is a skulker and best known for its raucous voice, not typical of its family. It is a resident in wooded parts of the country where it is a ruthless hunter of small birds and their eggs. We saw and heard it every day in the plantations around Jerusalem.

4. The Fan-tailed Raven, *C. rhipidurus,* is the rarest of them, for it is confined to the dry hills and mountains, and reaches just to the Negev and Sinai. It overlaps with the Raven but is smaller and also distinguished by its shorter tail. It becomes much more common east and south-east of the Dead Sea. It visits oases to settle on camels and remove ticks and other parasites.

5. The Hooded Crow, *C. corone,* is often considered a race of the carrion crow, with which it overlaps. Only this form, with its unmistakable grey mantle and underparts, is found in Palestine, where it is as much associated with roadsides and large towns as the carrion crow in Britain. It is by far the commonest resident crow and is frequently seen waiting near the verge to snatch any small animals knocked down by passing cars. It also joins gulls, egrets and storks in following behind the plough. The rather mournful call is heard everywhere, especially in the evening when large flocks gather in communal roosts.

6. The Raven, *Corvus corax,* is much the largest of this powerfully-built family; it is 25 in. long and black all over, including beak and feet. It is found in a number of slightly varying races over much of Europe and N. Asia.[1] The Raven is easily recognized by its huge size and, when flying

---

[1] Older works sometimes mentioned the Brown-necked Raven; this name was once given to a southern race in which feathers on the neck had a brown tinge, but it is now regarded as a true species. *C. ruficollis*

overhead, by its obvious wedge-shaped tail; it is usually first spotted through its deep note, often repeated and usually written 'pruk'. In Palestine the raven is less common than it was, and in recent years it has been hard hit by secondary poisoning; even so we saw it frequently and in many parts of the country – among the Judaean hills, in N. Galilee, on the Mediterranean coast, on the Red Sea shore and around tiny oases in the Negev. We found a Raven's nest with young almost over the road some twelve miles north of Eilat and in waterless desert. Presumably the pair got their food by scavenging around the mines at Timna, a few miles across the desert, or in the growing town of Eilat itself. The nest was at the top of a thorn tree and the birds took no notice of the passing traffic so we stopped the car and had a look. This seemed a fine opportunity to get some shots of the hen returning to the nest, which we tried to do from a reasonable distance, but although our car seemed identical with many others that passed, the ravens spotted it every time. They left the nest long before we were within range, nor did they return while we were anywhere near. The raven rightly has a reputation for intelligence.

The nests are built on crags or trees according to convenience; massive structures of sticks and twigs, they are lined with all sorts of scraps, including cloth and newspaper. Up to six eggs are laid, blue blotched and 2 in. long. They live in pairs during the breeding season and are thought to pair for life. Later in the year ravens gather in large flocks and migrate to some extent.

Like most other crows, ravens eat a wide range of food – locusts, frogs and lizards, and any fruit they can find, especially dates – but dead, dying or weak animals form the bulk of their diet. They often begin by picking out the eyes: e.g., 'The eye that mocketh at his father . . . the ravens of the valley shall pick it out' (Prov. 30:17). The massive three-inch beak could do this very easily. Their work as scavengers is useful, however unpleasant it sounds. The raven is the first bird to be named in the Scriptures; Gen. 8:8 records that Noah 'sent forth a raven which went to and fro'. The Heb. may mean that it kept going and coming, i.e., it rested on the roof of the ark but flew round in search of food, which would consist of carcases, etc.

The Raven appears in a variety of figurative passages. Cant. 5:11, 'his locks are bushy and black as a raven' seems to have no deeper meaning. When in good condition the plumage has a gloss of which the colour varies from blue and green to bronzy. Some authorities claim that the Heb. 'oreb, is from a root meaning 'black'. G. R. Driver regards it as descriptive of the call, which is certainly true of the Gr. korax, which is found in its specific name.

It may seem strange that the raven is mentioned three times as being the special object of God's care. 'Who provideth for the raven his food?' (Job. 38:41); 'He giveth to the beast his food and to the young ravens

which cry' (Ps. 147:9); 'Consider the ravens; for they neither sow nor reap
. . . and God feedeth them' (Luke 12:24). Perhaps the lesson is that God
cares for His creatures, however unattractive some of their habits may be.
In Isa. 34:11 the raven stands with the owl as a symbol of desolation and
Zeph. 2:14 (RSV), has it in a similar context; the Heb. of this passage is
in dispute and AV reads 'desolation' from *choreb* instead of *oreb*.

During Roman times ravens, and other crows also, became important
as omens, and they have been found on Egyptian and Assyrian monuments in similar connexions. No hint of this is found in the Scriptures
other than in the above verse. In early times Ravens were said to be able
to smell land and so were taken on board ship for use as guides. Presumably
this legend has its roots in Noah's raven.

Finally there is the passage in I Kings 17:4 ff., where we read of the
ravens appointed by God to care for Elijah. Some commentators have
suggested that the ravens were in fact a tribe known as Orebim who acted
as his suppliers. This is possible, but it is generally assumed that the birds
are meant. This incident is set during a period when miracles were a
familiar part of God's method of operation: the provision of food is said
plainly to have been organized by God and it is enough to leave it at that.

In early Christian times this passage was the inspiration of many pictures showing ravens with holy men and also several legends. For instance,
St. Anthony is said to have visited Paul the Hermit and found him
supplied with half a loaf of bread a day – a ration that was doubled for the
time of his stay!

XV

Birds

of Every

Sort

Swallows and Swifts, Hoopoe, Sparrow-like birds, Ostrich.

THE PRECEDING CHAPTERS HAVE DEALT WITH BIRDS THAT FELL INTO fairly logical, if not natural groups: the diurnal and nocturnal birds of prey; the migrants; birds that are important for food, which are mostly the game-birds and pigeons; the great assortment of birds closely associated with the marshes and waterside; and the crow tribe. No clear distinction could usually be drawn and many could well be included in several chapters; for instance the osprey, a migratory bird of prey catching its food only in the water, could have come under any of three headings. There remain a number that do not fall into any clear category, for the most part birds of the countryside and roadside that the ordinary person is likely to see. Precise identification of these in the Heb. text is not easy and the remarks that introduce Chap. XIII are also relevant here. Some species that can be reasonably recognized from their Heb. names will be discussed, and mention made of some of the numerous birds that live there and pass that way today.

Swallows and Swifts

These birds have been mentioned already under 'crane', where it was shown that an early transposition of two words caused extra confusion. There is general agreement that *sus* and *deror* stand for swallows and swifts; they are found in the following passages:

sus:
'As a swallow did I chatter' (Isa. 38:14).
'The crane and the swallow observe the time of their coming' (Jer. 8:7).

deror:

'The swallow a nest for herself, where she may lay her young, even thine altars, O Lord of Hosts' (Ps. 84:3).
'As the swallow by flying' (Prov. 26:2).

Driver (1935) points out that Arabic *sís* is cognate with *sus* and means swift, from its twittering call. He argues that the migratory habit of the swift confirms this identification and so allows a clear distinction to be made between *sus* (swift) and *deror* (swallow). This separation may well be correct but two points must be made that have usually been little stressed in this discussion. First, the swallows, with the closely related martins, are in a family separate from the swifts; the former are among the perching birds and the latter nearer to the nightjars and kingfishers, yet they have developed on similar lines and live in almost exactly the same way. All take their food in the air, where swifts spend most of the daylight hours and perhaps some of the night also, and they are at a great disadvantage on the ground. All over their range most nest in man-made situations such as buildings and culverts, or quarry-faces, into which Sand Martins tunnel. Even in countries such as Britain there is confusion between swallows, martins and swifts, all often being called swallows, which is the best-known of the three names. It seems doubtful whether the ancient peoples distinguished them clearly enough to give separate names. Second, the argument about migratory habits is not valid, for four of the six species of swallow are migratory and one of the three swifts is resident, the other two being in part summer visitors and in part passing migrants.

The Common Swift, with its habit of flying noisily in flocks, is often the most obvious of all, and Tristram reported a century ago that it arrived suddenly and in numbers; this is not markedly true today, for it may come in at any time from February onwards. In two months of spring there I heard the swifts regularly, but the swallows on the telegraph wires, making their way north, were even more conspicuous.

Another explanation of these names has been offered. Heb. *deror* means 'liberty' and it could be that this is a more general word embracing all birds that feed on the wing, which might also include shrikes, flycatchers, bee-eaters and rollers.

Either swallow or swift could fit the context of Ps. 84:3 and Prov. 26:2 equally well, but swift fits Jer. 8:7 no better than swallow. If the verb 'chatter' of Isa. 38:14 means a loud, harsh note it would apply to the scream of the swift rather than the gentle, singing notes of the swallows and martins. However, it is elsewhere tr. chirp and whisper, and RSV notes its meaning as uncertain so it gives no firm evidence.

The members of these families are few enough to mention briefly. Besides passing through in numbers, the Common Swallow, which is an eastern form of our British species, nests widely. We filmed a row of nests in a carpenter's workshop in Tiberias, one of them with a family of eight hungry fledgelings. The other true swallow is the Red-rumped, another summer breeder, which we noticed especially around the oasis of Ein Gev, opposite Tiberias. The Sand and House Martins pass right through Palestine, having wintered in S. and E. Africa. There are also two Crag Martins, looking something like the brown Sand Martin; in contrast to all the others they are solitary and found mostly in the rocky parts of the Jordan valley; we met them in a gorge just above Jericho. Apart from the tunnelling Sand Martin these all make nests of mud pellets; some are simple cups, but the Red-rumped Swallow makes an elaborate nest shaped like a retort and a foot long.

The three swifts are much longer in the wing and have short forked tails. The Common Swift seldom breeds away from buildings and its nest is made of scraps of wind-borne material collected and stuck together with saliva. The Alpine Swift is larger and visits Palestine to nest in rocky areas. The Galilean Swift is a resident in parts of the Jordan valley, where it sticks its nest of feathers and fibres to an overhanging rock face.

If the wider meaning of *deror* is accepted it would include the bee-eaters, with three breeding species and the European Roller. These, with the related kingfishers, are the most colourful birds in this part of the world, and they catch all their insect prey in the air.

Hoopoe

The Hoopoe is another conspicuous bird classified near these colourful families and it has long been identified with Heb. *dukiphat*, the 'Lapwing' of Lev. 11:19 (AV) but tr. 'Hoopoe' (RV and RSV). This has never been more than a rare bird of passage in Britain and the English word became current only in the late seventeenth century, which explains its absence from AV. The Coptic, Egyptian and other ancient names resemble the Heb.: these and other names, including the Arabic *hudhudu*, the scientific name *Upupa* and Hoopoe itself are all based on its unmistakable call, usually recorded as 'poo-poo-poo'. Its plumage is very striking; the general colour is pinkish brown, with boldly barred black and white pattern on the wings, which move in such a way as to show the details clearly. The crest is often erected and it protrudes noticeably when at rest.

After wintering in tropical Africa hoopoes return through Palestine and many stay there to breed, mostly in the northern half of the country, choosing the roofs of occupied buildings, old ruins and trees, etc., as nesting sites. The droppings foul the surroundings of the nest beyond description and this, with its habit of probing in rubbish and manure heaps for worms and insects, would make it unclean. The fact that it was a sacred bird to the Egyptians would have added force to the ban. The hoopoe features in many ancient legends, especially those of Arabic origin. One of these says that Solomon gave the bird a crest as reward for providing him with shade in the desert. The hoopoe is also said to have brought him a special worm for cutting the temple stones without using hammer or axe (I Kings 6:7). An equally fanciful tale is that it took a letter to the Queen of Sheba inviting her to visit Solomon. Much earlier than this the hoopoe was shown on Egyptian monuments representing gratitude, and for long it has been called the doctor-bird and its head used in witchcraft. On all counts it would hardly be part of the Hebrew diet.

Cuckoos cannot be identified in the Scriptures, the word *shachaph* of Lev. 11:16 being more probably tr. 'sea-gull', as discussed in Chap. XIII. Two separate species are found in Palestine; the European Cuckoo is rather an uncommon passing migrant and the larger and much more obvious Great Spotted Cuckoo comes to the more wooded parts to breed, returning to tropical Africa about August. Like its better known relation it is wholly parasitic, laying its eggs singly in nests of the much larger hooded crow; unlike the smaller cuckoo, its young do not eject the other chicks from the nest.

Sparrow-like birds

Heb. *tsippor*, is tr. 'bird', 'fowl' and 'sparrow', and the relationship between these English words is discussed in Chap. XII. It is suggested there that while *tsippor* generally means a small bird suitable for eating, and thus refers to a great range of species, there may be times when it has a more precise use, such as when it stands alone, or even more, where it is contrasted with another variety, e.g., 'the sparrow hath found a home and the swallow a nest' (Ps. 84:3). (In its original meaning 'sparrow' was perhaps very near to *tsippor*, for in Old English it referred to any small bird that fluttered).

It is seldom possible to suggest firmly whether the wider or narrower meaning should be taken, but the word sparrow (more strictly sparrow-like bird) could probably be used more often than in either AV or RSV, in each of which it is found twice. The EV agree in Ps. 84:3, above. In Ps. 102:7 'a sparrow alone upon the house top' (AV), becomes 'a lonely bird' (RSV), but in Prov. 26:2, 'a bird by wandering' (AV), is a 'sparrow in its flitting' (RSV).

A good example of its general use is in Gen. 15:10 where birds *(tsippor)* refer back to turtle dove and young pigeon in the previous verse. This is the word used throughout Lev. 14, describing the rites and sacrifice prescribed for the cleansing of the leper and it appears to be the only case where the birds and animals for sacrifice are not clearly specified. The inference is that the outcast leper could present two small birds trapped alive at little or no cost.

There are five separate references to *tsippor* being trapped or snared, e.g., 'a bird out of the snare of the fowlers' (Ps. 124:7). The nick-name *baal kanaph*, 'owner of a wing', is used only once, in the familiar proverb of Prov. 1:17, 'Surely in vain the net is spread in the sight of any bird'.

'*oph*, the more general word for birds, mostly larger birds and usually unclean, is never used in this connexion. Further confirmation that trapping these small birds was a regular practice is found in Job 18:8–10, where the words net, snare, gin and trap, from four Heb. words are employed. The use of decoy birds is mentioned in Ecclus 11:30, see 'Partridge'. Sennacherib, describing the siege of Jerusalem (701 B.C.), wrote 'the King was enclosed in Jerusalem like a bird in a cage'. The wide-spread use of such devices is suggested by the fact that up to fifteen different words, mostly in figurative passages, refer to various methods of taking wild animals, including birds. Birds were also shot with bow and arrow, as illustrated in an eighth century B.C. relief from Kharsabad, Iraq.

Such trapping continued through NT times and our Lord's reference to five sparrows being sold for two farthings (Matt. 10:29) was perhaps made as He pointed to a bunch of dead small birds being sold. This practice is still common in many countries around the Mediterranean and it largely accounts for the lack of singing birds in Italy. During the spring migration – and probably at other times too – small children wander into roadside restaurants in the Lebanon and Jordan selling strings of freshly-plucked sparrows, larks, finches, etc., to be grilled and eaten on the spot. Present-day Israel is in great contrast, for few of these birds are harmed, whether resident or on migration. Such ruthless killing was discouraged when the Hebrews occupied Canaan, as witness the humane and sensible law of Deut. 22:6 that forbids the taking of both the adult birds and the nestlings or eggs; the latter could be used, while the parent birds were left to breed again. The need for such reasonable conservation of wild life is still unrecognized in many parts of the world, where old and young are shot indiscriminately without regard for the future.

The few more specific renderings of sparrow are worth examination. The sparrow alone on the house top of Ps. 102:7 is something of a contradiction, for the House Sparrow is seldom solitary, and that applies to most true sparrows. Many commentators think the *tsippor* of this verse may be the Blue Rock Thrush, a resident in rocky places and on old buildings, with the interesting scientific name of *Saxicola solitarius* – the solitary rock- dweller. This is found over much of Palestine except for the desert; we saw it several times in the rocky *wadis* of Upper Galilee.

The House Sparrow is more likely to be the bird of Ps. 84:3, building its nest in the Temple, for few sparrow-like birds habitually nest in such places. On the other hand, the birds nesting in trees (Deut. 22:6 and Ps. 104:17) could be of many kinds. This may be true also of Eccl. 12:4, 'he shall rise up at the voice of the bird', but the inference is that the old man is woken up by birds around the house; these could be such a flock of chattering sparrows as woke me at dawn when we stayed at the Italian

Hospice on the Mount of Beatitudes.[1] Gr. *strouthion*, found four times and only in the context already mentioned, is always tr. 'sparrow'; the word is very close to *tsippor* in meaning.

The Palestine House Sparrow is slightly larger and paler than the European race but has almost identical habits, being closely associated with man at most seasons and making its untidy nests in and near buildings. The handsome Spanish Sparrow has benefited from the roadside planting of eucalyptus and its communal nests can now be seen on formerly treeless stretches inland from Gaza. There is also the Dead Sea Sparrow, a summer visitor which nests only in the lower Jordan valley and on the shores of the Dead Sea, and whose winter haunts are still unknown.

The birds of this area that can be classed generally as sparrow-like by the non-technical observer are far too many to list. The buntings and finches are their nearest relatives and most are close to sparrows in size, with similar strong beaks for seed-eating; most of the twenty kinds are migrants, the biggest group being winter visitors from Europe, but at least six are resident. There are nearly thirty members of the thrush family, most nearer in size to a sparrow than a Song Thrush; no less than ten of them are wheatears, six of them resident, and these take the place of the large thrushes in the desert and dry open country. These are mostly insect-eaters; alongside them are the larks, with eight species, and these feed largely on seeds. The warblers are smaller and more slenderly built; more than half of the thirty kinds are either resident or summer visitors to the moister areas of the north, or to the odd patches of denser cover that they demand. Those that stream through on migration are the despair of the bird-watcher, for many look alike and they are heading for, or coming from, almost anywhere to the north.

Armed with Collins' *Field Guide to the Birds of Britain and Europe* (which seems to be the only pocket-book covering this field), a pair of field-glasses and a reasonable knowledge of British birds, a visitor to the Holy Land today should be able to put a name to most species that he sees.

Ostrich

Our last subject is the biggest of all living birds. This huge bird was certainly known to the Biblical writers and the various VSS have tr. four different Heb. words as ostrich. There is still some disagreement but the general view seems to be that only two of these words are correctly translated. *bath ya'anah* is found eight times, first in the food lists and then being one of the names used in the prophetic passages to typify desolation. AV. tr. 'owl' throughout, which is probably correct. RV and RSV have gone back to some of the ancient VSS and used the traditional rendering of ostrich; this cannot be supported, for it does not fit the habi-

[1] The dating makes it most unlikely that the reference is to a crowing cock.

tats in which the passages are set. This word is discussed further under 'Owl' (p. 148). In Job 39:13 both AV and RV have 'ostrich' for the Heb. *chasidah*, elsewhere tr. 'stork' but rendered 'love' by RSV.

Two words are now generally accepted as referring to ostriches.

1. *ye'enim* is found only in Lam. 4:3: 'the daughter of my people is become cruel, like the ostriches in the wilderness'. (Heb. *midbar*, wilderness, is not necessarily actual desert; it can also mean steppe and dry pasture land, which are typical of the ostrich.) This is supported by LXX and Vulg.; the root meaning is sometimes said to be 'screamer', but it seems more likely to have come from a word meaning 'greedy', perhaps from its well-known habit of eating unsuitable objects; this is probably exaggerated in captivity but found in the wild also.

2. *renanim* occurs only in Job 39:13, a rather difficult passage, which has been so variously rendered that it is best to quote the three VSS.
AV: 'Gavest though the goodly wings unto the peacocks? or wings and feathers unto the ostrich?'
RV: 'The wing of the ostrich rejoiceth; but are her pinions and feathers kindly?'
RSV: 'The wings of the ostrich wave proudly; but are they the pinions and plumage of love?'
The two latter are close and may be taken as expressing the generally agreed meaning. Bodenheimer is exceptional in rejecting this view; he gives no alternative and only suggests that the whole passage may be a distorted version of an old Aram. fable. The details in these vv., which are discussed below, seem amply to confirm the identification.

The Ostrich, *Struthio camelus*, is unmistakable; standing between 6 and 8 ft. tall and weighing up to 300 lb. it is approached in size only by the giant flightless birds of the S. hemisphere – rheas, emus and cassowaries. The adult cock is most conspicuous, with black and white plumage and bare neck and upper legs, which in some races are pink. The hen is smaller and greyish brown. The wings are tiny and quite useless for flight; the cocks use their wings in their breeding display and these bear the plumes which have long been used for ornamental purposes and for which ostriches are kept on special farms. Their feet are adapted for fast running, each with only two toes, and they make formidable weapons. Though basically vegetarian the ostrich can best be described as omnivorous, eating such small animals as it happens on and like so many other birds, gorging on locusts when the chance offers.

Its habitat is open thornbush country and semi-desert with a fairly warm climate. Ostriches once extended, in a number of races and on suitable ground, from Mesopotamia, through Arabia to S. Africa; they may even have been found as far to the north-east as Baluchistan within the historic period. From the early beginnings of civilization their range has been progressively reduced, but in biblical times they were found widely in Palestine and in surrounding countries. A century ago there were still just enough in some parts for the Arabs to hunt them; this has been a favourite sport for many centuries and the ostrich was regarded as one of the great trophies of the chase. A few lingered on into the present century, and eggs were reported found in Kerah, Jordan, and in one or two other places as late as 1940. The Arabian race seems to have become extinct when the last known specimen was killed for food in Saudi Arabia during World War II. After that wild ostriches were confined to Africa, though they had disappeared from their former haunts around the N. African deserts and their numbers in other parts had been much reduced. In particular, they had been driven from most of their range suitable for cultivation, which is understandable, and now live only in the open dry country, mostly in E. Africa, where they are protected in Reserves and National Parks.

The ostrich was well known to the ancient peoples and it was widely hunted for food. It cannot be identified among the forbidden meats and it was probably eaten by the Hebrews, though there is a strange comment that the Roman emperor Heliogabulus (A.D. 218–222) prescribed the ostrich as Jewish food, thus inferring that it had formerly been prohibited. Its eggs (6 to 8 in. long and weighing 3 lb.) were eagerly eaten and the shells were made into a variety of utensils and also into beads, some of which have been found in Hyksos tombs. Ornamental cups from Assyrian graves are dated c. 3000 B.C. and about that time they were also being exported to China and other lands. Eggs were sent as tribute from Libya to Egypt, for the pharaoh's table; also plumes, which were made into fans and other ornamental objects. The Arabs made use of both eggs and feathers, and they also prepared the skins.

From the detailed description in Job 39 it would seem that the author knew the bird well and it is quite possible that Job had ostriches living tame around his tents, as they have been kept by Arabs into the present century. When taken young they grow up tame and will even live around an eastern bazaar, picking up scraps and begging fruit. They are still kept in this way in parts of central Africa. During my service in the W. African jungle my boy came in one day to tell me that a man wanted to sell me a very large fowl; standing outside the door was a well-grown ostrich, led on a piece of string, and it must have walked at least 500 miles, for none was found nearer than that! Ostriches were probably among the great collections of tamed animals kept in Ancient Egypt and Mesopotamia; perhaps not very early, for the first specific mention so far found is from the third century B.C., when a procession at Alexandria included eight pairs of ostriches in harness.

The following comments on the passage in Job 39 are based on the preferred rendering of the RSV:

v. 13: 'The wings of the ostrich wave proudly, but are they the pinions and plumage of love?' When displaying, the cock bird waves and shakes its plume-covered wings in a characteristic way.

v. 14: 'For she leaves her eggs to the earth.' The cock does most of the incubation, including through the night; during the day the hen often leaves the eggs partly or wholly covered with warm sand to a depth of several in.

v. 15: 'A foot may crush them.' In fact the eggs have such thick shells that they are not easily broken by accident. Only a few animals have mouths large enough to smash one of these eggs. Among birds only the Egyptian vulture can do so and it has been filmed throwing large stones at an ostrich egg till it was cracked.

v. 16: 'She deals cruelly with her young,' cf. Lam. 4:3, above. Perhaps this is an echo of v. 14, but it could refer to what happens when a pair of ostriches and their brood are chased by hunters; the adult birds often run away, hoping to draw off the intruders, while the chicks lie flat on the ground, their mottled down and feathers providing a good camouflage.

v. 17: 'God has made her forget wisdom.' This charge of foolishness is very old; it comes partly, perhaps, from its habit of eating hard objects, which are actually taken to serve as grinding stones in the gizzard. It is mixed up with the myth that it hides its head in the sand, but this cannot be traced back with certainty. Pliny, in his *Natural History*, spoke of ostriches hiding head and neck in a bush, believing themselves safe and unseen because they could see nothing. Oppian, of the early third century A.D., suggested that the ostrich bent its head down to the ground, and more recent observers have said that a distant ostrich may crouch on the ground, with neck outstretched and parallel to it. From these have grown the legend that the ostrich buries its head in sand that would quickly suffocate it!

v. 18: 'she laughs at the horse and his rider.' The ostrich can afford to do this, for on its own ground it can leave the horse behind, maintaining fifty m.p.h. for at least the first half-mile, but that is not to say it cannot be caught or killed by the skilful use of horses on land favouring the hunters.

XVI

The Serpent in the Wilderness and Other Reptiles

The problem of identification. Crocodile, Tortoises, Lizards, Snakes in general: Cobra, Desert Vipers, Fiery Serpent, Palestine Viper, Python, Frog.

SEVERAL FACTORS COMBINE TO MAKE REPTILES A DIFFICULT GROUP TO study and name at any time and in any country. Palestine is no exception, with at least eighty kinds of snake, lizard and tortoise already recorded. Two or three of the lizards are seen often enough, and among the fish-ponds and water channels of the Jordan valley terrapins are common, but the ordinary folk and most visitors today seldom see any others and this must always have been the case. Many of them are small and secretive, which even experts must examine closely before suggesting a name. The nature of the climate means that most reptiles of the open steppe and desert are safely out of sight for most daylight hours, except in winter. In the more temperate conditions of the scrub, woodlands and farms in the northern half of the country they are more active by day but equally hard to see in the denser cover.

It is therefore obvious that we cannot expect to find many of these species clearly recognizable in the Scriptures, where they are referred to generally as creeping things, though this term is used not only for reptiles.

Reptile is an old word meaning 'creeping thing' but it was hardly used until the seventeenth century, and is found only in RSV. In I Kings 4:33 Solomon spoke of 'birds, and of reptiles and of fish'. This is from Heb. *remes* which RSV elsewhere tr. 'crawling thing', 'creeping thing', etc. *Remes* cannot be properly tr. 'reptile', for in Gen. 9:3 it is promised that 'every moving thing *(remes)* shall be food for you' and no reptile was allowed for food. RSV is more consistent in NT, where Gr. *herpeton* is always tr. 'reptile', though in fact its meaning is wider than this.

194

The reptiles form a class of the Vertebrates, i.e., they all have backbones. They are cold-blooded, which merely means that they have no internal method of temperature regulation. They breathe air at all stages of their lives even though some, like the terrapins, live in the water and find their food there. They differ widely in shape and covering. Snakes and lizards are covered with separate scales, the surface of which is renewed at intervals. In the crocodiles the hard scales are more or less joined together to form armour plating. Tortoises and terrapins are enclosed in the familiar shells. Fertilization is always internal; most kinds are egg-laying but in a few lizards, including chameleons, and a few groups of snakes, principally the rattlesnakes, some vipers and sea snakes, the eggs are retained in the body of the female until they hatch. Although called viviparous (live-bearing) they are more correctly known as ovi-viviparous, to distinguish them from the true live-bearing mammals. Reptiles vary in size from minute worm-like burrowing lizards only 2 in. long to crocodiles weighing over a ton. The long-extinct reptiles were very much larger, perhaps up to thirty-five tons. Snakes and crocodiles are entirely carnivorous, as also are the great majority of lizards and water tortoises; land tortoises are basically vegetarian.

Some eighteen Heb. names are thought to represent reptiles: each of these will be mentioned and some discussed in detail, though few can be tr. with complete certainty, even in the light of modern knowledge of the animals, and with the help of philology and archaeology. Most reptiles are named only vaguely by the great majority of people, even in countries where literacy is general and adequate reference books are easily available. It is unrealistic to expect specific naming by the biblical writers so many centuries ago.

Crocodile

We may begin with the Crocodile, for the case is simplified by there being only one species for consideration. Heb. *liwyathan* is found six times and is so rendered in all EV except Job 3:8 where AV alone tr. 'mourning'. This is better read as RSV 'who are skilled to rouse up Leviathan'. It seems probable that this word, like a number of others, may have both a wider and a narrower meaning. In Ps. 104:25, 26, 'This great and wide sea . . . that leviathan whom thou has made to play therein,' it seems to have a general meaning of large sea creatures. 'Playing' would indeed describe the movements of the porpoises and some of the giant fish which leap out of the water from time to time. In most other passages where it occurs 'leviathan' seems to have a more precise meaning and RSV mg. gives 'crocodile' for Job 41:1.

'Thou brakest the heads of leviathan in pieces' (Ps. 74:14), is figurative, like the other passages, but it may well refer to the crocodile. The remaining two occurrences are in Isa. 27:1, 'The Lord . . . shall punish leviathan the piercing serpent, even leviathan that crooked serpent.' This is another highly figurative context in which the description of serpent need not preclude the meaning of crocodile, for *nachash* (serpent) is a general word for snakes and, probably, for other large creeping things as well, which would include crocodile. The only passage calling for detailed comment is discussed below.

The setting of the epic of Job remains uncertain; even so it is worth while considering the crocodile's former distribution around the eastern Mediterranean, where only one species has been known – the Nile Crocodile, *Crocodylus niloticus*. This is, and always has been, the commonest and most widely distributed of the four African species, and the only one north of the Sahara. Within historic times it was found from the mouth to the source of the Nile; by the mid-nineteenth century it had almost gone from Egypt; and everywhere its range and numbers have been reduced by power river-craft, rifles and hunting of all kinds. Like the leopard it is destroyed both as a potential killer of stock and for its skin.

In Ancient Egypt the crocodile was venerated as a symbol of sunrise and it became a hieroglyph for this. At Thebes a young crocodile used to be reared in the temple and decorated with jewels of all kinds; at Ombi it was worshipped and its mummies have been found in the catacombs there and elsewhere. In contrast, the crocodile was hunted in other parts of Egypt. Although not specifically banned as food to the Hebrews there is no doubt that it was regarded as utterly unclean, partly because of its position in pagan worship, partly for its food habits. These reptiles are entirely carnivorous at all stages, taking animals varying from aquatic beetle grubs to fish, birds and mammals, the type of prey depending mostly on size. Larger crocodiles take carrion, especially cattle and sheep drowned in floods, and occasionally become man-killers.

Its status north of Egypt is hard to determine. Remains have been found in the Mount Carmel caves dating from the Pleistocene period, when climatic conditions were different, and the only definite locality for the biblical era is the Zerka river; this runs from the hills around Samaria and flows into the Mediterranean, near Caesarea. These crocodiles were mentioned by Pliny and Strabo; a thousand years later the early Crusaders saw them and just after World War I the Bedouins claimed that sheep were still being taken. The drainage of the marshes on the coastal plain destroyed their last refuges and crocodiles are no longer found wild north of Africa, but the Zerka is still known as the Crocodile River. There are less substantial reports for their existence in the Kishon river. It is possible that crocodiles were once found in the Tigris-Euphrates area; if so, they were probably exterminated very early, otherwise it is unlikely that Tiglath-pileser I of Assyria (eighth century B.C.), would have received one as a present from the pharaoh. It therefore seems that the Hebrews knew the crocodile both in Egypt and on the coastal plains of Palestine, where it probably once had a wider distribution than just the one river valley.

The crocodile is largely aquatic, coming ashore to bask in the sun and to lay its eggs, which are carefully buried in the soil and then guarded until they hatch. The eyes and nostrils are so placed that the crocodile can see and breathe while lying almost completely submerged. There is no evidence about the size of the Palestine specimens; a maximum length of 20 ft. is possible in optimum conditions but today anything over 12 ft. is big.

A few scholars also see the crocodile in the dragon of Isa. 51:9 and Ezek. 29:3: 'Behold, I am against thee, Pharaoh, King of Egypt, the great dragon that lieth in the midst of his rivers' (also Ezek. 32:2). However, most commentators prefer to regard this as a reference to the chaos dragon of Babylonian mythology. The two words *tannin* (dragon) and *nachash* (serpent) are used in connexion with the rods that became serpents in Exodus 4 and 7. It is interesting that Moses's rod became *nachash* and those of Aaron and the Egyptian magicians *tannin*. The suggestion has been made, without much support, that the latter refers to the crocodile and that this incident had symbolic meaning in that Aaron's rod destroyed the objects of Egyptian worship. (This is discussed further on p. 205.)

The whole of Job 41 is poetic and full of imagery; nevertheless there are several points that could hardly be made about any other animal and it seems impossible for such a passage to be written without personal knowledge, e.g., v. 7, 'Canst thou fill his skin with barbed irons? or his head with fish spears?'; v. 26, 'The sword of him that layeth at him cannot hold'. An adult crocodile's skin is hard to penetrate with a bullet unless it is carefully directed, and the weapons used then would have been inadequate. Vv. 13, 15 are better read in RSV, 'Who can penetrate his double coat of mail? . . . His back is made of rows of shields'. These phrases well describe the armour which covers the sides and back of a crocodile. The problem of catching a large one is well portrayed in v. 1, 'Canst thou draw out leviathan with a hook?' and v. 5, 'Wilt thou play with him as with a bird?' And the result of hooking one is emphasized in v. 31, 'He maketh the deep to boil like a pot'. A wounded crocodile, lashing with its powerful tail and throwing its whole body about can make a tremendous disturbance. Wherever it is set this can scarcely refer to any other animal.

Tortoise

Tortoises are found plentifully in Palestine and surrounding countries. The name is found just once in the Scriptures in the AV only, and it forms part of the list of forbidden animals in Lev. 11:29. It is tr. from Heb. *tsab*, which is discussed below, for it is much more likely to be the Spiny-tailed Lizard.

Land tortoises cannot be confused with any other animal. The whole body is protected inside a horny box, the upper part of which is the carapace, with a pattern of shields peculiar to each species and more or less fused together, out of which head, tail and legs can be protruded. This shape varies but in the land species the carapace is usually well rounded, in contrast to the more flattened outline of the water tortoise or terrapin. In both groups the under-surface, called the plastron, is fairly flat, and also smoother than the often rugged carapace. Land tortoises live in a wide range of habitats outside the actual desert and they are normally vegetarian, though they sometimes chew bones and small dead animals, presumably to get the calcium needed for their massive shells. Two rather similar species occur in Palestine. The commoner is properly known as the Mediterranean Spur-thighed Tortoise, *Testudo graeca*, and this is widely found in countries along the northern shores of the Mediterranean; this is the kind usually imported into Britain for keeping as pets and it may reach a length of 12 in. The other is Leith's Tortoise, *T. leithii*; it is without the heavy spur on each thigh, near the tail, that marks the first kind, and it is smaller and sandy-coloured. It extends through into Lower Egypt.

Land tortoises are most active in spring and early summer when the vegetation is greenest; except in the lower Jordan valley they normally hibernate in the ground for up to several months, while the height of the summer may also be too hot and dry for much activity. These tortoises are regularly eaten by the Arabs, as they are also in parts of Africa; the pigeon-sized eggs are also widely enjoyed. The near extermination of some of the giant tortoises from the Indian Ocean islands was the result of taking them on board sailing ships for use as fresh meat; like many reptiles, tortoises can survive long periods without food and these were kept alive until needed. Though perhaps not forbidden by name the tortoise would not have qualified as food for the Hebrews, nor, as far as can be understood from the Mosaic code, would any other reptile.

Terrapins of the genera *Emys* and *Clemys* are found widely in the area and these are carnivorous, eating almost any kind of small water life, starting with insects and tadpoles when first hatched, and going on to fish, frogs and even small birds. These were very common in the former swamps and we saw them in great numbers, sometimes literally in heaps, in the drainage channels of the Huleh valley, and less plentifully in the actual fishponds, where the fishermen regard them as a nuisance but make no great effort to exterminate them. These terrapins, with longer neck and tail, are more active than the land species; their webbed feet carry them easily on land, where they come to bask, dashing back into the water and hiding in the mud when alarmed. They are foul-smelling and probably not eaten widely.

Finally a mention of the largest and most aquatic of all the freshwater turtles found in this area – the Nile Soft-shelled Turtle, *Trionyx triunguis*. It reaches a length of over 2 ft. and its rather flat back is covered with leathery skin that makes it invisible when lying on the bottom. Its range and numbers must have been reduced drastically by tapping to extinction the rivers running into the Mediterranean and, earlier, by the drainage of the coastal marshes.

Lizards

Throughout the world the lizards far out-number all other reptiles and they are sighted even more frequently by comparison. In Palestine lizards are the most conspicuous vertebrates other than birds and there are at least 40 species. These range from the desert monitor of up to 4 ft., down to tiny geckos of perhaps 2 in. The problem of naming them is considerable for although they are seen all the time they may be hard to approach closely, and even in the hand the exact identification is usually a matter for the experts. Lizards vary widely in appearance but many people would regard them as forming a rather vague family for which there would be a name in most languages. This might not be so in Palestine where the variation in size, shape and habit is so great, and the Hebrews may well have had different names for the several clearly marked sections. In addition there could have been names for the more conspicuous genera and species, which would be less generally known and perhaps used only by those connected closely with the land.

Seven Heb. names have been tr. as one or other of the lizards in various VSS and of these one is found in Prov. 30:28 while the others are used only in the Mosaic food lists. With one exception they form a section of the food list of Lev. 11:29, 30 which has often been thought to refer to reptiles and is so rendered in RV and RSV, though mixed in its AV form. This exception – *tinshemeth* – also appears in the bird section of forbidden foods. The other words, found once each, can yield little data except their root meaning, if known, and suggestions must therefore be largely conjectural.

This list is now discussed; except in the second use of *tinshemeth*, these are tr. the same by RV and RSV:

tsab: 'Tortoise' (AV); 'Great Lizard' (RV and RSV), 'Land Crocodile' (LXX). Tortoise is not correct. Tradition has long identified this with the Mastigures or Spiny-tailed Lizards of the genus *Uromastyx*; reaching a length of nearly 2 ft. they are second only to the monitor lizards in size and so perhaps merit the title of great lizard, which has no precise meaning. The Arabic *dhubb* or *dhabb* is sufficiently like the Heb. to give some confirmation. There are several species; perhaps the commonest is *Uromastyx aegyptius*; a smaller and more brightly coloured one is *U. ornatus*. These live in the desert and all are heavily built, with a powerful spiny tail, shorter than the body, which is used in defence; the lizard takes refuge in a hole which it then blocks with the sharp-edged tail. Unlike most other lizards this is largely, or even entirely, vegetarian. These Dab Lizards, as they are sometimes called in zoos, are eaten by the

Arabs, who regard them as lawful meat and actually fatten them in captivity specially for eating.

'anaqah: 'Ferret' (AV); 'Gecko' (RV and RSV). The AV is incorrect, as also are older suggestions of shrew mouse and hedgehog. Gecko is more likely. This Heb. word is also tr. sighing, moaning and crying out, and it is interesting that the geckos are the only lizards with a truly voiced note. The name is from Malay *gecoq* in imitation of its two-syllable call and many native names are based on these notes, which vary in quality and volume with the numerous different species. The most remarkable feature of typical geckos is their ability to cling to smooth surfaces of walls and ceilings with the aid of rows of microscopic hairs on the under-surface of their toes; these are so fine that they can engage with the tiniest irregularities of the surface.

The Rock Gecko, *Ptyodactylus syriacus*, is the most frequently seen, especially in Galilee, where it lives among the rocky outcrops and boulders and is mostly active at night; in spring, when the nights are still cool, it suns itself in the early morning and it is then that it is most easily observed. Other species are found in other habitats, including the desert, and some are closely associated with houses here as in other parts of the world. Partly for this reason the *semamith* of Prov. 30:28 is thought not to be the spider of AV (*q.v.*) but the gecko, as in RV 'The lizard taketh hold with her hands, yet she is in kings' palaces'. This makes better sense than RSV 'the lizard you can take in your hands'. Solomon must have known this strange little lizard that the description fits so well.

koach: 'Chameleon' (AV); 'Land Crocodile' (RV, RSV). The expression land crocodile is now meaningless but it was once given to the giant of the lizard family now properly known as the Desert Monitor, *Varanus griseus*. So named for its greyish colour, it is at home in the dry country and desert, and it is carnivorous, eating animal prey of many kinds, including those already dead. The even larger Nile Monitor lives near water and was once found in suitable places all over Africa but there is no reason to accept some travellers' claims that it has been seen in the desert around the Dead Sea. These monitors are big enough to provide useful meat and they are eagerly hunted in many parts of Africa and also by the Arabs. One would therefore expect such a conspicuous member of the desert fauna to feature in the food list and this could be *koach*.

The common Chameleon, in contrast, is an inhabitant of the greener parts of the north and the Jordan valley, among vegetation where its effective camouflage makes it hard to see. Only the AV mentions it, and the only possible confirmation of this tr. might be found in the fact that *koach* is from a common root meaning 'strength'. While this could apply to the larger and very powerful monitor, it could equally well refer to the strong grasping claws of the chameleon, which are unlike those in any other lizard, for they are gripping pincers, with two claws on one side opposing three. A chameleon firmly attached to a small branch can hardly be pulled off without danger of doing it damage. *Chameleo chameleon* is a small species and reaches a length of only 6 in. It could not have been known to the Hebrews on their desert march but its many strange features should have made it familiar to the tribes living in the wooded hills.

Chameleons are widely regarded with unreasoning fear, especially in W. Africa. Best known for its power of changing colour it uses this to show emotion as much as to match its surroundings, and the familiar round-backed shape, with prehensile tail curled downwards like a catherine wheel, can also be varied beyond recognition. Its eyes too are unique; the lids are fused over each ball, leaving a small aperture, and each eye moves independently, like a gun turret. Seen close up this is perhaps its most unnerving feature. Finally, the tongue is also without equal, for it is an extraordinary muscular structure which can be projected to about the length of the body so that the mucus-covered tip can catch the insect prey. It is not surprising that the chameleon is thought to have magic properties.

Other ancient authorities have suggested chameleon as a tr. for *tinshemeth*, discussed below, from its root meaning of breathing or panting. The chameleon has huge lungs and air sacs and when fully expanded it becomes almost transparent, a phenomenon that gave rise to the old belief that it lived on air.

There is yet a further possible tr. for *koach*. The Vulg. rendered it *stellio*, which is now part of the Latin name *Agama stellio*, the *hardoun* of the Arabs and often called the Rainbow Lizard. This is the commonest large lizard in most of the inhabited parts of Palestine and like its close relatives all over Africa it is often closely associated with man, feeding around houses, on the roadsides, etc., where insects are often easier to catch than in thicker cover. This lizard may be nearly 2ft. long and it is easily recognized by its bobbing movements, best described as doing press-ups!

leta'ah: 'Lizard' (AV, RV, RSV). There is general agreement that this is correct and this is confirmed by the use of this Heb. name in the Talmud for what is thought to be the Lacertid family of lizards; these are the typical European lizards and they include the beautiful Green Lizard of France and the Channel Islands and the less obvious Sand and Viviparous Lizards of Britain. It is more likely to be a general name for medium-sized and small lizards of typical lizard shape.

chomet: 'Snail' (AV); 'Sand Lizard' (RV, RSV). The former is impossible. While the term sand lizard does not refer to any precise species it is meaningful in that some lizards are adapted for living in sand, which is the root meaning of this Heb. word. Such a name would fit the skinks, sometimes called snake-lizards from their smooth, stream-lined build. Their legs are short, sometimes absent, and their tapered heads allow very easy entry into the dry sand, through which they move with a swimming motion. These are typical of the desert and the Israelites must have known them on the journey from Egypt. Today these are avoided by the Jews but considered good eating by the Arabs. The skink family is sufficiently distinct to merit a name in many languages.

tinshemeth: This is a difficult word. In Lev. 11:30 it concludes the list of unclean animals under the name 'mole' (AV), but this is certainly wrong, nor is there any firm basis for the tr. 'chameleon' (RV, RSV), and it is thought to be a lizard solely because of its position in the list. Further discussion is not profitable but it must be noted that the same word is also found in the earlier section of the list generally regarded as a catalogue of birds of prey (Lev. 11:18 and Deut. 14:16) and discussed under 'owl'. This may be an error of transmission but it could be that the one word stands for two different animals, like the English word turtle.

It must again be stressed that these identifications are no more than hesitant suggestions, except perhaps for *leta'ah* which has firmer support. However, the list does seem to have some semblance of order and, with the various alternatives, it would include the major groups of lizards plentiful in Palestine.

Two fabulous reptiles are mentioned in older VSS which have rightly been replaced by 'adder' (RSV). 'Cockatrice' and 'basilisk' are very old words originally given to crocodiles and snakes through a series of tr. and other errors, and they are now obsolete in ordinary use. Cockatrice features in heraldry, as a hybrid cock and serpent. Basilisk is derived from Gr. *basileus* (king), because the head was said to be marked with a crown. This name is now applied to a group of small lizards of the Iguana family.

Serpents

Before any attempt is made to identify individual snakes it seems best to review the various Heb. and Gr. words that have a rather general meaning. Throughout this chapter the more precise word snake will always be used, except in quotations; the absence of this word from the RV and RSV is surprising, as is also the retention of the archaic 'serpent'. Snake was in general use long before the AV was made and it is found in Shakespeare. Serpent is seldom used today other than metaphorically, but it is seen in *Serpentes*, the sub-order of reptiles comprising the snakes.

Four Heb. and two Gr. words are rendered 'serpent' (AV):

1. *zachal*. Once only in Deut 32:24, 'with the poison of serpents of the dust'. This is in a prophetic passage and perhaps better tr. 'crawling thing' (RV) or 'creeping thing' (RSV). This word is discussed under 'worm'.

2. *nachash*. Tr. 'serpent' in most VSS and found more often than the total of all other Heb. words for snakes. It is a general word and the contexts suggest that while it usually means snake it could sometimes include other

creeping reptiles also. Its first mention is in Gen. 3:1, introducing the fall of man, the discussion of which is a theological matter, while the punishment given to the serpent 'dust shalt thou eat' (Gen. 3:14), can hardly be interpreted biologically. In NT Gr. *ophis* is used in the four references to the Fall.

3. *saraph*. This is a common root usually tr. 'fiery' or 'burning'. In Num. 21:6 it is used to qualify *nachash*, to give 'fiery serpent'. It stands alone as the fiery serpent that Moses was told to make in v. 8, i.e., make it by fire, and this is described in v. 9 as the brazen serpent. *Saraph* is also used for the fiery flying serpents of Isa. 14:29, 30:6; and the same root is in *Seraphim*.

4. *tannin*, usually tr. 'dragon' (see App. A) is rendered 'serpent' only in the incident of Aaron's rod (Exod. 7:9 ff.). This is discussed under 'Crocodile' (p. 195).

5. *ophis* is properly tr. 'snake'; it is 'serpent' in all EV.

6. *herpeton*, tr. 'serpent' throughout is a more general word; this is shown by the only common English word derived from it – herpetology, the study of reptiles and amphibians.

The relation of these words one to another is not easy to work out, especially in the incident of the rods and serpents. In the narrative of the fiery serpent, *nachash* is used everywhere except in v. 8 which has *saraph*, and the former is clearly the more general word. There seems to be some parallel with English, where snake refers to all species, which are referred to individually as vipers, mambas, cobras, etc.

Some contexts provide useful clues, but in most cases precise identification is difficult. The great majority of the seventy or so mentions of snakes are in figurative passages and the two principal literal narratives are those concerning the miracle of the rods into serpents and the fiery serpents. Comment has several times been made about the difficulties of tr. resulting from inaccurate or inadequate naming by folk ignorant about animal life. With snakes a new element is introduced – they have long been the subject of superstition and irrational fear, and many people suffer from something near a phobia, usually acquired early in life. For many years snakes have been my special interest, so this problem is familiar to me, and I receive occasional requests for help in overcoming this paralysing fear from folk going overseas. Some of these people cover their eyes when a picture of a snake is thrown on the screen. This is no new thing and it is widespread; this dread is not inherited but taught by one generation to another, and snakes become not merely potentially dangerous, i.e., they *may* be poisonous, but universally terrifying. This is somewhat reflected in the biblical snakes, where there is no suggestion that a snake may be harmless! Their poisonous nature is inferred some fifty times, though many Palestine snakes are non-venomous. The snake thus becomes a picture of evil and danger, whether personally, as in Matt. 3:7 where the Pharisees are called vipers; or nationally, as in Isa. 14:29, where the adder and fiery flying serpent are promised as punishment on Philistia.

Because of this ignorance and fear few snakes were probably known by name except to the hunters, shepherds and so on, who came in closer contact with them and made it their job to name those that were conspicuous or dangerous. This is the position in most parts of the world today, perhaps one could say it is true everywhere. Most names used by the writers would thus be general rather than specific, and we should also expect to find many traces of the myths that result from this ignorance and deep-rooted fear – myths that are believed today. Ps. 140:3, 'They have sharpened their tongues like a serpent.' Many well-educated people still regard the tongue as a poison fang! Prov. 23:32, 'it stingeth like an adder'. This reflects another ancient misunderstanding – that a snake stings. The poison is in fact injected through the hollow fangs, though the act is described as striking rather than biting in the sense that most animals bite.

Mention of the snakes eating dust in Isa. 65:25 and Micah 7:17 must be an echo of Gen. 3:14, but it is a sign of changed conditions in a restored kingdom rather than punishment. The specialized feeding habits of all snakes make comment on this point difficult. They feed only on animals swallowed whole with no chewing, and this applies to all snakes big and small; their jaws can dislocate and dilate enormously to engulf prey much thicker than themselves. They can also pass long periods, sometimes over a year, between feeds.

The lands around Palestine have an assortment of snakes far too big to describe or even list; they include all the main families except rattlesnakes and they range from some never reaching a foot in length to several exceeding 6 ft. and a girth of perhaps 6 in. Most are quite harmless; some six species can give a potentially lethal bite but only a low percentage of these bites will prove fatal. Snakes are found in every region from desert to closed woodland and marsh, some widely like the Palestine Viper; some confined to narrow habitats, like some of the desert snakes. Palestine, near the meeting point of Europe and Africa, has both elements in its snake fauna, which is probably true of most groups of animals.

Some snakes are mainly nocturnal and others diurnal, but this activity pattern is affected by the interaction of their cold-blooded system and the locally extreme climate of Palestine. Without the automatic temperature regulator built into birds and mammals, snakes are dependent on external heat sources, and they bask in the sun or move out of it to keep their bodies within suitable limits; while for many species this is between 60 and 80° F, those in cold temperate zones have a lower bracket, and some tropical snakes can tolerate greater heat. In much of northern Palestine and in the hills, snakes must hibernate under cover for part of the winter, but in parts of the Jordan valley they can remain active then. In some parts the summer temperatures may rise so high that food becomes scarce and conditions unfavourable and snakes are forced to stay underground for perhaps weeks at a time. At some seasons the diurnal temperature range, especially on high open ground, is so great that activity may be confined to early and late periods, between the heat of the day and the bitter cold of the night.

Snakes are entirely carnivorous; some take only one or two kinds while others are catholic. This food includes worms, insects, fish, frogs, lizards, other snakes, birds and their eggs, and mammals.

Most biblical writers were interested in snakes only as potential dangers and it is not surprising that we cannot identify any harmless species. These include typical non-venomous snakes of the genus *Coluber*, of which *C. jugularis*, the Syrian Black Snake, reaches well over 4 ft.; slightly venomous snakes such as the Cat Snake, *Tarbophis syriaca,* and the Tree Snake, *Psammophis schokari*, with their fangs at the rear of their upper rows of teeth where they cannot hurt humans: these snakes are of African origin. One member of the python/boa family is found in and around the desert – the Sand Boa, *Eryx jaculus.*

The only three comments on snake behaviour are from the pens of Solomon and the herdsman Amos, both noted for their knowledge of animals. 'The way of a serpent upon a rock' (Prov. 30:19), was one of the things that Solomon found wonderful. This is a profound truth, for the snake's normal locomotion, in which the power is applied by individual scales, is most complex and hard to describe. Eccl. 10:8 and Amos 5:19 both warn against resting one's hand where a snake may be hiding. In the former this is the loose stone wall around the sheepfold; in the latter, the rough wall of a house. When surprised in such a situation the snake feels threatened and its natural reaction is to strike.

Some passages will now be examined where it may be possible to identify the species concerned. The linguistic problem of the incidents in Exod. 4 and 7 is outlined above, where the possible alternative of crocodile is mentioned. This trick was clearly part of the court magicians' repertoire, so that conjuring and probably snake-charming were practised very early in Egypt. For a long time the Egyptian Cobra, *Naja haje*, has been the stock-in-trade of the charmer and it could have been in use then. All kinds of cobras are well known for their ability to expand the upper neck into a disc shape by spreading the ribs, which are long in this region. This is usually done when the cobra raises vertically the front part of the body and thus takes on its unmistakable outline. The cobra then symbolized immortality and was regarded as a protecting deity, being frequently illustrated on Ancient Egyptian monuments.

Scarab amulets show cobras being held suspended by the neck, which is in fact the correct way to grasp a venomous snake, except that it is wise, with heavy specimens, to support most of the weight with the other hand.

The significance of this portrayal has only recently been confirmed; charmers have been filmed holding snakes in this way until a state of rigid unconsciousness is induced, a trick of which Tristram had heard rumours a century ago without being able to find any proof.[1] Cobras eat other snakes – and also smaller cobras – which favours this tr. in the incident; here, too, swallowing up the magicians' cobras would be a serious insult to their religion.

One of the words obviously representing a venomous snake is Heb. *pethen* and this is traditionally associated with the cobra; this word did not appear in English until the nineteenth century, so it is hardly surprising that no VSS use it. Found six times the AV tr. 'adder' twice and 'asp' four times. Its Gr. equivalent is *aspis*, which occurs once and is rendered 'asp'. The Egyptian Cobra extends into the drier parts of Palestine; a second species, the Spitting or Black-necked Cobra is found in Egypt. The former may reach a length of 8 ft.; the latter, which is less heavily built, seldom exceeds 6 ft. Several deductions from the contexts seem to confirm the identification.

1. All references are to venomous snakes.

2. In Egypt the bite of the asp was once used to commit suicide. For this purpose they would be more likely to use a snake of the neurotoxic type (cobra) which can kill quickly, rather than a viper whose haemolytic venom acts more slowly and often causes a lingering death.

3. Isa. 11:8 speaks of the hole of the asp. Cobras are often found in holes in the ground.

4. 'The deaf adder (asp) that stoppeth her ear; which will not hearken to the voice of charmers' (Ps. 58:4, 5). As discussed above, the cobra is the main subject of snake-charmers. The first clause records another early snake myth that is still current. It is now agreed that all snakes are deaf, though they have some capacity to sense vibrations received through the ground, and the charmer holds their attention by the movement of his pipe, not its music. A further reference to snake-charming is in Eccl. 10:11, 'Surely the serpent will bite without enchantment'.

The fiery serpent of Numbers 21, which is the serpent in the wilderness of John 3:14, is of great metaphorical importance. The location was the Negev desert on the borders of Edom, probably to the south-east of the Dead Sea, and although cobras might be found here they would not occur in the numbers required by the narrative, nor do they fit the picture generally. The *saraph* seems to be one, or perhaps more than one, of the four desert vipers. Two are known as Sand Vipers, *Cerastes cerastes* and *C. vipera*; the former may reach 30 in., the latter less than 15 in., and they are well adapted to desert life, matching the sand closely and quickly

[1] This is documented in H. S. Noerdlinger *Moses and Egypt* (1956) p. 26. (*E. Brit.* ii., vi. p. 613).

sinking into it with a shuffling movement until only eyes and nostrils are showing. They feed on small rodents for which they wait lying unseen in the sand, and the bite of the larger one can be dangerous to man.

The False Cerastes, *Pseudocerastes fieldii*, is a highly specialized form with a valve-like structure inside the nostril to exclude driven sand. Its venom is the least potent of the group and in the wild it may feed partly on dead migrant birds, which is unusual, for few wild snakes will take dead prey. All these are typical vipers, rather stoutly built, with flat head markedly broader than the neck, and stubby tail ending in a point which is not poisonous, though widely believed to be so. As in all vipers the two long curved fangs hinge in the front of the upper jaw and normally lie against the roof of the mouth; they are needle-sharp and hollow to the tip. To swing the fangs down and forward into position the mouth is opened wide and this whole action, ending with the fangs penetrating the victim, is too quick for the eye to see any details.

However, the species most likely to have been the fiery serpent is a very different viper of the genus *Echis*, which has two species, *carinatus* and *coloratus*. In this area it grows to around 24 in. long; for its length it is thinner than the other vipers and its head is smaller. Known as the Carpet or Saw-scaled Viper it is found from W. Africa right across the continent to SW. Asia and through to central Asia. In some parts of this vast range it is very common; for instance in NW. India, over an area not stated, the fantastic total of about 200,000 was killed annually for bounty for six years, and several thousand have also been taken in Kenya in a short period. No other snake is known to exist in such numbers. Three other points are valid. The venom of *Echis* is more potent, weight for weight, than in any other viper; it is notorious for being aggressive and easily provoked and is described as 'bad-tempered', whereas most of the large vipers are placid; and it seems to tolerate hotter conditions than most, so it would be more active by day. The late Karl P. Schmidt, of the Chicago Museum, who died of snake-bite, regarded the Carpet viper as one of the most dangerous of all venomous snakes.

When gliding over shingle or rock the carpet viper moves normally but for travelling over loose sand it has developed the same method of loco-motion as the sand vipers and one of the desert rattlesnakes; this is known as side-winding and consists of throwing a loop of the body sideways and then bringing the other part over to it, resulting in a diagonal move-ment and leaving a characteristic track of parallel lines. The viper venom breaks down the capillaries and ruptures the blood corpuscles, finally causing death by massive internal haemorrhage. My experience with this most unpleasant snake in W. Africa was that the patient often died after several days and that treatment was difficult. Prognosis depended on the site and severity of the bite, and other factors, including the health of the victim. This medical fact is relevant to the incident for it must have taken

Moses some time – certainly many hours – to cast a serpent in bronze and publish news through the host, which amounted to many tens of thousands at even the lowest estimate. This provides one of the clearest biblical pictures of man's salvation and there is one further practical point; the injection of this venom does not always cause intense pain but the internal destruction goes on steadily. The victim may even feel better for a while, but after a severe bite left untreated, the process continues until death. The timing shows Divine over-ruling, and the results of looking in faith at the brazen serpent were wholly miraculous, but the setting needs no metaphysical explanation.

It seems that this brazen serpent was kept – or perhaps a copy of it was made later – and it became a focus for heathen worship, so that Hezekiah destroyed it in his reformation (II Kings 18:4). Serpents had long been venerated in other countries and the miraculous incident of the brazen serpent could easily lead to this. There is much other evidence of a snake cult in early Palestine. There is a flat relief stele of the serpent goddess at Beit Mirsim. A bronze snake, dated c. fifteenth century B.C., has been found at Gezer, with the expanded neck typical of the cobra, and an iron serpent of the Israelite period was dug up in the valley of Ayalon. There are many examples of jars and incense vessels with snakes forming relief patterns on the outside. Snake worship is still widespread in Asia and Africa.

Five further Heb. words are also tr. viper and adder, as follows:

tsiph'oni: 'adder' and 'cockatrice' (AV) 'adder, asp, basilisk', (RV); 'adder' (RSV). These are found only in figurative passages where no facts can be inferred. This is also true of tsepha', which is used only in Isa. 14:29 and tr. 'cockatrice' (AV); 'basilisk' (RV): 'adder' (RSV).

shephiphon: 'adder' (AV, RV); 'arrowsnake' (AV mg.); 'viper' (RSV). Found only in Gen. 49:17, where the context is more helpful. 'Dan shall be as an adder in the path that biteth the horse heels.' This description would fit one of the desert vipers that lie hidden in the surface and strike out when disturbed.

These three words are all thought to be onomatopoeic, suggesting both the hissing so characteristic of some vipers and also the noise made by rubbing together the rough scales that give Echis the name of saw-scaled viper and which are found on the others also. The sand viper was the origin of the hieroglyph of the sibilant 'F' in Ancient Egypt.

The English words adder and viper are now almost synonymous but this was not so when the AV appeared. Adder is an Old English word related to German Natter, and quite early a nadder became an adder, and was used for snakes rather generally. Viper, from viviparous or live-bearing, was first used by Tyndale early in the sixteenth century, and gradually the two became equated.

A ROUGH BOULDER on the roadside covered with thistles provides a basking and look-out point for a Rainbow Lizard. This is a familiar scene in many parts of Palestine (p. 201).

HONEY BEES at the entrance to a nest in a hollow tree. Most of the Hebrews' honey was taken from the combs of wild bees in trees and among rocks (p. 245).

NEARLY ALL of the forty or so Wading Birds on the Palestine list are migrants. Here are three of the most typical, photographed in spring on the fish-ponds at Ma'agan Mikhael, on the coast south of Haifa. The Kentish Plover, rare in Britain, has small breeding colonies in many parts of Europe. The Wood Sandpiper is on its way to the forests of northern Europe. The conspicuous Black-winged Stilt nests in marshes across southern Europe and some stay to breed in Israel (p. 178).

The remaining two Heb. words are:

'eph'eh: 'viper' (AV, RV, RSV); *'akshubh*, 'adder' (AV, RV); 'viper' (RSV). Together they occur four times in figurative passages that give little help. *'eph'eh* seems to be Arabic *afa'a* or *efa*, which is sometimes applied to *Echis*, sometimes to snakes generally or to vipers as a whole. In all cases the snake is assumed to be venomous. 'The viper's tongue shall slay him' (Job 20:16). Again the writer records the old myth of the poisonous tongue. In Isa. 30:6 the viper is one item in a list, but 59:5 needs comment even though the text is not clear – 'that which is crushed breaketh out into a viper'. This could refer to a characteristic of this family, most of which bear living young, the eggs having been retained within the body of the female till they hatch. If a gravid viper is crushed these may emerge and such an accident could give rise to the old tale that the viper swallows her young in time of danger. *'akshubh* is found only in Ps. 140:3, 'adders' poison is under their lips'. This is a figurative verse which records, probably quite unwittingly, an interesting truth; the poison glands are related to the salivary glands and are situated between the eye and the lips.

Palestine's largest viper cannot be identified with any of these; this is *Vipera palestina*, related to the British Viper but much larger and more dangerous. It is found from the woodlands of the north almost to the desert edge, and it is now thought to be responsible for more bites than any other species, if only because it is often found where people live. It is common in the parts of Galilee where our Lord had His ministry and we can perhaps regard this as the main species to which the Gr. *echidna* was given. Four of its five mentions are in the phrase 'generation of vipers' (AV), 'brood of vipers' (RSV), used by our Lord and John the Baptist (Matt. 3:7, etc.) when indicating the Pharisees. These words clearly picture the batch of young that emerge from the mother fairly quickly. The smaller species have a dozen or so, the giant vipers upwards of fifty each.

The remaining reference is the only literal one, in Acts 28:3. The snake which bit St. Paul is traditionally held to be the common viper which is still found on Sicily and other islands, though not on Malta. The intensive occupation of this island for many centuries could have exterminated it since those days, but it is also possible that this snake was not venomous. In many undeveloped countries all snakes are still regarded as deadly poisonous and I have known an African carried to hospital and treated for severe shock after merely stepping on a harmless one!

Gr. *ophis*, always rendered serpent, occurs fourteen times in NT and deserves comment for the variety of its contexts. The serpent in the wilderness features in the key passage of John 3:14 and Paul refers to it in I Cor. 10:9. The serpent of Genesis 3 is said plainly to be the devil in Rev. 12:9 and 20:2, and also mentioned in II Cor. 11:3 for his subtilty. This quality is echoed in Matt. 10:16, 'be ye therefore wise as serpents' though this is at once qualified by the end of the verse 'but harmless (innocent, RSV) as doves'. Two further proverbial sayings are discussed under 'scorpion'. In Matt. 23:33, the Pharisees are called both serpents and vipers. Only two references are literal and current, where disciples are promised immunity from snake poison (Mark 16:18; Luke 10:19, the former being in a section generally considered a postscript). Finally there are three purely symbolic occurrences in the Revelation.

Python

There is no suggestion that the giant snake now known by this name was ever found in Palestine or even in Egypt, though it was sometimes brought alive to lower Egypt from the higher reaches of the Nile. However, the name *python* is given as a mg. reading in Acts 16:16, while usually tr. 'spirit of divination'. The giant mythical serpent which later received this name first appears in Homer; it lived in caves on Mount Parnassus and was killed by Apollo, who was given the surname Pythius. The Greeks believed that Python was a spirit of prophecy which possessed certain persons unconsciously and its chief oracle was at Delphi. The girl whom Paul exorcized at Philippi was one of these. The snakes now having *Python* as their scientific name have no connexion with this legend and it can only be coincidence that in Dahomey, in W. Africa, the python deity is regarded as the god of wisdom and earthly bliss.

Frog

Although it belongs to the class of Amphibians the frog can be included here. Like reptiles frogs are cold-blooded but they are restricted in their range by their breeding habits; with a few exceptions the eggs are laid in water, where the young, in the form of tadpoles, spend from a few weeks to a year or more, and at this stage they breathe through gills. When they change into the adult form these gills are lost and they then have lungs. All adult amphibians are carnivorous, taking mostly insects, worms and small aquatic prey. The commonest kind in Palestine is the Edible Frog, *Rana esculenta*, which is about 3 in. long. It is found right across Europe and is also plentiful in parts of Egypt and Mesopotamia. It spends much of the year in the water, and not just the breeding season. The pale green Tree Frog, *Hyla arborea*, with its rhythmic musical note, lives in the Jordan valley and the Green Toad, *Bufo viridis*, is widely distributed· Strikingly marked salamanders occur in the north and newts are now common, having greatly extended their range in recent years.

The only OT mention of the frog (Heb. *tsephardea'*) is as the cause of the second plague. Many people dislike the clammy feeling of a frog's skin but the frog was unclean to the Egyptians and their invasion would be abhorrent. This aspect finds an echo in the only occurrence in the NT

(Rev. 16:13). The frogs followed closely on the first plague, and the serious pollution of the Nile can be seen as the immediate cause of the frogs leaving the river and entering the houses. The court conjurers could produce frogs by their tricks but they could not stop the invasions. In the hot dry air the frogs quickly became dehydrated and died, the resultant decay in and around the houses being very unpleasant. It is ironical that these frogs would have been useful in controlling the insects involved in some of the following plagues.

XVII

All the
Fishes
of the Sea

Fish and Fishing methods in and around Palestine and Egypt.

ALTHOUGH THE RIVERS AND LAKES OF PALESTINE ARE LIMITED IN extent, the warm climate and slightly alkaline water give them a good potential for fish production. Fishing villages have grown up all around the lake of Galilee and little boats are busy day and night bringing in the harvest. On odd patches of level land, and especially in the upper Jordan valley, series of fish-ponds have been made, the total area of which exceeds 12,000 acres, and they now produce more than half of Israel's catch.

The lakes and streams have been fished since antiquity, and there were fish-ponds well over 2,500 years ago, yet fish occupy a rather strange position in the OT. Heb. *dag* (masc.) and *dagah* (fem.) are always tr. 'fish' but they have a far wider meaning than this, and they can include shellfish, crustaceans, etc., and even sea mammals such as seals. They occur some thirty-five times and in only two of these passages is there any reference to fish being eaten. The first of these is Num. 11:5, where the Israelites on the desert march looked back wistfully and longed for the fish 'which we did eat in Egypt freely'. The second is Neh. 13:16, where the Tyre merchants were breaking the law by selling fish on the Sabbath day. As will be described below, several vv. in figurative contexts refer to methods of catching fish, and the Fish Gate at Jerusalem is mentioned three times; fish, though not specifically named, are included in the aquatic animals allowed for food under the Mosaic law, in fact they are the only ones to qualify by having fins and scales.

It is the more remarkable that the eating of fish is never mentioned favourably in the OT, although twenty-five of the twenty-six NT mentions concern fish as food, exactly half of the total being found in the accounts of feeding the four and the five thousand. None of the three Gr.

words is found in a wholly figurative context, even in I Cor. 15:39, where Paul is discussing the resurrection body and points out that 'there is another flesh of beasts, another of fishes', and the proverbial saying quoted by our Lord (Matt. 7:10, etc.) speaks of fish being requested for eating. With this one exception, the word fish is found only in the Gospels, in incidents involving catching and then eating them.

The Greek words are: *ichthus*, a general word for fish which we find today in ichthyology, the natural history of fishes; and *ichthudion* and *opsarion*, which refer to small fish of more or less any kind. The latter is found only in the Gospel of John where it is used for fish about to be or already cooked, as in 6:11 and 21:10. This is consistent with its use in classical Gr., where in some contexts it may also mean food.

Fish are also included in group names, e.g., 'let the waters bring forth abundantly the moving creature that hath life' (Gen. 1:20, AV, RV). Young gives its meaning as 'teeming thing' and RSV has 'swarm of living creatures'. Clearly these expressions refer to the great assortment of marine life. In the following verse two different words are used to indicate the results of this divine creative command. 'And God created great whales and every living thing that moveth, which the waters brought forth abundantly, after their kind' (AV); 'great sea monsters . . . with which the waters swarm' (RV, RSV). The Heb. words used here are *tannin* (which is discussed on p. 253), and *nephesh*, a common word very variously tr. with the basic meaning of living.

The clean and unclean aquatic life is described in the Mosaic law in Deut. 14:9, 10 as 'All that have fins and scales shall ye eat', i.e., all typical fish. 'Whatsoever hath not fins and scales ye may not eat.' This would exclude water snakes and lizards, which have scales but no fins, and such fish as eels and mud-fish, which have either no scales at all or minute ones hidden in the skin. This definition also cuts out all aquatic invertebrates, many of which are nourishing and tasty and thoroughly enjoyed today; these are shellfish, like mussels and oysters; crustaceans like shrimp, crab and lobster; also octopus and squid, though these are not taken by everybody. The prohibition of this group was wise on hygienic grounds, for both shellfish and crustaceans can easily cause food-poisoning and may also carry disease.

The marine mammals might also be excluded, of which the dugong was once common in the Red Sea, though very rare now, and the Monk Seal, which has always been scarce in the Mediterranean. Among the sea fish the shark family, including the rays and skate, would be barred as having no scales; this is not strictly correct, for the tiny spiked plates buried in the skin are technically scales. The evil-looking Moray Eels, later reared in marine fish-ponds and a great Roman delicacy, would have been disallowed as apparently scaleless.

During biblical times **fish** came from four sources and these will now be considered.

Marine

At different times varying lengths of the Mediterranean coastline were occupied by the Israelites, not with any great enthusiasm, for they were never sea-faring people. It is quite clear that most of the maritime shipping mentioned in both OT and NT, often all of it, was owned and manned by foreigners, the main nation concerned in this trade being the Phoenicians, who had excellent ports at Tyre and Sidon. These two ports were never in Israelite hands, and Joppa was their only harbour on which a fishing fleet could possibly have been based. Some authorities claim that Sidon (Zidon) means a fishing-place, and that this was the earliest industry of the Phoenicians. Ezekiel's prophecies foretelling the destruction of Tyre refer to this trade. Tyre 'shall be a place for the spreading of nets in the midst of the sea' (Ezek. 26:5); 'I will make thee like the top of a rock; thou shalt be a place to spread nets upon' (v. 14). This was literally fulfilled. Any sea-fishing was most probably done close inshore and there is no evidence that the Hebrews themselves did any at all. In fact, the only possible reference to sea fish is in Neh. 13:16: 'Men of Tyre ... which brought fish ... and sold ... in Jerusalem.' This was presumably fish brought from the coast and because of the distance – over 100 miles – it must have been preserved by salting, smoking, sun-drying, etc., methods which are of great antiquity. Jerusalem is about forty miles from the coast and it is hard to see how fresh fish could have been carried to Jerusalem by animal transport without deteriorating in the heat of the plains.

The Mediterranean Sea is very poor fishing ground and even with modern methods the potential is low. This is confirmed by the catch made by the Israeli fishing fleet based on Haifa and Jaffa; the total for 1965 was less than 60,000 cwt., when Britain landed 300 times as much. This difference is due not just to the greater length of coastline and area of sea to be fished but rather to the sea depth. A glance at a contoured map shows hardly any coastal shelf: most water in the E. Mediterranean is deeper than 1,500 ft., much of it deeper than 3,000 ft. Such waters are of little use for commercial fisheries; in fact, more than half of the above catch was of sardines, which are surface fish of the open sea, and grey and red mullet, which live in shallow water and estuaries, came next. In contrast, thousands of square miles of sea around Britain are shallower than 150 ft., and this is where the important food fish live.

At several periods, especially during the reigns of Solomon and Jehosaphat, Israel occupied the northern tip of the Gulf of Eilat/Aqaba, which is an arm of the Red Sea, and had ships based there. A wide variety of tropical fish is found in these warm waters and there may have been some fishing for local use only. The potential cannot be very great, for the present annual catch by the small Israeli commercial fleet is only about 14,000 cwt.

Egypt

The Nile has always been a rich source of fish to both man and a great host of water birds, and various methods of catching them are illustrated in Ancient Egyptian art. This yield is in part due to the high average temperature of the water, which allows a much longer growing season than in temperate countries, and there is also a further factor; the dense population of lower Egypt was made possible by intensive irrigated cultivation, which meant the construction and maintenance of large areas of water channels also available for fish. Provided that it does not reach the stage of pollution, which would be likely only around large concentrations of people, manuring can feed the minute organisms on which the fish ultimately depend. Over 100 species are recorded for the lower Nile, many of them edible, and they include the valuable perch, carp and Cichlids. Their distribution may have altered, but in general the fish fauna has probably changed little since the Children of Israel were in bondage there. In those days fish was the main, perhaps even the only meat available to the poorer people, who could seldom afford to kill one of their few livestock. Fish must have been plentiful, for the Hebrews looked back remembering the fish that they used to eat 'freely'.

Fish was also important to the Egyptians as food, though forbidden to the priests – who presumably had plenty of red meat when they wanted it! The First Plague that turned the water into blood and killed all the fish would therefore have been a serious blow to food supplies; what is more, the fish population was such that the dead fish polluted the whole river, even though it was probably high at the time. The importance of the Nile as a fishing ground is also suggested by the judgement pronounced on Egypt in Isa. 19:8: 'The fishers also shall mourn, and all they that cast angle into the brooks shall lament, and they that spread nets upon the waters shall languish.' These fishing methods and others mentioned in the two following vv. are discussed below.

Lake of Galilee and River Jordan

Through much of its history Israel had control over the whole Lake of Galilee, which has gone by many names, including Sea of Tiberias, from the town on its western bank founded during the time of our Lord; the Lake of Gennesereth or Chinneroth; and today, by the modern Israelis, as Lake of Kineret. It is roughly fourteen miles by eight miles, and has an area of 112 square miles. Its surface is about 680 ft. b.s.l. and its maximum depth is 150 ft. It seems to be mentioned only three times in the OT, solely as marking a boundary, e.g., 'from the plain to the sea of

Chinneroth on the east' (Josh. 12:3). Not a single direct reference to its fish or fisheries can be found, though it is inconceivable that it remained unfished throughout all those centuries. The NT position is different. Much of our Lord's ministry was based on the towns around the north-east of the lake, which was then of such importance that the word sea is virtually synonymous with it through the Gospels. At least seven of the disciples were fishermen from the lake, and it is partly for this reason that its fishing has so much emphasis. Except for the Common and Mirror Carp, which from time to time escape from the fish-ponds and make their way through drainage channels and the Jordan to the lake and grow large there, and some Grey Mullet, from brackish water, which are now reared to finger-size and introduced as food fish, the fish are just about the same as they were when St. Peter practised his craft there.

There are at least twenty-five native species, of which only seven or eight are important. Since World War II much research has been done and modern methods have been introduced, as well as regulations to ensure that the fish stocks are exploited soundly, with maximum sustained yield. The output for 1965 was:

Tilapia spp.	304 tons
Bleak or Lake Sardine,	
Acanthobrama terrae sanctae	787 tons
Barbel, *Barbus canis* and *longiceps*	123 tons
Grey Mullet, *Mugil cephalus*	55 tons
Other kinds	9 tons
	1, 278 tons

The remark made in connexion with the lower Nile is relevant here. With more intensive agriculture in the drainage basin of the Jordan more nutrient salts, especially nitrates and phosphates, should find their way into the water and eventually increase the yield of fish.

The catfish, *Clarias lazera*, only yields 3·4 tons per annum; it is reckoned good eating today but was earlier forbidden as food. It is a typical bottom-feeding fish, with wide mouth and barbels for finding food in the darkness. The Lake Sardines are taken by a specialized night fishing technique described below. The *Tilapia* spp., known locally as St. Peter's fish, belong to the family *Cichlidae*, which include many tropical aquarium fishes. This fish is now too expensive for anything but the luxury trade and it is a regular dish at the lakeside hotels and special seafood restaurants at Tel Aviv. In April we found whole fish being sold on the quay for 3s. 6d. (40c. U.S.) per lb.; this was just before Passover and perhaps prices were higher than usual. These are known as mouth-breeders, from the habit of taking the fertilized eggs into the mouth of one of the parents, which protects them until they hatch and the fry are free-swimming. *Tilapia* is a genus typical of the Nile system, including the central African lakes, where they are the most important edible fish.

Until about 1950 the lake of Huleh, though silted up in parts, was still a rich fishing ground worked by *kibbutzim* such as Kfar Blum, and the fish were the same species that now live in the Jordan and the lake. The lake has been drained, but the fish-ponds ringing the reclaimed area more than compensate for the loss of production. Between this point and the lake of Galilee the river drops some 900 ft. in eleven miles, and for most of this stretch it is too swift-flowing to be suitable for commercial fishing. The yield from this part of the Jordan, and from the other rivers subject to big seasonal changes of level, would probably have been small, but such tributaries as the Jabbok are said to have held good stocks.

The small fish of the two miracles of feeding are variously called by the three Gr. names; none of these is specific and the fish cannot possibly be identified, but it can certainly be assumed that they came from the lake. Many fish of all sizes are cleaned, salted and spread in the hot sun to dry; they can then be stored for a short period or sold for eating as described. They could have been Bleak, which are now largely taken for canning locally and have obviously always been a common fish.

Both OT and NT contain interesting details of fishing methods. In the OT at least four different kinds of nets are referred to in figurative passages, as well as comments about line fishing and the use of spears; in contrast the NT features two types of net as the tools of the disciples as they earned their living, and a third kind is mentioned just once in a parable (see below).

The OT nets are not easy to differentiate clearly. The most frequently used word *resheth* appears in a range of situations, all figurative, mostly on land, and the word 'spread' normally describes how they were set. It is a favourite metaphor with Ezekiel who once (32:3) uses it in a passage which shows that it could refer to a fish net, and probably a cast net. The picture is generally of a net that is thrown at the critical moment, perhaps the kind that fowlers use to trap a flock of birds enticed within range by decoys or food. But this can be a very general word for net and it is twice used of the ornamental design for the base of the brazen altar of the Tabernacle (Exod. 27:4, 5).

Ezekiel also refers four times to *cherem*, a much larger net used by the fishermen at Tyre, who spread it on the shore for drying and mending; this could well be the long seine net that is described below as the Gr. *sagene*. There are several forms of the word *matsod*, which is from the root 'to hunt'; this was used on land and in the water but no details can be inferred from the contexts. This group of words is more frequently tr. 'stronghold' or 'fortress'. The fourth Heb. word, *makmor* has the root meaning 'to cover': it is net erected in the desert to catch the Arabian oryx. In Isa. 19:8 the related word *mikmar* is the net used by Egyptians and rendered 'net' or 'drag' (AV): the RSV has 'seine', which may be more correct.

The net which Peter and Andrew were casting when our Lord met them at work on the lake shore (Matt. 4:18) is mentioned only in this incident, which is also recounted in Mark 1:16. This is the Gr. *amphibles-tron*, and it is usually taken as equivalent to the cast net which can still be seen in many less-developed parts of the world, especially in shallow waters and coastal lagoons. This is circular, with small weights set at regular intervals around the perimeter, and it is thrown with a spinning motion so as to fall spread and flat on the surface. It is mostly used by fishermen wading naked in the water and watching for a shoal of small fish or perhaps a single larger one. The weights sink quickly to the bottom and as the cord attached to the centre is pulled the perimeter is drawn in, entangling in the mesh any fish that have been covered. In countries such as Israel this method of working is quite uneconomic today but it is still demonstrated by request in the shallow waters of the lake, so that tourists can take photographs!

Gr. *diktuon* is probably a general term for net and may include all other types. This is found in Matt. 4:20 'and (Peter and Andrew) straightway left their nets and followed Him'. They had just been throwing their cast nets and it must be assumed that as professional fishermen they would have a set of all the standard types.

This general use is probably seen also in the references to washing and mending their nets. Much of the fishermen's time ashore was taken up with this maintenance, which also included spreading out and drying (Ezek. 47:10). As has been common practice all over the world, they are likely to have made most of their own nets; the only possible reference to this is in Isa. 19:9, 'they that weave networks' (AV) from a disputed Heb. text that other VSS render differently. Much of this work is now made much easier and lighter by the use of artificial filaments, most made up by machine; these fibres are 'drip-dry', which means that most of the water runs off as the net is hauled.

The *diktuon* occurs in some passages where it could refer more precisely to what today is called a gill net, e.g., 'launch out into the deep and let down your nets' (Luke 5:4). This instruction was given after they had been fishing all night and presumably still had their nets on board; it sounds very like the method used today well out in the lake for catching medium-sized *Tilapia* and other species. Long nets hang from a row of floats, often right through the night, before being hauled into the boat. There are occasions when it is possible to shoot this type of net around a shoal but it is mostly used in a more passive way and takes fish of only one size. The smaller specimens pass right through, while the larger cannot insert their heads into the mesh. The fine monofil materials now obtainable makes this net easier to use and also more effective. If a really large shoal entered the net it would be almost impossible to haul it into the boat; the fishermen would have to draw it slowly towards land and beach the full net before removing the fish.

Gr. *sagēnē* is mentioned only once – in the parable of Matt. 13:47, where the Kingdom of Heaven is compared to a drag-net. This is now generally thought to be a type of seine net which can be several hundreds of yards long. With one end held on shore the other end is taken by boat around a semi-circle and back to shore, preferably when a shoal has been located. This is most effective when the water is shallow enough for the foot of the net to be on the bottom for most of the operation. Such a net takes all kinds and sizes, which are then sorted into edible and otherwise, as described in the parable. Because of the waste caused by catching immature fish these nets are forbidden in some fisheries.

The visitor to the lake today may also see other modern methods of netting for the market, and on our 1962 visit we were given special facilities for studying them in detail while making the B.B.C. 'Adventure' film, 'A Draught of Fishes'. The trammel is so called because it was originally a fishing net having three layers; this has been modified to a double net for local use, though still called trammel, and it is especially effective in spring when the large *Tilapia* enter the reed beds for spawning. This net is taken by hand around each area to be worked and this is a most uncomfortable job, for the reeds are sharp and the fisherman has to protect himself thoroughly with old clothes. The two nets are of different mesh, the inner one fine and loose, the outer very coarse and rather tight. Once the circle is complete the reeds are disturbed until all the fish are driven out; as one hits the fine net it pushes a pocket of it through the large mesh and there it stays, its rather spiny dorsal fin helping it to get well entangled. Then the net is hauled aboard but the mix-up is often such that it must be taken ashore before the fish can be removed and the net prepared for relaying. We watched numbers of fish between 2 and 4 lb. being taken in this way.

Officials of the Israeli Fisheries Department kindly arranged for us to spend a night with the boats working on the lake sardines. Unless the night is calm the operation is almost impossible; it must also be moonless, otherwise the 4,000 c.p. pressure-lamps are not fully effective. Soon after dark the foreman stations three of these lamp boats at suitable points on the lake, the lights shining down into the depths. We set out with him about 11 p.m. in his patrol boat, and his echo-sounder showed that the fish had already started to gather. When he reckoned that the shoal was dense enough he signalled for the net boat to go into action, encircling the lamp boat with a very fine net, the top fitted with cork floats, and both top and bottom capable of being hauled. When the sardines were safely enclosed the resulting purse was lifted by an electric winch, which poured the fish into a keep-boat alongside. The other lamp boats were visited in turn and, if the sounder showed that it was worth while, the net boat would go the rounds again before dawn. As much as 10 tons may be taken in one night. A similar method is used in suitable weather in the Mediterranean off Jaffa.

We noticed another strange method of gill net fishing being used by some Arab fishermen based on Akko (Acre) harbour. The net is shot in a circle and any fish enclosed are then driven into the net by splashing and throwing in large boulders. The total catch for the operation we watched was about two rather small fish per man!

Several references in the OT show that catching fish with hooks was widespread. In Isa. 19:8 'they that cast angles into the brooks' (AV) is modernized into 'the fishermen . . . who cast hooks in the Nile' (RSV). The word 'angle' is from a very old root meaning bend and at first it meant a fish-hook; then it was applied to fishing generally and finally to sport fishing alone. The use of a primitive gorge made of flint, around which a bait was wrapped, began in the Stone Age; this gradually took shape and by the time metal came into use it had become a barbed hook which could be applied as soon as the bait was in the fish's mouth. Some early hooks were made from natural materials and Heb. *sir dugah*, meaning fish thorn, reflects this. It is found in Amos 4:2: 'He will take . . . your posterity with fish hooks.' There are remote tribes in several parts of the world which still make their hooks from non-metallic materials.

Ancient Egyptian art shows many fishing scenes, including the use of rod and line by important men, which suggests that fishing for sport had already begun. The earliest reference to this in Gr. literature is in the *Odyssey*. An Assyrian relief dated about 700 B.C. shows fish being taken from a fish-pond by a line held in the hand, and the three scriptural references to hooks make no mention of rods. Heb. *chakkah*, tr. 'angle' in Isa. 19:8, is also found in Job 41:1, 'Canst thou draw . . . Leviathan with an hook?', and in Hab. 1:15, 'They take up all of them with the angle.' Assyrian monuments show captives being led away with fish-hooks in their noses, and the prophetic reference in Amos 4:2 suggests that this may indeed have been done. These passages may all be figurative but the use of such technical terms shows that catching fish by baited hook and line – and also by various nets – was regularly practised.

A different use of the hook is suggested in Job 41:2, which is better rendered by RSV, 'Can you put a rope in Leviathan's nose or pierce his jaw with a hook?' It was usual in Egypt to keep alive any large fish not needed for immediate use; a rope or hook was put through the gills and the fish then tethered in tanks or streams.

The single NT passage in Matt. 17:27, 'cast an hook and take up the fish that first cometh up', seems to refer to a baited hook. Another method of hook fishing is still practised on the lake, mostly by children, in which a large treble hook, unbaited, is thrown into a shoal and snatched, very occasionally hooking a fish. A harmless water-snake is sometimes caught by mistake and this is taken locally as a commentary on Luke 11:11, 'will he for a fish give him a serpent?'

Fish-spearing is another very old technique, illustrated in a painting in the tomb of Simut at Thebes, about 1500 B.C. In Job 41:7 there are two Heb. words, tr. 'irons' and 'fish spears' (AV, RV), 'harpoons and fishing spears' (RSV), and the prey is a crocodile. This method was regularly used in shallow waters for taking fish, especially in the rivers in the north of Palestine and in the Lebanon. In spring the large *Tilapia* are very vulnerable to such weapons when they enter the reed beds to spawn, but the Jews prefer to take them undamaged in the trammel nets.

The keeping of fish in artificial ponds and pools is also ancient, remains of such structures having been found in Mesopotamia and Egypt, and they are illustrated on Assyrian reliefs. The Hebrews probably practised some form of fish farming, to which there is a reference in Cant. 7:4, 'fish pools of Heshbon'. This old Moabite city is in trans-Jordan, more or less level with the northern point of the Dead Sea, and excavation has revealed remains of ponds and conduits which apparently collected the water from a little stream running around the base of Mount Nebo. While the main purpose may have been water storage against the dry season, they seem also to have been used for the raising or holding of fish. Another passage seems to make even clearer reference to this work – Isa. 19:10 'all that make sluices and ponds for fish' (AV); unfortunately the Heb. text is far from clear and other VSS tr. it differently, so that no firm conclusion can be drawn.

The Romans later became experts in the design and management of fish-ponds; in particular they showed great skill in raising several species of sea fish, including mullet and wrasse and, above all, Moray eels. They also made freshwater ponds in many countries which they occupied, and the 'fish stews' kept by monks in medieval Europe were their successors. There is no evidence about the kinds that they kept in these ponds; presumably they were local fish, especially the *Tilapia*, which make excellent eating.

Since World War II fish farming, which has already been referred to in several connexions, has become an important industry in several Mediterranean countries, especially in Israel, which now produces some 10,000 tons per annum, mostly carp for the preparation of specialized Jewish dishes. This is an ideal pond fish, for it will tolerate more brackish water than many species, and so uses some water that would otherwise be wasted. It originated long ago in E. Europe but its extensive use for this purpose can be traced back only to the Middle Ages. The revival of fish farming in recent years sprang from the increased need for animal protein, and research work has brought a high degree of efficiency to the production of carp; other desirable fish for which there is an even greater demand, such as *Tilapia* and grey mullet, have also been the subject of much work, so far without complete success, and they still make up only about 10 per cent of the total.

Production of carp is highly mechanized and a tiny labour force runs a large complex of ponds. Even feeding is now done by a specially designed 'blower' drawn by tractor. Petrol-driven elevators move the carp, very much alive and kicking, from the nets to the grading tables or aerated tanker wagons which will carry them to the market, whence they are distributed to the retail shops for sale – still alive! Only the hardy carp could survive such treatment.

Fish markets are no new thing. The existence of the Fish Gate in Jerusalem, which was one of the NW gates of the city, suggests that the fish market was near by. In those days only preserved fish – smoked, salted, sun-dried, etc. – would be sold, as is still the case in many inland markets in Asia and Africa today.

Comment has already been made on the very largely figurative position of fish in the OT. Of six Heb. words for net, the four listed above are fish nets and all are used metaphorically for the catching of men, in particular men trapping others with evil intent (e.g., Mic. 7:2). Jehovah is pictured as acting in judgement on nations in Ezek. 32:3, using two types of net, which the RSV renders 'I will throw my net over you . . . and I will haul you up in my dragnet'. In Ps. 66:11 God is taking action against individuals, 'Thou broughtest us into the net'. In a similar strain Jer. 16:16 contains the warning to Judah, 'I will send for many fishers, saith the Lord, and they shall fish them'. The warning in Amos 4:2 is to Samaria, 'He will take you away with hooks and your posterity with fish hooks', using yet another Heb. word for hook in the first clause.

The metaphorical use in the NT is very different. In a parable (Matt. 13:47) our Lord compares the Kingdom of Heaven to a drag or seine net which brings in fish of all sizes and sorts, both good and bad, for sorting after the catch is landed. In the following v. this is likened to the position at the end of the world, when the wicked will be divided from the just. The only other figurative use is in a passage too well-known to need comment – Matt. 4:18, 19; Simon and Andrew were fishermen and our Lord's call came to them, 'Follow me and I will make you fishers of men'.

The fish became a common symbol in early Christian art, almost a code word, because the Gr. *ichthus* spelled out the initials of a simple creed 'Jesus Christ the Son of God, Saviour'.

The fish very early became an object of worship, probably connected with a fertility cult because of its fecundity in laying so many eggs. Fish-worship was already forbidden in general terms in the Ten Commandments, being included in 'anything . . . that is in the water beneath the earth'. This is repeated more specifically in Deut. 4:18, where the Hebrews are warned against making an idol in the likeness of any fish.

The fish-tailed deity shown on coins found at Ashkelon has been identified with Atargitis, the fish-goddess whose cult originated in Syria and was probably spread by merchants who traded over much of the civilized world of that time. It is interesting that although the Hebrews dabbled in most cults favoured by neighbouring nations there is no evidence that any shrines were ever set up in Israel to the fish-goddess.

The often repeated statement that Dagon, the principal deity worshipped by the Philistines over a long period, was a fish deity is now regarded as doubtful, and no definite association with fish has yet been found. The confusion has come from the apparent connexion of Heb. *dag* (fish) and *dagon*. In fact the latter is more likely to be related to Heb. *dagan*, corn or grain.[1]

[1] This point is discussed more fully in N.B.D. p. 287

XVIII

Winged Creeping Things and Others

Animals-without-backbones. Scorpion, Spider, Clothes Moth, Silk Moth, Beetle, Flea, Fly, Gnat. The Third Plague – Lice, Ticks or Gnats? Snail, Onycha, Tyrian purple, Pearl, Sponge, Leech, Coral, Worms

THE ANIMALS-WITHOUT-BACKBONES, AS THIS GROUP IS PROPERLY called, include some well-known animals, easily recognized and important in the life of the Hebrew people; the Bible mentions other names which undoubtedly refer to these invertebrates but which, for reasons suggested below, prove hard to identify. These lowly animals are far more numerous than the vertebrates (those with backbones) and they make up some 97 per cent of the million or so species of animals so far named by scientists. Except for a tiny proportion of conspicuous kinds these are known only to specialists, even though some are unbelievably plentiful, with normal populations of many thousands to the acre. Most have only their Latin names and are lumped into all sorts of groups, natural and otherwise, even by educated Westerners. Among underdeveloped peoples, and in pre-scientific times everywhere, naming is a practical matter and depends on the animal's importance – usually as a pest!

This is generally true of the Heb. names. The clothes moth, scorpion, coral and sponge are well known from their damage, shape or use; the honey bee is valued for its produce, but 'bee' is everywhere a portmanteau word and several species are probably included in the Heb. name; locusts should be unmistakable, yet their names are hard to sort out.

It is not surprising that the word 'insect' is absent from earlier VSS for it appears first in 1601; it has always had a fairly precise meaning – a small animal divided into segments. RSV uses it four times (Lev. 11:20, etc.) to tr. Heb. 'oph where AV has first 'fowl' and then 'flying creeping things', and RV has 'winged creeping thing'. RSV is technically correct, for insects

224

FISHING SCENES. (*above*) On Lake Galilee; the small fish are being carefully removed from the fine nylon gill net (p. 218). (*below*) Work in the fish-ponds. The netted carp are being transferred, alive, to a transporter on the right (p. 221).

LOCUSTS have been a plague to man since earliest times. No amount of waving and beating can save crops in the path of such a swarm (p. 238). The lower picture shows adult locusts on a stalk of maize.

are the only invertebrates that fly, and in this passage the contrast is with other insects that are edible – the locusts (see Chap. 19).

Only those invertebrates that can be reasonably recognized in the Bible are discussed but it must be emphasized that many conspicuous kinds, such as butterflies and beetles, are never referred to simply because the writers did not consider them relevant to the narrative.

No logical order is possible for such a diverse collection. A start is made with the scorpions and spiders, most of which are at least recognizable as such. Insects important as food – the locusts and honey bees – are described in the next chapter.

Scorpion

This is one of the animals-without-backbones about which there is no problem. Its well attested Heb. name 'aqrab is still used today, while one of the few routes up the great Negev escarpment has long been known as the Ascent of the Scorpions[1]. Even though scorpions vary in size, colour and proportions, with some reaching nearly 10 in., the outline is unmistakable – the forward-pointing, sting-tipped tail, and the pair of heavy pincers which, in some forms, give almost the impression of a lobster. Scorpions are among the *Arachnids* and they are entirely carnivorous. The prey is seized with the strong claws (which are a pair of highly modified mouth-parts) and the sting is used to paralyse or kill it. This is then eaten by a method peculiar to this and related orders; powerful digestive juices are pumped in to break down the soft body tissues, which are then sucked out. Scorpions eat a range of animals, mostly invertebrates such as beetles, locusts and millipedes, but some may kill small mice.

Of the world's 500 or so kinds about twelve are found in one or other of the various regions of Palestine, from the Negev desert to the moist woodlands of the north. Size itself is no indication of potency of venom and though at least one local species has a most unpleasant sting none is likely to kill a healthy person. The only two species known to be potential killers are from around Mexico and they are by no means the world's largest. Like so many ground animals in hot countries, scorpions are largely nocturnal, and towards nightfall they emerge from their hiding places and wander in search of prey. They would never attack human beings, but if trodden on or handled foolishly they react instinctively and painfully. When making camp in scorpion-infested areas it is as well to search stones and other hiding places, and also to check boots and shoes before putting them on.

With more intensive use of the desert and other marginal areas, scientists have realized the need for fuller knowledge of scorpions and their venom. At the Laboratory for Venomous Animals, in the Hebrew

[1] This is Maaleh-accrabins which marked the southern border of Judah (Josh. 15.3).

P

University at Jerusalem, Professor Shulov and his team have worked out a method of persuading scorpions to eject their venom into tiny tubes, where its volume is measured before being tested for toxicity.

Most Scriptural mentions refer to the scorpion's unpleasant and dangerous nature. It comes first in Deut. 8:15, 'that great and terrible wilderness, wherein were fiery serpents, and scorpions and drought'; this is literal, but most contexts are figurative. The reference in I Kings 12:11, 'I will chastise you with scorpions' is probably to a many-thonged whip armed with pointed metal knobs. Our Lord's comment in Luke 11:12, 'If a son . . . shall ask an egg' could well have been made as He indicated a scorpion (Gr. *skorpios*) under a roadside stone. The contrast is striking, for the main segment in some kinds is fat and almost egg-shaped. This saying may be a modification of the Gr. proverb, 'a scorpion instead of a perch'.

Spiders

Spiders also belong to the *Arachnids*, being related to scorpions and ticks and quite separate from insects; they have four pairs of legs and a complicated set of mouth-parts, including a pair of poison fangs which are seldom big enough to hurt anything but their normal prey, though some can be very painful or even dangerous to man. Some are so small as to be seen properly only with a lens; others have bodies as large as a walnut. Proportions and habits are just as varied. Palestine has numerous species, including the Trap-door Spider which has worked out this novel method of catching prey. Many kinds must have been known to the Hebrews, and the more obvious may have had their own group names, for their relationship would probably not have been noticed, but Scriptural references are few and one of the only two words commonly tr. 'spider' is disputed. However different their ways of using it, all spiders have a set of special glands for extruding silk in continuous strands. This is most obvious when woven into complex and beautiful webs by the Orb-spinners, but the same material is also made into nests, egg cases, the lining and hinge of the trapdoor and many other strange devices.

Heb. '*akkabish* is found in Isa. 59:5 'weave the spider's web', which confirms the identification. A somewhat similar phrase occurs in Job 8:14, which AV and RSV both tr. 'whose trust shall be a spider's web' (RSV mg., 'house'). A common Heb. word is used here *(bayith)* which is nearly always tr. 'house', and here only as 'web'. This latter may be what the writer intended, but many spiders make flimsy shelters of silk and reference could be to such. Most modern VSS following LXX and other old VSS render Job 27:18 'he buildeth his house as a moth'. RSV regards the Heb. text as indefinite and in need of reconstruction, and suggests 'the house which he builds is like a spider's web, like a booth which a watchman makes'. This may portray an orb-spinner, which watches its web from a vantage point alongside, where it controls certain strands that give warning of prey entering the mesh.

The Heb. word in dispute is *semamith*, found only in Prov. 30:28, where AV tr. 'spider' but RV and RSV prefer 'lizard'– this latter is more probable. See 'lizard' (p. 260) for discussion.

Clothes Moth

Moth in the Scriptures has a narrow meaning and refers only to the clothes moth; e.g., 'as a garment that is moth-eaten' (Job 13:28). The *Tineidae* are a family of small moths now almost entirely associated with man and his surroundings; they have developed what can best be described as perverted habits and now feed only on prepared or preserved materials. As a result they have been destroyers of fur and feathers, leather and clothes almost since man started wearing them. The term moth-eaten is descriptive but not strictly true, for the damage is done by the larvae. Soon after emerging from the pupae the female moths ($\frac{1}{4}$ to $\frac{1}{2}$ in. long) lay their eggs among clothes; hatching time varies with the temperature, but the damage has, in effect, started before the moths are seen flying. The grub-like larvae make a silk-lined case, covered on the outside with debris, out of which only the head protrudes. They feed on a variety of fibres, but clothes are seldom damaged if they are stored thoroughly dry and clean.

There is some dispute whether this Heb. word *'ash* occurs in Job 27:18 and this is discussed under 'spider'. (See 'Worm' [p. 235] for discussion of Isa. 51:8).

Many of the more typical members of the order *Lepidoptera* are found in Palestine, including such conspicuous species as the Swallowtail Butterfly and some of the large Hawk Moths, but none is mentioned in the Scriptures.

Silk Moth

Silk is the product of a number of moths, in particular of *Bombyx mori*, of which China held a closely-guarded monopoly until almost the beginning of the Christian era. Small quantities of silk, worth its weight in gold, were brought to the Western world many centuries earlier and it is likely that Solomon knew it. Some critics believe that Heb. *meshi*, from a root 'to draw out', refers to it in Ezek. 16:10, 13; but this is disputed and in older VSS this is sometimes tr. 'fine linen'. Several centuries B.C. silk from other species of moth was being produced in a small way on the island of Cos; by NT times silk was more widely known, though still an extravagant luxury (Rev. 18:12). Chinese silk moths finally reached the Mediterranean area in the sixth century A.D., by which time silk-farming had spread through India as far as Persia. The caterpillars of the silk moth feed on mulberry leaves and tolerate only certain climates, so that not by any means all countries are suitable.

Beetle

Beetles are the *Coleoptera*, which make up nearly half the known number of insects. They are easily recognized by their thick leathery forewings under which the membranous hindwings are kept folded up when not in use. Palestine has a wealth of species, from most of the important families; the scarab dung beetle, sacred to the Egyptians, is common, and several kinds could easily become serious pests in the intensively cultivated areas now found in Israel. Among the edible insects listed in Lev. 11:22 (AV) is the beetle, but this tr. is not now accepted. The RV and RSV rendering of 'cricket' is nearer the mark, but still rather unlikely, and it is generally agreed that Heb. *chargol* is a locust or grasshopper. No kind of beetle is known to be eaten in Palestine though some are considered delicacies in parts of Africa and Australia; they are usually eaten in grub form, either roasted or deep-fried.

Flea

The dry countries of the Middle East are notorious for the fleas, flies, ticks and other pests that can make life almost unbearable for strangers, though many of them are accepted stoically, as something which is always with them, by most of the local people. Several of these find mention in the Bible but with the exception of the Flea (Heb. *parosh*) their precise identification is never easy. The AV speaks of this in two passages (1 Sam. 24:14; 26:20) but RSV omits it from the latter. They are both metaphorical but the tr. is clearly correct. David, speaking to Saul, suggests that he is hunting something small and contemptible and in the second verse the force of the metaphor is doubled, for David also compares his pursuit to that of a partridge in the mountains; this well describes the hunting of a flea as it leaps time and again trying to escape.

The common flea is *Pulex irritans*, but various other species are also parasitic on man, while many others live on a wide range of other furred and feathered animals, each normally having one main host species. Fleas belong to a small and highly modified insect order (*Siphonaptera* – wingless suckers). The third pair of legs is enormously enlarged for jumping and the adults are blood-suckers, but the larvae are not parasitic; they live on rubbish, so that fleas preying on humans thrive only in dirty surroundings. In the dry conditions of Palestine fleas are so plentiful and universal that the nomads, who try to regard them with indifference, must sometimes abandon camp and move to a clean site. Although fleas are usually known for the discomfort they cause they are also specific carriers of disease, in particular of bubonic plague, which is passed on by the flea of the black rat. This is discussed more fully under 'Mouse' (p. 132).

Fly

The term 'fly' is properly applied to members of the order *Diptera*, the two-winged insects, but popularly it is given to many other insects also, e.g., Dragonfly, Fire-fly, Sawfly and Crane Fly, all belonging to different insect orders – and the usage is even wider among primitive peoples and in old languages. Of the two Heb. words tr. fly, one ('arobh) is used only for the mass appearance of flies in the Fourth Plague and in subsequent references to it. Flies of many kinds swarm in Egypt – House Flies, Mosquitos and various other blood-sucking flies. Some are very troublesome merely because of their numbers: some are dangerous because they spread diseases, as the Anophelene mosquito does malaria; others just carry infection on the feet and proboscis and so pass on the various filth and eye diseases. There is nothing in the context to identify these swarms of flies but the fact that they are described as being actually on the people suggests that they might have been biting flies like *Stochomys calcitrans*. Commentators like Hort see a logical connexion between Plagues Four and Six with the fly carrying a skin disease, perhaps a modified form of the anthrax that had struck the cattle in the previous plague, according to this theory. (N.B.D., p. 1,002.)

The other Heb. word is *zebub*, best known in the name *ba'alzebub*, the god of the flies, invented by the Phoenicians to control the flies that they found such a nuisance, and sarcastically changed by the Hebrews to *Ba'alzebul*, the god of the dunghill. *Zebubh* itself is found only twice. The proverb in Eccl. 10:1 is still used. Ointments of those days were basically grease, mostly vegetable, scented with spices and other perfumes, and used more for regular skin treatment than for medicinal purposes. If left unprotected they were soon covered with flies and spoilt. The same word is found in a figurative passage in Isa. 7:18, 'The Lord shall hiss for the fly,' of which the meaning is not clear. This is discussed under 'Bee' (p. 245).

Gnat

In most EV this word is found only in the passage where our Lord quotes, or perhaps adapts, an earlier proverb and accuses the Scribes and Pharisees of 'straining out a gnat and swallowing a camel'. (RSV here corrects a confusing phrase in AV which has 'strain *at* a gnat') (Matt. 23:24). This is characteristic eastern hyperbole and refers to the orthodox Jewish practice of straining wine before drinking, or actually taking it through a piece of cloth to avoid ritual defilement by eating forbidden meat, which is how any fly swallowed inadvertently would be classed. Gr. *kōnōps* seems to be a general word for small flies and the root is today found in *Conopidae*, a family of two-winged flies. Gnat is also used in RSV as the cause of the Third Plague in Egypt.

The Third Plague

Heb. *kinnim* is rendered 'lice' in AV, where it is used only in connexion with this plague. It is always pl. and comes from a root 'to establish or fix'.

It clearly refers to parasites able to multiply rapidly and cling to both man and beast. Various arguments support the RSV tr. 'gnat' but Rabbinical commentators, and also Josephus, agree with the older tr. 'lice'. There is also a third possibility which is not found in any EV. These are all discussed below in the light of modern knowledge about the habits and spread of these parasites and also bearing in mind the important comment in Exod. 8:16, 17 'It became lice in man and beast; *all the dust* of the land became lice'.

1. *Lice:* (AV, RV and many old authorities). These are degenerate wingless insects of the order *Anoplura* and they live exclusively by sucking blood. They flourish on dirt and over-crowding everywhere and they are still all too common in parts of SE. Europe and the Middle East. Lice have been closely associated with man since antiquity and their preserved bodies have been found in Egyptian mummies. They are often regarded as just a nuisance but they are far more than that, for they are vectors of diseases such as typhus fever, which in many wars has caused more deaths than the fighting. A peculiarity of lice is that very few groups of animals, outside humans and cattle, are attacked. Each species is strictly confined to one kind of host, sometimes to one part of a host, with perhaps one form on the head and another on the body. However, their breeding pattern does not really fit the Bible narrative, for lice breed only on the host and cannot spread explosively, as the verse implies; nor can they survive where there is scrupulous personal hygiene. Herodotus described how Egyptian priests shaved the hairy parts of both head and body every third day to combat lice, and there is evidence that this practice is an old one. These priests also washed their clothes frequently and should have been immune.

2. *Ticks:* These are not insects but classified as Arachnids, so they are allied to spiders and scorpions, with four pairs of legs but no wings at any stage. Like lice, at all stages they feed only on blood sucked from a host, and having fastened on with their special mouth-parts they finally become so engorged that head and legs almost disappear. When nearly pea-sized they drop off and burrow into the surface of the ground where, some weeks later, they lay numerous eggs. The minute ticks that hatch can survive in dry sand and soil for perhaps a year waiting for a suitable host to come along; in some arid lands they seem as plentiful as dust and it is impossible to take a few steps without being invaded. Some kinds live on one species only but some are not fussy. Like lice they can transmit dangerous diseases to man and stock, including relapsing fever and Texas cattle fever. Their breeding pattern and way of seeking hosts make ticks a likely cause of this plague and it is strange that the only authority who seems to have made the suggestion is J. G. Wood in his *Bible Animals* (1869), where he quotes Sir Samuel Baker's opinion.

3. *Gnats and Mosquitoes:* (RSV and Hort in ZAW LXIX pp. 84–103, cited

in NBD.) Lands like Egypt, with rivers that flood periodically and leave temporary stagnant pools, provide almost unlimited breeding places for gnats and mosquitoes. In popular usage these words are interchangeable, but the word gnat is a more general one and better applied to a group of two-winged flies, mostly smaller than true mosquitoes. Eggs are laid in water, rarely in damp places, and at certain seasons, in the high prevailing temperatures, breeding is rapid and the gnats hatch in clouds. The larvae feed in water, mostly on microscopic organisms, but when they emerge as adults they go in search of blood, and some kinds are indiscriminate in their choice of hosts. Mosquitoes transmit some of the world's worst diseases, including malaria and filariasis. The detail of the narrative RSV v. 17, 'all the dust of the earth became gnats,' is clearly figurative to some extent and perhaps need not preclude the gnat, but this tr. does seem less likely. The theory of Hort referred to above sees the first nine Plagues as a logical and connected sequence in which natural phenomena are used by God to fulfil His purpose, the miracle being in the timing, extent, intensity and, above all, in their control. This hypothesis is an interesting one deserving consideration, and it does not in any way belittle the supernatural content. If this is correct the gnat would best fit into the sequence, but there is much to be said for the rendering 'tick' on both philological and biological grounds.

Snail

In the various EV two Heb. words have at times been tr. snail, of which only one is now accepted as correct. (The other; *chomet*, is found only in Lev. 11:30, 'snail' (AV) and 'sand lizard (RSV); it is almost certainly one of the lizards and is discussed under that name.) Ps. 58:8 speaks of the snail *(shablul)* 'which dissolves into slime' (RSV), 'which melteth' (AV). The former is the better tr. for it describes, in non-technical terms, the trail of slime left behind a snail or slug as it crawls along; this is formed of the snail's secretion, which makes a sort of track on which it glides along. The predominantly limestone rocks of Palestine make it easy for snails to find the calcium for shell-building, with the result that many kinds live in most regions, even in the desert. They have a wide range of food habits, and while some are carnivorous and eat other snails, most are vegetarian. These may become pests in irrigated fields, where the moist conditions, even in the dry season, allow them to be active for a longer period than usual. On the high ground and in the north the winter becomes cold enough to make snails hibernate, when they hide away after sealing the open end of their shell with a thin plug of dried secretion. The hot summer weather is a more vulnerable period for them, when they also have to hide away sealed up against desiccation, but many of the thinner-shelled kinds fail to come through. The verse quoted is purely figurative and refers to no particular species.

Three shellfish are mentioned by the name of the product obtained from them:

Onycha

This is found in Exod. 30:34, where it is one of the substances used for compounding the incense used in the Tabernacle, and again in Ecclus. 24:15 in a similar context. Heb. *shecheleth* is the same word as onyx but was not recognized by the translators as merely an inflexion of it. One small part of the live shellfish is used, known as the operculum, a horny shield by which the opening to the shell is closed when the soft body has been drawn into it. The species concerned belong to the genus *Strombus* and were found in the Red Sea, but this genus is widely distributed and includes the giant conch of the West Indies, which can be over 10 in. long. The operculum once featured in medicine under the name of *Blatta byzantina*, and until the end of last century, and probably later still, it was being used in the east for preparing incense.

Tyrian Purple

In the case of *Murex* spp., from which the famous Tyrian purple was obtained, the name is synonymous with the colour. It was manufactured in Phoenicia from a formula now long lost, though it was once known through much of the civilized world and Pliny the Elder left some account of its preparation. Many efforts have been made to reproduce the old method of extraction, none very successfully. The exact identification of the shade is impossible, for precise definition of colours is a modern concept. In ancient languages their few colours were vaguely described and brightness may have counted for more than actual shade. Thus our Lord's robe is described as purple (*porphurous*) by John and scarlet (*kokkinos*) by Matthew. This extract was mostly used for drying raw wool for export. It seems that the finest dye, which sold for a very high price, came from an organ so small that the yield was one drop per shell, and a second leaching, from the crushed whole shell, was of poorer quality. The volume of this trade is suggested by the extensive banks of crushed shell which can still be found around Tyre. *Murex* belongs to the same order of shells as *Strombus* (See above). Some marine shells were used for ornamental purposes; necklaces and pendants have been found in graves. (Heb. *'argaman*).

Pearl

The single OT reference is generally agreed to be incorrect (Job 28:18) 'no mention shall be made of coral, or of pearls'. Heb. *gabish* is used for 'ice' and RSV now properly renders it 'rock crystal'. But there is no doubt at all that Gr. *margaritai* is the pearl that is so precious and has been so regarded since early times; in fact pearls were relatively more valuable then, for techniques for cutting and polishing the hard gemstones had not been invented and most of their jewels would today be regarded only as semi-precious stones. Pearls are produced by a number of different bivalves and consist of concentric layers of shell secreted around some object that has found its way into the cavity. This is usually a hard substance like sand, but the oyster reacts similarly to a deliberately introduced foreign object and this is made use of in the production of cultured pearls, in which the starting point is round and of fair size.

The main pearl-bearing oyster, well named *Avicula margarifera,* is collected by divers from many parts of the Indian Ocean, including the Red Sea. The shell itself yields the mother-of-pearl used commercially for making a range of ornamental goods. In NT the pearl is something very precious e.g., Matt. 13:45. When our Lord spoke of 'casting pearls before swine' (Matt. 7:6), He was reflecting an ancient eastern metaphor, apt sayings and words of wisdom often being referred to as pearls.

Sponge

The almost universal modern custom of using synthetic materials as 'sponges' makes it easy to forget that the word is derived from the Gr. *spongos.* This is the sponge that lives in great numbers in the shallow warm waters of the E. Mediterranean where it has been the object of well organized fisheries since antiquity; larger quantities now come from the Caribbean area. Sponges are lowly marine animals that were once thought to be plants; there are many kinds and it is the horny sponges whose 'skeletons' are prepared for a variety of domestic purposes. Sponges grow very slowly and a large specimen may be fifty years old. The word is found only in one context (Matt. 27:48 etc.) where the soldier gives our Lord a drink of vinegar on the cross. This was apparently a normal method, for Pliny the Elder reported that Roman soldiers regularly carried a piece of sponge for use as a drinking vessel, just as described in the Gospels.

Leech

Heb. *'aluqah* is found only once, in a difficult v. rendered 'The horse-leach hath two daughters crying, give, give' (Prov. 30:15). RSV is similar, with the more modern spelling 'leech', but the mg. points out that the meaning is not certain. The sense of the v. is hard to make out but there is no reason to query the tr. of the word itself. It comes from a root meaning 'to adhere or suck', and the Arabic *alaq* still means horse-leech. These annelid worms are widely distributed and in the wet tropics they are found on land at some seasons, sometimes in great numbers, but in most places they are confined to water. The characteristics to which the v. probably refers are bloodthirst and tenacity. Leeches normally fasten on the skin but some can invade the throat and nasal passages after being taken into the mouth with water, and this may have fatal results. In Palestine both horse-leech and medicinal leech were once very abundant in the swamps and small streams, but swamps have been drained and the rivers are tapped to exhaustion, so many of their haunts have disappeared. However, the new fish ponds may offer homes and there the leeches may have to be controlled. This habit of sucking blood, their only food, led to their early use by physicians for 'letting' blood, and until about the middle of last century great numbers were still being used, especially to remove blood from swellings hard to treat by other methods. Even now they are still applied occasionally in orthodox medicine. At least two centuries ago physicians became known as 'leeches' because of this practice, but this use is now obsolete.

Commentators have sometimes identified 'aluqah with an Arabic word tr. 'blood-sucking vampire bat', but this is quite impossible, for the only bats known to feed on blood, i.e., the vampires, are found in Central and S. America.

Coral

Two Heb. words are usually tr. 'coral' and there is general agreement that both refer to precious or semi-precious stones of animal rather than mineral origin; i.e., they are coral, or perhaps even pearls, and not rubies, which is the suggestion made in RV mg. There is no difficulty about *ra'moth*, from a root meaning growing high or like a tree, but it could be either black or red coral, probably the latter, which was expensive and in greater demand. In the Scriptures coral is always something of great value, e.g., Job 28:18, and in tombs in Ancient Egypt coral objects are found alongside other jewels and gold.

Coral is strictly the name given to animals of the class *Anthozoa* (flower-animals), which are lowly organisms living in vast colonies in seas not colder than about 68°F. Some 2,500 species have been described; all are individually minute and they vary widely in the size and shape of the structures which they make. Some are reef-builders and their cal-cereous remains form many islands in the warm seas; others grow in ornamental shapes and it is a few of these that are suitable for making into jewellery. To ancient writers, and to most people today, coral is just the dead 'skeleton'. Some pieces are used, after cleaning and bleaching, for decorative work, especially in tropical marine fish tanks, but this is a modern and limited application. Personal ornaments are made from carefully cut and polished pieces, and red coral, in particular, was so used long before it finds mention in OT. Its main source was in the E. Mediterranean, where it was once plentiful in the shallow coastal waters and exploited by well organized fisheries. About the beginning of the Christian era large exports of red coral were being made to India, where it was believed to have sacred properties. Heb. *peninim* is almost certainly a reddish stone but the context is of little help and it may have been of mineral origin (Job 28:18 etc.).

Worms

We must expect a range of lowly Biblical animals to be referred to as *worms* in English, where the word also has a non-specific figurative use, as when a person is just called 'a worm'. This is also Heb. usage in several passages, such as Isa. 41:14, and there is no point in trying to recognize any particular species. Five Heb. words and one Gr. are tr. 'worm' in the various EV and although in all cases the word is used without qualification, in contrast to what might be done today, the contexts give some useful clues and some attempt will be made at identification.

1. Heb. *zachal* is a general word rendered variously in different passages and VSS. Tr. include 'serpent' and 'creeping thing', as well as 'worm', and we can perhaps regard this as equivalent to our 'creepy-crawly', i.e., a popular name for a vague group of rather unattractive animals. This word is discussed further under 'Serpent' (p. 202). Micah 7:17, 'move out of their holes like worms of the earth,' suggests to some commentators the earthworm with its habit of lying on the surface of the ground at night when dew has fallen. Earthworms are found in Palestine, though they are not so important in soil processing as they are in temperate lands, but this reading of the v. is unlikely in the light of the RSV, which attaches 'crawling things' to the preceding clause and begins a new sentence, 'They shall come trembling out of their strongholds'. This confirms the non-specific nature of the word.

2. Heb. *rimmah* is tr. 'worm' in all EV with the exception of two passages in RSV (Job 25:6 and Isa. 14:11) which have 'maggot'. The only literal use is discussed below; in addition it is found six times in figurative contexts so varied that this must be compared with English worm used generally.

3. Heb. *sas* occurs only in Isa. 51:8 'The moth shall eat them up like a garment, and the worm shall eat them like wool.' Most commentators and naturalists see here the clothes moth and then its caterpillar, and while this may be so there are reasons against it, for it is usual to speak of the moth as the actual destroyer though all the damage is done by the grub. Under 'Moth' (p. 227), this grub is described as living in a small felted case, with only the head exposed; it does not look at all worm-like and it is doubtful even today if people often see it or identify it, for the trouble is generally found after the grubs have pupated and the moths have emerged. So it seems unlikely that this non-typical larval form would even be called worm. There are other insects that destroy fibres used by man, including cockroaches and the larvae of some beetles, and it seems possible that the v. refers to the clothes-moth and some other house pest.

4. Heb. *tola'* is only once tr. 'worm', in connexion with the manna kept over to the next day in disobedience to God's instructions – 'it bred worms and stank' (Exod. 16:20). It is interesting to compare v. 24 concerning manna that had been kept over to the Sabbath, where it states that 'it did not stink, neither was there any worm therein'. Here the more general word *rimmah* is used. It could be that the former refers to a more specific infestation; in the high temperatures experienced in the desert for much of the year maggots would quickly turn such nutritious material into a seething mass.

This is elsewhere tr. 'crimson' and 'scarlet', showing relation to, or perhaps confusion with, the next word.

5. Heb. *tole'ah, tola'ath*: tr. 'worm' seven times, but only once used literally (Jonah 4:7) for the grub that killed the gourd shading Jonah. The other contexts are all figurative and it seems that this could be the term for a different group of worms, since in two vv. this word and *rimmah* are used as contrasting pairs 'Maggots are the bed beneath you and worms are your covering' (Isa. 14:11 RSV).

However, *tole'ah* has a different and more interesting use. It occurs some twenty-seven times, sometimes alone, and sometimes qualified by *shani* (red), and it is everywhere tr. 'scarlet'. It is noted elsewhere (see *Murex*, p. 232) that colours were seldom named accurately in ancient languages. Scholars have suggested that the need for a full and precise vocabulary had not yet arisen and that such colours as were recognized took their names from the materials providing them. This is still true of Central African languages, where the range is being extended by using English colours, suitably modified phonetically. In these passages, therefore, *tole'ah*, the worm, becomes synonymous with the scarlet made from it.

The insect from which this dye was prepared belongs to the *Coccidae*, the Scale Insects and Mealy Bugs. This family includes several other dye-producers, e.g., the cochineal insect and lac insect of India (from which came the name crimson lake), but it has a different economic importance today because some of the worst insect pests of the Citrus belong to it. This scarlet dye of the ancient world came from *Coccus ilicis*, whose host plant is the Holm Oak, *Quercus coccifera*, once widespread and abundant in N. Palestine, but now much reduced. Great numbers of this insect attack the twigs, piercing the thin bark to suck the sap; a waxy scale is prepared to protect the soft bodies against enemies and desiccation, and the dye is in this scale. The Arabic name for this insect is *kermez*, from which comes kermesic acid, the active ingredient. This is one of the anthroquinones, which is yellow in water and becomes the typical violet-red when acid is added. About a century ago this began to be replaced by the nearly related *Coccus cacti*, which feeds on the introduced prickly pear, but now this in turn has largely been superseded by synthetic dyes. All these insects are small, about the size of Aphids, or plant-lice, to which they are related, and this may suggest that the basic meaning of *tole'ah* is a very small grub.

6. *skōlēx*, the only Gr. word, is found twice only. The first passage (Mark 9:48) is purely figurative and therefore non-specific, but there is no need to regard the other as anything but literal, 'He was eaten of worms and gave up the ghost' (Acts 12:23). Josephus describes the death of Herod in a parallel account 'and (Herod) was eaten of worms and died'. There is a further account in II Macc. 9:9 'so that the worms rose up out of the body of this wicked man . . . his flesh fell away.' This is the subject of comment by Prof. A. Rendle Short in *The Bible and Modern Medicine* (1953), who points out that there are several ways in which intestinal worms can cause fairly sudden death even today. A further suggestion is that Herod had a hydatid cyst, which is the alternate host stage of the dog tape-worm and, when it forms in man, is usually fatal. *skōlēx* is a general term, but it is an interesting coincidence here that it is now the technical name for an embryonic tape-worm.[1]

The manna provided on the wilderness journey is perhaps beyond the scope of comment here but one theory is that it was a substance of animal origin. This is discussed in some detail by Prof. F. S. Bodenheimer, the well-known Israeli zoologist, in pp. 217–225 of his book *Insects as Human Food*, his suggestion being that manna is the exudate of insects related to aphids and therefore analogous to 'honey dew'.

[1] A passage well-known through being sung in the aria 'I know that my Redeemer liveth' in the *Messiah* is not a correct tr. In AV 'worms' is in italics, and Job 19:26 is better rendered 'after my skin has been destroyed' (RSV).

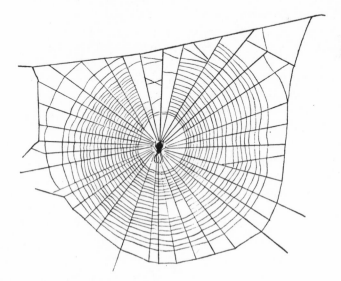

XIX

Locusts, Bees and Ants

Locusts as a plague and as human food. Bees, honey and wax. Hornets and Wasps. The Harvester Ant.

LOCUSTS ARE BY FAR THE MOST IMPORTANT INSECTS IN THE BIBLE; WITH some fifty-six mentions, under nine different Heb. names and one Gr., they appear more often than all other insects together. While to the Hebrews the locust was first and foremost a destroyer, both literal and metaphorical, it was also a useful source of animal protein at some seasons, so that the cause of the Eighth Plague also helped to feed the crowds on their desert march, for this seems to have been the only type of invertebrate allowed as food.

Although locusts appear in seventeen different books of the Bible, and in a wide variety of contexts, both literal and figurative, these give almost no incidental information that might help identify the types involved. The single exception is *chagab*. Although this may come from a root 'to hide' (and some commentators infer 'to hide the sun', suggesting a swarming species) yet this is three times used to denote something rather small and insignificant, e.g., 'we were in our own sight as grasshoppers' (Num. 13:33). Elsewhere it appears once as an insect allowed as food and once as a potential danger to crops; it could therefore refer to one of the smaller kinds, perhaps a non-gregarious grasshopper, of which there are many species.

There is little uniformity in the EV, either within any one VS or among recent VSS. For instance, AV tr. three Heb. words both 'locust' and 'grasshopper'. However, one word – *solam* – is given the quaint name 'bald locust' in all VSS, based on Talmudic and Rabbinical statements that its head is smooth or bald in front; such a description would fit some of the

238

Tryxalinae, a family with long smooth heads, though otherwise they are typical grasshoppers.

One other problem of identification must also be mentioned. How far do these varied names refer to separate species? Could they be the stages through which a locust passes towards the adult condition, or the phases, both solitary and gregarious, which some species show? Could some of these names be 'nick-names'? From the food list in Lev. 11:22 it is implied that *'arbeh, solam, chargol* and *chagab* are different kinds. There is another list in Joel 1:4 from which it would seem that *'arbeh, gazam, yeleq* and *chasil* are all different.

These two lists are tr. as follows: Lev. 11:2. Locust, bald locust, beetle and grasshopper (AV, RSV). RV differs only in having cricket instead of beetle. These are all discussed. Joel 1:4. Palmer worm, locust, cankerworm and caterpillar (AV, RV). Palmer worm was used in the Geneva Bible (1560) and then meant a processional caterpillar, being derived from 'palmer', a pilgrim returning from the Holy Land with a palm branch. Both words are now obsolete. Cankerworm (16th. Cent.) was once the name for destructive caterpillars and is also obsolete. Since the 15th. Cent. 'caterpillar' has been used for a larva of butterfly or moth (its true meaning today), but it once had a wider meaning of 'plunderer' and the second part of the word may be cognate with 'pillage'. It is quite impossible to give these words any specific value either here or in other texts, as RSV seems to suggest when tr. cutting, swarming, hopping and destroying locusts.

Some commentators regard Joel's striking description of a locust plague as detailing the progressive stages as the locust swarms develop and move on. Many authorities have regarded *'arbeh,* which is the word most used and the only one applied to the Eighth Plague, as the Migratory Locust, and the other names in Joel may be its phases and stages. *Solam* and *chagab* are discussed above, and we know nothing of the root meaning of *chargol,*[1] found only in Lev. 11:22, but the other names all refer to one or other attribute of the locusts and it seems possible that some, at least, are virtually synonyms for locusts generally. Such Heb. usage is seen in other animals such as lion and ass, and it is common today in other countries. When I lived in Ghana I compiled a glossary of animal names in the main languages and I recorded what could be a close parallel. The Ground Squirrel has invaded large areas of farms within the forest country and at times does some damage to root crops but is also hunted eagerly for food. It has its own precise names in the forest languages but farmers and hunters more often refer to it as traveller, road-crosser or pea-

---

[1] Heb. *chargol* is tr. 'beetle' (AV) and 'cricket' (RSV). Neither is likely to be correct, if only because they would not be classed as suitable for food. Crickets belong to another family of Orthoptera and some of their species have long been associated with human surroundings, as for instance, 'the cricket on the hearth.'

nut thief, all names descriptive of obvious habits. Such could easily be true also of the locust in Palestine. Perhaps the most logical treatment is that found in the *Jerusalem Bible*, which makes no attempt to name the varities but simply has 'the solham, hargol and hagab locusts in their several kinds'.

Locusts and grasshoppers belong to the easily recognized family *Acrididae* (Gr. *akris*) of the order *Orthoptera* (straight-winged). They vary in size from under 1 in. to 3 in. or over, and are mostly in browns and greens, with perhaps some colour on the under-wings or legs. The fore-wings are straight, narrow and parchment-like; the hind-wings are much larger, thin and membranous, and when not being used in flight they are folded, fan-wise, and hidden under the fore-wings. The main distinguishing feature is the third pair of legs, enormously enlarged for jumping. Their antennae are short and the female has a short, stubby ovipositor. They have mouths with powerful mandibles with which they cut up leaves and other herbage; locusts and grasshoppers are entirely vegetarian in all their stages, which is one reason why they were allowed as food to the Hebrews.

The term locust is variously applied. In America it is almost interchangeable with grasshopper and to make confusion worse, even cicadas, of another insect order, may also be called locusts. In Europe locusts are often the larger members of the family and grasshoppers the smaller, but a better criterion is that locusts swarm and migrate while grasshoppers are more or less solitary, for the real characteristic of locusts is that they can multiply at a frightening rate and move in vast swarms over great distances.

However, much recent research on this serious pest suggests that the definition is not quite so simple as this, for locusts are now known to exist in two phases, solitary and gregarious, with intermediate forms; these phases differ in appearance and within each phase there is variation in colour, size and proportions. It is hardly surprising that the Heb. names are difficult to sort out! Swarming is now seen as a physiological response to conditions, and a way of colonizing new areas. The only direct biblical comment on the locusts' biology or habits is by Solomon in Prov. 30:27, where he refers to their extraordinary co-ordinated mass-movements. These are still a mystery to scientists.

It seems unlikely that locusts have changed their habits since biblical times and we assume that the same species are active in the lands around Palestine now as then. The main change has been brought about in recent years through locust control, and this has affected numbers rather than species. Only three kinds are likely to do damage. The Migratory Locust, *Locusta migratoria*, in many races, is found in most parts of the world other than America; this is perhaps the commonest and most important. The others are the Desert Locust, *Schistocerca gregaria*, and the

Moroccan Locust, *Dociostaurus maroccanus*. The breeding biology of all
is roughly the same. Eggs are laid in small packets near the surface of
the soil, and hatching may depend on moisture – a safety device to
prevent the emergence of hoppers in a drought. The eggs of some
species, e.g., South African Brown Locust, have been known to
survive for three and a half years in dry ground, yet they hatch in ten
days when the soil is damp. Unlike most insects, which pass through
several entirely different stages (i.e., grub, pupa, adult), the young
locusts that hatch have the same general shape as the adults, but no
wings. They moult five or six times, growing and gradually acquiring
full wings; temperature, moisture and food supplies all affect the rate of
reaching maturity.

In their early stages the young locusts can move only by crawling
or hopping and are then known as hoppers; these are less mobile and
therefore easier to destroy, so the control organizations aim at forecast-
ing first the formation and then the movements of swarms in order
to do this. Some swarms fly out to sea or into great stretches of true
desert and so destroy themselves. Numbers in these swarms can be
astronomical; for instance, a Desert Locust swarm that crossed the Red
Sea in 1889 was estimated to cover 2,000 sq. mls. Like many large
insects they have comparatively little control over their flight and
wind is probably the main factor in determining the direction taken,
cf. Ps. 109:23: 'I am tossed up and down as the locust.' Locusts usually
approach Palestine from the Arabian deserts to the south-east, but they
can also come from other directions. They have been a scourge from
time immemorial, especially in regions where agriculture is marginal,
but modern chemicals, transport and communications, based on a
degree of co-operation rare in that part of the world, have greatly
reduced the damage done.

The locust's place in the biblical narrative is best discussed in its
three main settings: (the figures in brackets show the number of references).

1. The cause of the Eighth Plague (nine);
2. A destroyer, both literal and figurative (twenty-five);
3. A source of human food (six).

The remaining sixteen references are in a wide variety of contexts, most
of them purely figurative, and comment has already been made on the
more important; all Heb. and Gr. words are included in these counts,
however they are tr.

1. The Eighth Plague

The details of the record in Exodus 10 amply confirm the cause though
the actual species is not known; it could have been either the Desert or the

Migratory Locust. Four points, in particular, stand out; the complete stripping of the crops and greenstuff; swarms dense enough to hide the sun (locusts are the only insects of which this is ever true); they came with the east wind, the direction from which swarms have often come; and they were carried away by a 'mighty, strong west wind', which is what people pray for to take away the pest. Hort's theory about the natural sequence of plagues is discussed under 'Lice' (p. 230). It is suggested that the unusually heavy rains that began the chain of events would finally create the conditions necessary for mass breeding and swarm formation. It is perhaps ironical that the cause of this devastating plague, whose effects lasted perhaps a year after the swarms had left, should provide food on the desert march.

2. The Destroyer

The locust has always been a symbol of wasting and destruction. This is well expressed in the familiar words of Joel 2:25, 'the years that the locust hath eaten' which is now a world-wide proverb. In 1546, not long after the Bible began to be circulated in English, a greedy, devouring man was known as a locust. To the inhabitants of Egypt and Palestine, and many of the ancient lands to the north-east, the locust swarms that came at unknown but all too short intervals were classed with drought and pestilence as utter calamities against which man could do nothing. On nearly half the occasions when these words are used it is in this connexion. Joel 1 may contain the accurate account of an actual plague (see p. 239) but some authorities regard it as figurative. It does not call for comment here and those interested should consult commentaries. In at least three cases, apart from the Eighth Plague, locusts are sent or threatened by God as instruments for the direct punishment of wrong-doing. Deuteronomy 28:42 lists the curses which would result from disobedience in Canaan, 'All thy trees and fruit of thy ground shall the locust consume'. (See also II Chron. 7:13; Amos 4:9).

3. As Human Food

In most literature on the subject this aspect of locusts is hardly mentioned; interesting work has been done in recent years on their nutritional value and this section will therefore be in rather more detail than the previous ones. As is made clear when this is discussed regarding other animals, there were sound reasons behind the Mosaic food laws; they could not be compared with the arbitrary food taboos still found in some parts of the world. When I worked in W. Africa in the 1930s some of my workmen, according to their clans, were forbidden to eat such ordinary foods as chicken, beef or certain fish, which might well be the only meat they could get while working in the forest. In contrast, the Mosaic code gave divinely inspired, rough and ready guides to the easy recognition of safe kinds of food. These people were not competent naturalists and they were travelling from the intensively cultivated Nile valley, with few wild animals, through the desert to the partially occupied land of Canaan.

The rules are especially interesting in the case of insects, a huge and diverse class of which only a tiny proportion can be eaten. The first ' instruction is in Lev. 11:20: 'All winged insects that go on all fours are an abomination to you' (RSV). This at once excludes many that spend most of their time on the ground – beetles, cockroaches, crickets, etc. Many of these feed on carrion or dung, or live in domestic rubbish; they are often associated with dwellings and therefore liable to spread human diseases. Few of these are, in fact, edible but it is essential to avoid them, even in hungry times. Insects are six-legged so that 'all fours' here must be taken as a technical term for 'creeping or running', as opposed to jumping, which characterizes the grasshoppers and locusts, the group clearly referred to in v. 21, 'which have legs above their feet, to leap withal upon the earth'. The anatomy sounds strange in all tr. but the meaning is clear; it refers to the section of *Orthoptera* sometimes called *Saltatoria* – the jumpers. In all phases the third pair of legs is enlarged and when the adult is at rest these legs extend far above the body, in a big inverted V. Any of the family answering to this description, and in particular the ones actually listed, were allowed, though there are some too bitter to be edible and these would be rejected on taste.

It is not actually stated that the Hebrews ate locusts in the desert, but there is little doubt that they did so. The instructions were given at Sinai, early in their wanderings, and as regards locusts this probably codified a practice of long standing, for these insects had early been recognized as good human food. The Exodus route must have crossed the line taken by many swarms and though the desert would offer no green food at most seasons, the locusts would literally run out of fuel and be compelled to land eventually unless they were entirely wind-borne. Then they would be easy prey.

Except for termites (white ants) in some parts of the tropics, locusts are more important than any other insect as a source of food. Carvings in the palace of Asurbanipal (eighth century B.C.) show locusts impaled on sticks being carried to a royal banquet. Diodorus of Sicily (second century B.C.) among other historians, refers to the *Acridiphagi*, or locust-eaters, of Ethiopia. Locusts have always been permitted food for Muslims and tradition has it that Mahommed himself used to eat them. Some African tribes still largely depend on locusts for their animal protein for parts of the year, and after eating as many as possible roasted or boiled they preserve quantities by drying or grinding into flour. Until recent years great numbers were eaten in N. Africa; the nomads of Algeria aimed at storing as much as 4 cwt. per tent. The recent influx of wealth from oil and natural gas is changing many old habits in parts of N. Africa and the Middle East, and much more food is imported; even so, in poor areas, locusts are still welcome as a tasty addition to an often marginal diet.

Locusts are now known to be a valuable source of protein, fat and calories. They also have a fair amount of mineral salts but are not rich in vitamins, and at all stages they are considered palatable, especially when freshly-killed and cooked. Europeans have reported them good eating when fried in butter, Arab style. Dried locusts contain over 50 per cent protein; the fat content varies, sometimes reaching 20 per cent. John the Baptist is the only biblical character said to have eaten locusts, and also wild honey (Matt. 3:4). He may have been on a simple and monotonous diet, but at least it was fairly well balanced; the honey would supply carbohydrates in the form of sugar, with some pollen and perhaps bee-grubs in the comb as well.

Bee

Five whole families of *Hymenoptera* have this general English name and they include the Leaf-cutting, Carpenter and Mason Bees, which are more or less solitary; the Bumble Bees, which are the biggest of all but whose small colonies last only a year; and the widespread family *Apidae*, the Honey Bees, which are world-wide and form highly organized, long-continuing societies. Although Heb. *deborah* refers to the honey bee, all these other families are also found in Palestine and it is likely that all were known by the same name.

Honey bees have queens, drones and worker-females which are winged all the time, though the first two fly only occasionally. The society depends entirely on pollen and nectar which are collected only by the workers; this is fed in various forms to the queens, drones and grubs, and the nectar is processed within the workers' bodies to make honey for storage in cells made of beeswax. This activity makes bees the most important agent in cross-fertilizing flowering plants, carrying pollen from one flower to another in their search for nectar.

Domestication of the honey bee began in Ancient Egypt some 5,000 years ago and it occurred independently in other countries also, based on the local races or species. The various nations in Mesopotamia were no good at bee-keeping but the Hittites in Asia Minor, to the west, were experts and in their code of laws dealt with such matters as the valuation of swarms of bees. The Hebrews should have known about bee-keeping from both Egypt and the surrounding nations, but there is no clear biblical or other evidence that they went in for it. Canaan was well described as 'flowing with honey' and large quantities were collected from wild bees making their homes in rocks and hollow trees, e.g., 'With honey out of the rock' (Ps. 81:16); this seems to have been the only source until the Romans introduced their method of keeping them in simple clay pipes of similar pattern to those still in use today. This idea had come from Egypt, where trees were scarce and clay plentiful. Around the Mediterranean wild bees are still abundant in the *maquis* country. The scrubby vegetation has many flowering shrubs from which nectar is obtainable for a long period, and travellers in Greece and Turkey today are surprised at the density of roadside hives, in a range of colours.

Honey production has become a highly organized industry in many countries, and modern techniques cannot be compared with the crude plundering that often killed much of the colony. Until the eighteenth century A.D. honey was man's basic source of sweetening. The Heb. word *debash* is found forty-eight times and Gr. *meli* four times. Six other Heb. and Gr. words describe honey in the comb. One or two passages may refer to a kind of treacle made by concentrating grape juice, but most to actual honey. Often honey is used in a purely literal sense, as a household commodity or article of trade; sometimes almost to denote fertility and abundance, referring to Canaan as a land flowing with honey; and in a purely figurative way, when it is compared to God's Word as sustenance for man, e.g., 'Sweeter than honey and the honeycomb,' (Ps. 19:10).

Wax is another valuable product of the honey bee and this is mentioned four times, always in connexion with melting. It had many uses in the ancient world – for writing tablets and candles, for medicines and embalming, but to the archaeologist its most important use was in the *cire perdue* process of bronze- and gold-casting, whose results have yielded so much data about the culture of those days.

Deborah was already a popular girl's name in the time of the Patriarchs (Gen. 35:8) and as such the word appears ten times, against only four meaning bee. Two of these clearly refer to the swarming habit; e.g., 'The Amorites . . . chased you, as bees do' (Deut. 1:44), suggesting the action of bees whose hive had been raided (also Ps. 118:12).

Some authorities regard the bees in Samson's lion incident (Judg. 14) as other than honey bees, but the general opinion now is that a dried and mummified skeleton, which it would have become in the climate of the desert edge, would make a suitable shelter for a swarm. Herodotus records how bees and honeycomb were found in the skull of Onisilos.

The remaining passage, Isa. 7:18, is figurative; 'The Lord will hiss for . . . the bee' (whistle', RSV). This is an obscure v. and while most commentators see it as calling for the hosts from Egypt, there is some evidence that 'whistle' here refers to the noises made by bee-keepers trying to make a swarm settle when it has left the hive.

Hornets

Hornets are well enough known by name, though few people in Britain will have seen live specimens of this ferocious, out-sized wasp measuring over 1½ in. in length. Four species are found in Palestine, similar to but not identical with *Vespa crabro*, the British species. There is no doubt that Heb. *tsirah* is correctly tr. 'hornet' in three parallel passages. 'I will send hornets before you, which shall drive out the Hivite,' (Exod. 23:28; also Deut. 7:20; Jos. 24:12). Hornets are unmistakable for their size, but they resemble wasps in having a conspicuously banded black and yellow abdomen separated from the thorax by the typical narrow 'wasp waist'. With bees these all belong to the *Hymenoptera* (membranous-winged insects); they all have sharp stings. Because of its large size, and therefore greater volume of poison, the hornet is the more unpleasant and it can even be dangerous.

The tr. 'wasp' is found in some older VSS; this is not correct but it is possible that the Heb. covers both. In contrast to honey bees, which are specialized flower feeders, both hornets and wasps are largely carnivorous. On our 1962 Israel journey we were filming bees drinking from a leaking irrigation pipe and found them being raided by several hornets, which pounced on a bee, stung it and carried it off. Classical writers often reported similar raids. Hornets are still found over much of Palestine and in all regions, including the desert alongside the Dead Sea, where I have watched them drink at a tiny trickle of water flowing out of the Massada hills above. Of these Palestine hornets two species nest underground or protected by rocks; the others, like some British wasps, make large round nests suspended from trees or shrubs. Either type could easily be disturbed by soldiers and their mounts going through woodland or scrub, with possibly serious results, for in that warm climate these insects become very active. Instances have been recorded of hornets becoming so plentiful as to be a dangerous pest, and they are known to have caused such panic among cattle and horses that they have stampeded and been killed.

Several letters to *The Times* in January 1953 listed modern instances of the use of bees as weapons. A Turkish ship saved itself by hurling skips of bees into the pirates' boats. From N. Nigeria came the account of native hives being overturned to deter pursuit through a village. It was also reported that in the 1914/15 Cameroon campaign columns advancing along narrow paths were seriously held up when hives were upset by distant trip-wires.

All this suggests that these passages might be intended literally. Massive interference by swarms of infuriated hornets might well affect the outcome of a battle, especially if the troops were inexperienced. This would be another example of God using natural means to serve His purpose. On the other hand Garstang (*Joshua-Judges* [1931], pp. 112 & 258 ff.) considers that the hornet here is figurative, identifying it with the sacred symbol of the pharaohs and seeing the fulfilment of this promise in successful Egyptian campaigns prior to the Exodus. However, this view is not generally held, largely because it raises big problems of chronology.

Ant

Ant is the name correctly and poularly given to insects forming another family of the *Hymenoptera*, the *Formicidae*. Nearly 100,000 kinds have been described and they vary in size, shape and, above all, in habits, yet they are distinguished by several unique characteristics. Only the sexual forms are winged and these are produced only at certain limited seasons; the bulk of each colony is made up of sexless workers and soldiers. Most important, all kinds are social – in contrast to bees and wasps which may be either solitary or social – and live in colonies ranging from a few dozen to perhaps millions, in the case of driver ants. Some ants are entirely tree-living; others nest underground and travel widely in search of food. Palestine has many species, including some that have been introduced accidentally in cargo or food and have now become house or garden pests.

The ant is referred to only twice in the Scriptures (Heb. *nemalah*), both times in Proverbs (6: 6–8; 30:24, 25), where it is commended as an example of industry and wisdom. The context suggests that one particular species is meant – the Harvester Ant. Other species may be said to provide their meat in the summer, but none quite so obviously as this ant, which is found from the edge of the beach, by the Mediterranean, right through to the hills of Galilee, though not in the desert. The nest is underground, the entrance made conspicuous by a series of well-worn paths leading to it from several directions. These ants are of uniform size – under $\frac{1}{4}$ in. long – and during the harvest season, which varies with the region, they spend the day collecting seeds of both cultivated and wild plants, from a wide area around the nest. The husks of those with a loose kernel are removed in the nest and the rubbish is brought to the entrance, and thrown out, to be carried away by the wind and formed into long plumes, thus making the nest even more visible. These ants are also opportunists. We studied one colony that had set up house in a compound of the Zoology Dept. at Tel Aviv University and was busy stealing grains of wheat from one of the bird enclosures. These stores are used in winter, which may not be too cold for the ants to be active but is a time when little suitable food can be found, and also in the heat of late summer, when everything dries up and plant growth usually stops for some weeks.

PALESTINE DIURNAL BIRDS OF PREY

THE FOLLOWING BRIEFLY ANNOTATED LIST OF DAY BIRDS OF PREY IS included to indicate the tremendous richness of the Palestine bird fauna, especially in a group which is now poorly represented in W. Europe generally. It is taken from the Israel check-list, which is not very different from that of the area as a whole, in *Birds of Israel*, by Paula Arnold and Walter Ferguson (Haifa, 1962).

The following abbreviations are used to show status:

p.m.   passing migrant.
r.   resident.
s.   straggler.
s.b.   summer breeder.
w.v.   winter visitor.

Shikra	p.m.	A small hawk found all over Africa and just reaching Palestine.
Goshawk	s.	A northern species which occasionally visits SW. Asia.
Sparrowhawk	w.v. and p.m.	From Europe.
Lanner	r.	A large falcon found mostly in northern half of Africa.
Saker Falcon	w.v. and p.m.	From SE. Europe.
Merlin	w.v. and p.m.	Smallest European falcon.
Sooty Falcon	r.	On Red Sea coast.
Lesser Kestrel	s.b.	Also in SE. Europe and W. Asia; winters in Africa.
Peregrine	p.m.	From Europe.
Hobby	s.b.	Winters in Africa.
Kestrel	r.	All Europe and W. Asia.
Red-footed Falcon	p.m.	Central Europe; winters in Africa.
Marsh Harrier	w.v. and p.m.	⎧ Breed in small numbers in
Hen Harrier	p.m.	⎨ suitable habitats over
Montagu's Harrier	w.v. and p.m.	⎩ much of Europe.
Golden Eagle	s.	Mountain areas of Europe. Some go south-east in winter.
Spotted Eagle	w.v. and p.m.	From Europe.
Lesser Spotted Eagle	w.v. and p.m.	From E. Europe.

Imperial Eagle	w.v. and p.m.	From Spain and Balkans.
Tawny Eagle	w.v. and p.m.	Mostly in NE. Africa.
Verreaux's Eagle	s.	From E. and S. Africa. Now also very rare s.b.
Short-toed Eagle	s.b. and p.m.	From S. and E. Europe.
Bonelli's Eagle	r.	Also in S. Europe and SW. Asia.
Booted Eagle	p.m.	Spain and Balkans.
White-tailed Eagle	r.	Very rare on coast and cliff faces.
Black Kite	w.v.	From Europe.
Red Kite	w.v. and r.	Also in parts of Europe.
European Buzzard	w.v. and p.m.	All Europe, some moving southeast in winter.
Palestine Buzzard	r.	
Honey Buzzard	p.m.	Nesting in Europe and wintering in Africa.
Osprey	w.v. and p.m.	European coasts and lakes; to Africa in winter.
Black Vulture	s.	Balkans and Spain. Vagrant to Palestine.
Lappet-faced Vulture	r.	Local and rare.
Lammergeier or *Bearded Vulture*	r.	Mountain ranges only.
Griffon-Vulture	p.m. and r.	Parts of S. Europe, moving southeast in winter.
Egyptian Vulture	s.b.	Winters in Africa.

ON THE USE OF THE WORDS 'ANIMAL', 'BEAST', 'CREATURE', 'DRAGON'

Animal

This word forms part of the title of this book and must therefore be discussed. As pointed out below, animal is a newer word than beast and was coming into use only as AV was being prepared, but it is strange that it is not found in RV. Strictly, an animal is any living being endowed with sensation and voluntary movement, in contrast to 'plant'; i.e., the animal kingdom as opposed to the vegetable kingdom, and it is so used in the title. In popular use it refers primarily to four-footed animals, often only to four-footed mammals, in contrast to man, fishes etc.

RSV uses 'animal' thirty-four times in OT and seven times in NT, but the treatment is far too complicated to justify detailed analysis ; e.g., the first twelve occurrences of animal in RSV are rendered as follows in AV: 'beast' (5), 'cattle' (4), 'of the herd' (1), 'of the flock' (1). In one case there is no word for it in Heb. or AV. These are derived from five different Heb. words: *behemah*, *chaiyah* and *miqneh* (beast or cattle); *baqar* (oxen); *tson* (sheep) and *nebelah* (carcase).

The NT position is similar and four different Gr. words are tr. 'animal': *therion* (wild beast); *tetrapous* (quadruped); *ktēnos* (beast of burden); *zoon* (creature).

Beast

Although found widely in modern EV, including RSV, this word is now obsolete in its general sense and in this respect can be compared with 'fowl' (see p. 163). 'Beast' is still used semi-technically in such combinations as 'beast-wagon', the living quarters for circus animals, and the term 'beast of burden' is still current; otherwise it has only literary and metaphorical uses, e.g., a cruel or uncouth man is a beast and his behaviour beastly or, worse, bestial. 'Beast' came from Old French and was in general use when the basic Bible tr. was being made; 'animal', beginning to appear in written works during the sixteenth century, was not widely known until later and is not found at all in AV.

Lack of uniformity in OT tr. causes considerable confusion and in general both RV and RSV follow AV; this is a case where RV does not render the Heb. as consistently as is its general practice. The two Heb. words most often tr. beast are *behemah*, which is elsewhere tr. 'cattle' (q.v.): *chaiyah*, with fem. *cheva*, is tr. 'beast' ninety-six times but is elsewhere used some thirty-five times tr. by ten different words: *be'ir*, with the meaning of 'brute', is usually tr. 'beast', but occasionally 'cattle', and the VSS are not uniform.

It is often hard to distinguish between *behemah* and *chaiyah*; e.g., in the same chapter and in almost identical contexts both words are used for clean animals. Lev. 11:2 'the beasts *(chaiyah)* which ye shall eat,' cf. v. 39, 'any beast *(behemah)* of which ye shall eat.' In Lev. 11:47 *chaiyah* is used first for clean and then for unclean animals. *Chaiyah* is generally wider in meaning than *behemah* and as such is sometimes tr. 'living thing' (RV and RSV), yet the contrary is true of its use in Lev. 11:2 'these are the living things *(chaiyah)* which you may eat among all the beasts *(behemah)* that are on the earth.'

In NT both RV and RSV follow the Gr. more closely and are preferred to AV. Gr. *zoon* which AV always tr. 'beast' is rendered 'living creature' RV and RSV in Rev. 4:6 *et seq.*

Except for RSV in Acts 23:24 (mounts), I Cor. 15:39 (animals), Rev. 18:13 (cattle) and Acts 28:5 (creatures), all VSS retain 'beast' for *ktenos* (domestic animal, especially beast of burden) and *therion* (wild beast). RV and RSV thus make a proper distinction between the Four Living Creatures on the one hand and the beast of Rev. 11:7 and all literal passages on the other.

Creature

This is another general word whose usage has changed and, in consequence, its treatment in the different VSS. In OT it is seldom used by AV and RV. Heb. *nephesh*, most often tr. 'soul', is rendered 'living creature' and 'creature' in some literal passages of Genesis and Leviticus. Heb. *chaiyah*, meaning 'living', is tr. 'living creature' in a long figurative passage in Ezekiel.

RSV uses 'creature' much more widely in literal passages than the earlier VSS. It agrees with the above renderings in AV and also tr. 'creature' at least ten other Heb. words rendered variously in AV. The first six occurrences of 'creature' in OT RSV are from six Heb. words. However, in spite of these divergences, 'creature' is used in OT and NT of AV, RV and RSV only in a literal sense except in the clearly prophetic passages.

Creature began by meaning anything created, whether animate or not, which is perhaps its strict meaning still. Mostly it is synonymous with animal; sometimes it is used for animals other than man in contrast to man. In the U.S.A. it often means cattle. The RSV treatment of this word is generally unhelpful and the more precise words 'animal' and 'cattle' are preferred.

Dragon

Two Heb. words are tr. 'dragon' (AV).

1. *tannim* (masc. pl. of *tan*) and *tannoth* (fem. pl.) are tr. 'dragon' fourteen

times and 'whale' once. RV and RSV are generally considered correct in having 'jackal' fourteen times and 'dragon' once. This has already been discussed under 'Jackal' (p. 124). It is tempting to regard the single exception (Ezek. 32:2) as a textual error for the following, which though apparently almost identical is not now considered cognate with it. (See NBD p. 322.)

2. *tannin* is less uniformly treated in all EV, viz:

AV	dragon (8)	serpent (3)	whale (2)	sea monster (1)
RV	dragon (7)	serpent (4)	sea monster (2)	jackal (1)
RSV	dragon (6)	serpent (4)	sea monster (2)	jackal (2)

In the two cases where RSV tr. 'jackal' it seems that *tannin* is read as *tannim*, e.g., Job 30:29, where AV has 'I am a brother to dragons and a companion to owls' the RSV tr. 'jackals' and 'ostriches'. The other v. where RSV has jackal is Lam. 4:3, which is discussed under 'Whale' (p. 137). These are mostly figurative contexts and *tannin* is found only twice literally:

(a) Gen. 1:12, 'whale' (AV); 'sea monster' (RV, RSV). This is the Creation narrative, fifth day, and the word is clearly a general one that might be better tr. 'giant marine animals'.

(b) Exod. 7:9; 10:12, 'Serpent' (AV, RV, RSV). This is the incident of the rods that became serpents (q.v.).

It could perhaps be argued that in Job 7:12 'Am I a sea, or a whale, that thou settest a watch over me?' a real animal is intended, but the poetic nature of the passage would allow almost any of these variants to stand. For the rest, perhaps the tr. 'dragon' in such pictorial and allegorical passages is as good as any. There is also some logic in giving *tannin* two senses, mythological and biological, for this is also true of the English word dragon. Coming from Gr. *drakon* it is first a mythological animal with wings and claws; it is also used currently in such animal names as Komodo dragon, which is a giant lizard, dragon fish, dragonfly etc.

Abbreviations

Aram.	Aramaic (language)
a.s.l.	above Sea Level
AV	Authorized Version
b.s.l.	below Sea Level
c.	circa (approx.)
cf.	compare
cwt.	hundredweight(s)
e.g.	for example
EV.	English Version(s)
fem.	feminine
ft.	foot, feet
Gr.	Greek
Heb.	Hebrew
i.e.	that is
in.	inch(es)
lb.	pound(s)
LXX	Septuagint
mg.	margin reading
masc.	masculine
NBD	New Bible Dictionary (1962)
N., E., S., W.	North, East, South, West; (also northern etc.)
NE., NW., SE., SW.	North-east, North-west, South-east, South-west
NT	New Testament
OT	Old Testament
oz.	ounce(s)
pl.	plural
RSV	Revised Standard Version
RV	Revised Version
sing.	singular
SOED	Shorter Oxford English Dictionary
tr.	translates, translated, translation, etc., as context
v, vv.	verse(s)
viz.	namely
VS, VSS	Version(s)
Vulg.	Vulgate

BIBLIOGRAPHY

This list is largely confined to titles of local importance. The natural history facts have been checked in a wide range of general textbooks. To save space reference is not made to more specialized papers, many of which are not easily accessible to the ordinary reader; brief notes on some of the entries suggest where these are listed in detail.

Arnold, Paula and Ferguson, Walter. *Birds of Israel* (Haifa, Shalit Publishers Ltd. 1960). Hebrew and English text, with beautiful illustrations of forty-eight typical birds and a complete Israel list.

Baly, Denis. *The Geography of the Bible* , A Study in Historical Geography (London, Lutterworth Press, 1957). The most useful book available on the physical background of Palestine; with numerous maps and comprehensive bibliography.

Bodenheimer, F. S. 'The Honeybee in Ancient Palestine' (*The Bee World* 15, 1934).

Bodenheimer, F. S. *Insects as Human Food* (The Hague, W. Junk, 1951).

Bodenheimer, F. S. *Animals and Man in Bible Lands* (Leiden, E. J. Brill, 1960). A book of great erudition, especially valuable for its detailed treatment of classical authors.

Cansdale, G. S. *Animals and Man* (London, Hutchinson, 1952). A consideration of all aspects of man's dealing with animals.

Driver, G. R. 'Birds in the Old Testament: 1. Birds in Law; 2. Birds in Life.' *Palestine Exploration Quarterly* (1955, pp. 5–20; 129–140). A most valuable examination of the Hebrew names of OT birds, with numerous technical references.

Harrison, David. *Footsteps in the Sand* (London, Ernest Benn, 1959). One of the few recent books with field notes on the small mammals and birds of Palestine and Mesopotamia.

Harrison, David L. *The Mammals of Arabia*. (London, Ernest Benn, Vol. I, 1964; Vol. II, 1968.) This is a definitive and comprehensive work, with very full bibliography. Vol. I deals with the Insectivores, Bats and Primates. Vol. II, which covers almost all the wild mammals of interest to Bible students, was published after the text of this book had been completed. One of the most useful features is a detailed list of occurences in the past 100 years or so.

Grimwood, Ian R. 'Operation Oryx' *Journal Fauna Preservation Society*

(1967, pp. 110–118). The latest account of the status of the Arabian Oryx and the work being done to preserve it.

Merom, Peter. *The Death of the Lake* (Tel Aviv, Davar Ltd. n.d., *c.* 1960). A fine pictorial record of the reclamation of Lake Huleh.

Moreau, R. E. 'Problems of Mediterranean-Saharan Migration.' (*Ibis* 103a, 1961, pp. 373–427). The most important paper yet published; with comprehensive references, including all notes relevant to the E. Mediterranean.

Mountford, Guy. *Portrait of a Desert.* (London. Collins, 1965.) An account of the 1963 Jordan Expedition. Very well illustrated by Eric Hosking, it states clearly the problem of nature conservation in arid countries with nomad peoples.

Parmelee, Alice. *All the Birds of the Bible* (London, Lutterworth, 1959).

Peterson, Roger, Mountford, Guy, and Hollom, P. A. D. *Field Guide to the Birds of Britain and Europe* (London, Collins, 1954). This covers all but a few Palestine birds and is the most helpful book for the visitor to take.

Tristram, H. B. *The Natural History of the Bible* (London, S.P.C.K.). First published 1867, with eleven editions in forty years but now hardly obtainable secondhand.

Wood, J. G. *Bible Animals* (London, Longmans Green, 1869).

Zeuner, F. E. *A History of Domesticated Animals* (London, Hutchinson, 1963). The most valuable book on this subject, with exhaustive bibliography.

While the *New English Bible Old Testament* was published too late to be of use in the present work, due reference has been made to the valuable work of Professor Sir Godfrey Driver, noted above, who was Convener of the OT Panel of Translators.

Maps and Indexes

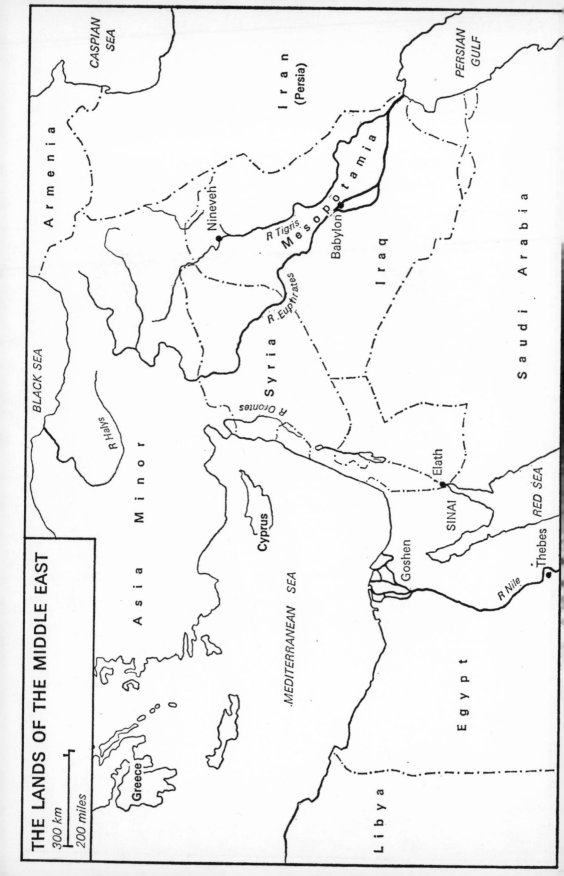

THE LANDS OF THE MIDDLE EAST

300 km
200 miles

CASPIAN SEA

Armenia

Iran (Persia)

PERSIAN GULF

Nineveh

R Tigris

Mesopotamia

Babylon

R Euphrates

Iraq

Saudi Arabia

BLACK SEA

R Halys

Asia Minor

Syria

R Orontes

Cyprus

Elath

SINAI

Goshen

RED SEA

MEDITERRANEAN SEA

Greece

Egypt

R Nile

Thebes

Libya

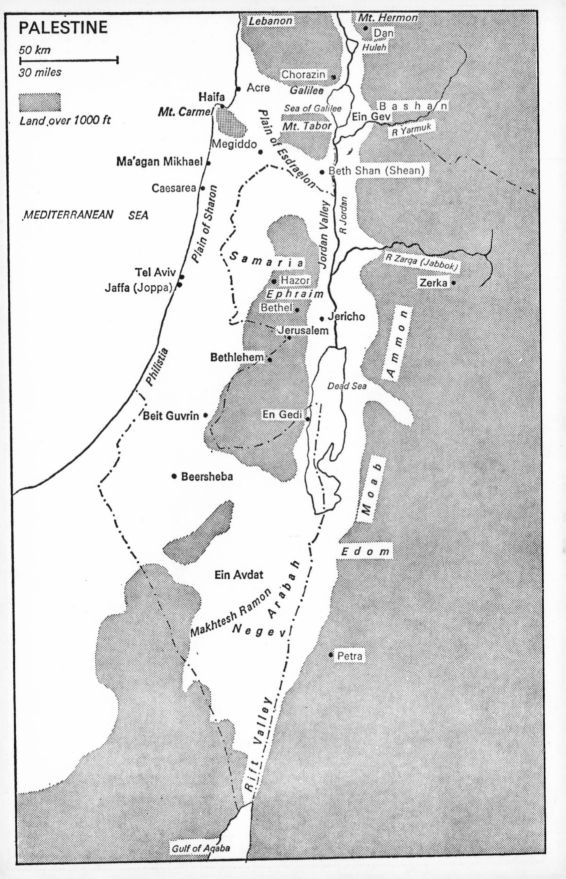

PALESTINE

50 km
30 miles

Land over 1000 ft

MEDITERRANEAN SEA

Lebanon
Mt. Hermon
Dan
Huleh
Chorazin
Galilee
Acre
Haifa
Mt. Carmel
Sea of Galilee
Mt. Tabor
B a s h a n
Ein Gev
Megiddo
R Yarmuk
Ma'agan Mikhael
Beth Shan (Shean)
Caesarea

Plain of Esdraelon
Plain of Sharon
Jordan Valley
R Jordan

S a m a r i a
R Zarqa (Jabbok)
Tel Aviv
Zerka
Jaffa (Joppa)
Hazor
E p h r a i m
Bethel
A m m o n
Jericho
Jerusalem
Bethlehem
Philistia
Dead Sea

Beit Guvrin
En Gedi

Beersheba

M o a b

E d o m

Ein Avdat
Arabah
Makhtesh Ramon
N e g e v
Petra

Rift Valley

Gulf of Aqaba

GENERAL INDEX

(Bold figures indicate principal entries)

INDEX OF HEBREW NAMES

INDEX OF GREEK NAMES

INDEX OF ANIMAL NAMES (ENGLISH)

INDEX OF ANIMAL NAMES (SCIENTIFIC)

INDEX OF SCRIPTURE REFERENCES